WRONG FIT, RIGHT FIT

"In a crowded field of books aimed at the future of work, *Wrong Fit, Right Fit* provides simple, practical, and sage advice to help companies build better workplaces and people to find a place where they can be at their highest, best use. This book is a must-read for anyone who wants to make work less work."

—**Prasad Setty**, Lecturer at Stanford; Advisor at BetterUp and Grab;
Former Google VP, People Operations

"If there is a book that can help companies build passionate and thriving teams filled with energized and happy people, or to help employees find these types of companies, *Wrong Fit, Right Fit* is that book. Filled with non-stop thought-provoking and actionable 'ah-has,' this book is a page-turner and a must-read for leaders, managers, and employees in any organization."

—**Wyatt Taubman**, CEO & Co-founder of Vive Organics

"In today's rapidly changing work landscape, *Wrong Fit, Right Fit* is essential reading. André provides a fresh perspective on today's challenges and offers practical tools to help all readers design a more intentional and fulfilling work life. Whether you're an intern or a CEO, this timely book offers valuable insights for navigating the evolving relationship between individuals and institutions."

—**Sandy Speicher**, Former CEO, IDEO

"*Wrong Fit, Right Fit* is a great fit for every C-suite leader to read and share with her or his team, and for every job candidate to read before accepting employment. [It] cuts through the miasma around workplace culture and 'fitting in' and focuses on whether the ways of working in the organization align with the values and natural work preferences of talent."

—**Mark D. Arian,** CEO Consulting, Korn Ferry

"Reading this book turned on a light bulb in my head, illuminating much more clearly and consciously why my own career experiences evolved as they have. It helped me to understand, in a practical and purposeful way, the elusive concept of 'fit' so often discussed in management today yet so little understood. . . . Andre Martin takes the concept of fit and moves it from generic to meaningful."

—**Jeanne Leidtka**, Professor, University of Virginia Darden School of Business,
and Author of *Designing for Growth*

"*Wrong Fit, Right Fit is* a powerful exploration of new ideas and practical insights that the global workforce and organizations need right now. The chaos and disruption that have marked the pandemic years, the renewed focus on well-being and culture, and the massive disengagement of employees are all signs that the way we've always worked isn't working anymore. André's fresh and insightful perspectives are needed today. This is a must-read."

—**Tony Bingham**, President and CEO, Association of Talent Development (ATD)

WRONG FIT,

RIGHT FIT

WRONG FIT,

RIGHT FIT

Why How We Work Matters More Than Ever

André Martin, PhD

IT Revolution

Independent Publisher Since 2013

Portland, Oregon

25 NW 23rd Pl, Suite 6314
Portland, OR 97210

First Edition
Printed in the United States of America
28 27 26 25 24 23   1 2 3 4 5 6 7 8 9 10

Cover and book design by Devon Smith/D.Smith Creative, LLC

Library of Congress Cataloging-in-Publication Data
Names: Martin, André, Ph.D., author.
Title: Wrong fit, right fit : why how we work matters more than ever / by André Martin, PhD.
Description: First edition. | Portland, OR : IT Revolution Press, LLC, [2023] | Includes bibliographical references.
Identifiers: LCCN 2023010083 (print) | LCCN 2023010084 (ebook) | ISBN 9781950508754 (paperback) | ISBN 9781950508761 (ebook) | ISBN 9781950508778 (pdf) | ISBN 9781950508778
Subjects: LCSH: Job satisfaction. | Employee motivation. | Employee selection. | Work--Psychological aspects. | Personnel management.
Classification: LCC HF5549.5.J63 M265 2023 (print) | LCC HF5549.5.J63 (ebook) | DDC 650.1--dc23/eng/20230602
LC record available at https://lccn.loc.gov/2023010083
LC ebook record available at https://lccn.loc.gov/2023010084

ISBN: 9781950508754
eBook ISBN: 9781950508761
Audio ISBN: 9781950508785
Web PDF ISBN: 9781950508778

For information about special discounts for bulk purchases or for information on booking authors for an event, please visit our website at www.ITRevolution.com.

To my wife, for loving all of me and all my nuance
To my mom, for being in my corner since day one
To my kids, for giving me a reason to be and do more
To my mentors, for opening doors and pushing me through them

To all my teams, for showing me the definition of brilliance
and inspiring me to help more talent find *right fit*.

CONTENTS

FIGURES & TABLES

There Is a *Right Fit* Company Waiting for You

Have you ever tried to write with your nondominant hand? If not, try it now. Grab a piece of paper and a pen, and write the following sentence first with your dominant hand and then your nondominant hand: *The quick brown fox jumps over the lazy dog.*

Take a look at the two sentences. How did it feel to write each sentence? Did one take more effort than the other? Is one better quality? Unless you're ambidextrous, writing with your nondominant hand likely took a lot more effort, required more concentration, induced more stress, resulted in much lower quality, and left you feeling less successful and satisfied with your work (Figure 0.1).

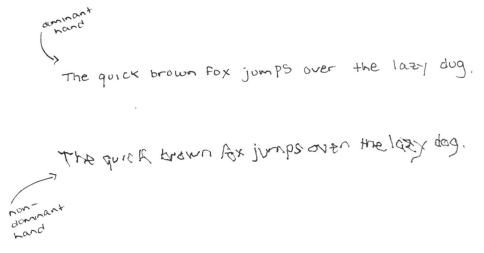

Figure 0.1: Handwritten Sentences with Dominant and Nondominant Hands

This metaphor is an apt descriptor of what many of us feel as we maneuver through our careers and choose the companies we join—it can often feel as though we are spending our days writing with our nondominant hand, leaving us less engaged, less confident, and more stressed. This is a shared experience, and it has a real impact on both our personal commitment to companies and the meaning we derive from work, as shown by the 2022 Gallup *State of Global Workplace* report. Gallup finds that businesses have lost an estimated $7.8 trillion[1] in productivity due to disengagement in the workplace and estimates that 60% of workers[2] are emotionally detached at work. If we need further proof, we need look no further than phenomena like languishing, the Great Resignation, and quiet quitting (more on these later) that have permeated our workplace conversations as of late. Additional studies have found that workers who are unhappy at work tend to experience poor health at twice the rate of satisfied workers[3] and that a lack of job satisfaction can lead to long-term mental and physical health problems.[4] It's clear that something isn't working at work.

The well of talent, all of the creative minds and capable knowledge workers who fuel the engines of businesses, seem to be increasingly disconnected from their companies, and companies are struggling to fuel the higher levels of dedication and commitment needed to succeed in these dynamic and uncertain times. Many have come to the conclusion that the only way to solve the issue is to transform the company culture or create new ways of working. Though this is a laudable idea, it requires more change and energy from talent and companies that are already above their cognitive and emotional limits. What if it isn't about changing how we work, but rather simply improving our chances of creating and finding better fit?

A Theory of Fit

It was the statistics from Gallup that first caught my eye and spurred my research for this book. As an organizational psychologist, my first impulse when reading something about productivity and engagement, or lack thereof, is to immediately consider what in our workplace cultures needs to change. This book originally was going to be about workplace culture in this new era of work—how to assess it, envision a better version of it, and transform it to create a better experience for all of the creative minds and capable individuals that fuel our companies. But, that isn't what happened.

Like any good researcher, I decided to gather data and insights. I began my process by interviewing talent within my immediate professional circle to help inform my working thesis and questionnaire. We talked about the places they worked, their thoughts on engagement, and what kind of cultures allowed them to thrive. Interestingly, those conversations weren't conclusive, meaning they didn't directly point to culture as the culprit—or at least not a single type of culture. What each person keyed in on or described was slightly different, subtly nuanced. These early conversations led me away from changing culture and toward this thing that kept popping up: *fit*, or more specifically, *right fit*.

The spark of something important was there, a potential space in the conversation that was not being talked about. So, I revamped my interview questionnaire to include *right fit* and *wrong fit* experiences at work. Once the questions were clear, I sought out over sixty-five in-depth interviews with talent ranging from twenty-two to fifty-five years of age, from CEOs to early career talent, from talent working in start-ups to global multinationals, and from talent working in Asia-Pacific to Europe to the US, all to see if my hypothesis was correct:

> Could **right fit** help talent discover more meaning and satisfaction at work and help companies find lost productivity?

What is *fit*? For the purposes of the book, *fit* is defined as a deep and authentic connection to how a company works day-to-day. To return to the metaphor, *right fit* feels like you are writing with your dominant hand the moment you walk through the door and most days after. When *right fit* is there, the days feel easy, the work is more meaningful, and our connection to our company grows exponentially. As one interviewee described it, "In my *right fit* experience, it felt like putting on my favorite outfit. I was more me." Another interviewee said, "You are putting in the hours, but it doesn't feel like work." Perhaps even more compelling are the feelings talent have when fit isn't there. One of our interviewees described *wrong fit* as if "everyone has a secret decoder ring for success, except for me." Another was much rawer about the feeling when they said "it was like being punched in the face every day in a different way."

Where talent looks at *right fit* from the perspective of the alignment of their personal way of working with that of the company they have joined, companies must view *right fit* as the clarity, communication, and practice of a consistent way of working that showcases the company at its best. This, unfortunately, is where many companies fail. You see, while companies have become adept at defining their mission, articulating their strategy, sharing their values, and crafting inspiring leadership expectations, few have put in the effort to understand and train talent on how work, done well, happens day in and day out at the company. How does the company actually run? How does the company prioritize work, solve problems, innovate, manage conflict, or socialize projects? Each company does this in a unique and natural way at its best. Those ways of working are innate in the fabric of the company and often emanate from the early days of its founding.

Not surprisingly, I found *right fit* to be elusive among the interviewees, meaning it was hard to find and then retain over time. From a talent perspective, the way a company works is often undervalued during recruitment compared to brand, bigger titles, better pay, or even a little flattery. Further, the current approach to everything from job descriptions to employer branding to recruiting makes it nearly impossible to assess *how the company works day-to-day*. So, many talent end up in experiences that are vastly different from their early interactions and expectations of the company.

On the company side, a lack of clarity, consistency, and transparency about the company's work principles, practices, and platforms during the hiring process and onboarding tamps down *fit* for extended periods. To complicate matters even more, companies do not often require newly acquired leaders to adopt the ways of working that drive the rest of the company, which becomes a recipe for a bureaucratic, slow, and confusing hairball of coordination costs, context shifting, and confusion.

Remember that $7.8 trillion of lost productivity? I am guessing a lot of it lies right here.

Something else became clear early on as I explored *right fit* with the interviewees: the pressure many of us feel to "fit in." "Fitting in" is about a person trying to become something they aren't in the hopes of one day being successful. In this context, "fit" has a negative connotation, especially among diverse or marginalized groups who have often been overtly told (due to their race, ethnicity, gender, sexual orientation, etc.) that they don't "fit in" or who have been subtly biased against when they try to find a place in any established community—neighborhoods, schools, companies, etc. This exploration of "fitting in" is important, and many tremendous minds have written about and are working on the subject through the lens of diversity, equity, inclusion, belonging, and how to create unbiased and equitable systems. I applaud that work and believe it is vital for all organizational leaders to lean into it as we create the future of work. For the purposes of this book, I am asking you to hold a new and nuanced definition of *fit* that is focused on helping talent and companies align on how work gets done day-to-day.

Finding *right fit* inside a company has three key dimensions, as shown in Figure 0.2. *Fit* is fully realized when *who* talent is (all of the characteristics and experiences that make them unique) and *how* talent prefers to work aligns with what the company values are and how the company works day-to-day. If there is only alignment on two of the three circles, then, at some level, talent is being asked to "fit in." That feeling of "fitting in" centers around three key misalignments:

- **Total mismatch:** The company does not value who the talent is or how they prefer to work. At the most simple level, talent might feel this mismatch as, "Nobody at the company 'looks' like me or works like me."
- **Person Mismatch:** The company values the way the talent works but does not value who they are as a person. The talent might experience

this mismatch as, "Nobody at the company 'looks' like me, but many people I have met work how I prefer to work."

- **Way of Working Mismatch:** The company values who the talent is, but doesn't value how the talent prefers to work. The talent might experience this mismatch as, "People at the company 'look' like me but nobody here works the way I prefer to work."

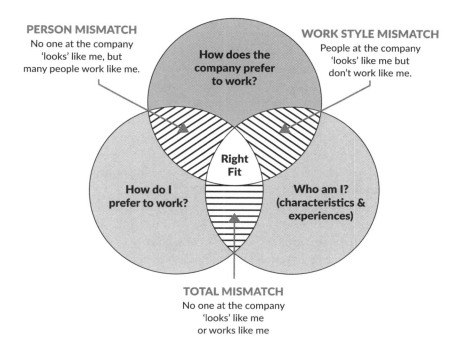

PERSON MISMATCH
No one at the company 'looks' like me, but many people work like me.

WORK STYLE MISMATCH
People at the company 'looks' like me but don't work like me.

How does the company prefer to work?

Right Fit

How do I prefer to work?

Who am I? (characteristics & experiences)

TOTAL MISMATCH
No one at the company 'looks' like me or works like me

Figure 0.2: The Elements of *Right Fit* and Fitting In

Though much work is being done to understand and alleviate the "fitting in" related bias and inequitable practices, very little attention has been paid to the misalignment of how work gets done on a daily basis. This book attempts to shed light on this subject and offer strategies to find *right fit* with greater frequency. When you have *right fit*, doing your best work comes easy, with seemingly little effort. When you are in a *wrong fit* experience, much of your available creative energy goes to context (fitting in) over craft (the core skill or capability you've built up over time).

Many gifted and motivated talent have lost the opportunity to show their full potential due to ending up in a *wrong fit* situation where they are left endlessly trying to gain the "secret decoder ring" to success. The cost is staggering both to talent and to the company. The company doesn't get the lift of captured discretionary effort (the extra productivity that comes with deeper commitment or engagement) or the unique brilliance of the person they hired. Even worse, talent walks out of these "fitting-in" experiences feeling less confident, less capable, less cared for, and less themselves.

Is *Right Fit* the Cure for What Ails Us?

From the interviews combined with over twenty-five years of leading culture, engagement, and talent initiatives in and with some of the most revered companies in the world, I have come to the conclusion that there is no one silver bullet to the crisis of commitment we are facing in the modern workplace—where talent doesn't fully feel seen or valued by their employers and company leaders struggle to get the level of engagement and commitment they need from their talent to sustain growth. There truly might not be one silver bullet, but *right fit* does offer a step in the right direction. Let's start by looking closely at our companies.

Who a company says they are rarely matches how that company works day-to-day. That's not to say the ways of working are bad or misguided or nefarious. No, they are simply different from what is expressed through formal communication channels, expertly crafted mission/vision/values statements, breathtaking career sites and employer brand campaigns, and inspiring leadership town halls. A 2020 study by MIT and *Culture 500* found zero correlation between the cultural values a company publishes and how well the company lived up to those values in the eyes of their employees.[5]

This divergence happens because actual ways of working evolve organically out of the preferences of leaders who are hired from different companies, the nudges of HR and business processes that are built on the best practices of other places, the complexity and distance that often accompanies scale, and the human nature to interpret vision/values/expectations in a way that most beneficially serves ourselves or our teams. The end result is two versions of the company—what we once were or aspire to someday be and what we actually are day-to-day.

As a result, what a company says about who they are and how they work no longer matches the felt experience of talent. So, talent is forced to bump into ill-defined ways of working, use their creative energy to understand how things actually get done, and struggle, for longer than they should, to feel settled and fully committed.

The company isn't alone in making *right fit* elusive; talent plays a role as well. In my interviews, it became clear that landing in a *right fit* experience seemed to be the hiring equivalent of hitting a bullseye while throwing a dart blindfolded after being spun around three times super fast. It happens, but not frequently nor consistently enough. Upon reflection, many of the interviewees admitted that they hadn't thought hard enough about how they prefer to work nor had they asked questions in the interview process that would help them better understand the ways of working in the company. Further, in the *wrong fit* experiences, most admitted to knowing "something was off" during the process but found themselves being swayed by other signals— company reputation, pay, life circumstances, savvy recruiters, bigger scope, flattery, inspiring leaders, and the allure of a beautiful campus. Then, once they found themselves in a *wrong fit* experience, talent admitted to working harder and longer hours to make up for the feeling of misalignment, leaving them more stressed, less productive, disengaged, and lacking confidence.

Our solutions to this crisis, from companies and talent alike, have either been to simply make the best of an imperfect experience, refresh culture from the ground up, or cut bait and try our hand at the disoriented, blindfolded dart toss again—all of which are emotionally and cognitively draining, complex, and limiting to the productivity, growth, and impact our companies have. Maybe we could talk less about aspirational culture and talk more about how the company works day-to-day. We could seek to know ourselves better and our preferred ways of working before we look for a new gig or hire more talent. We could make the interview process more vulnerable and authentic by showing who we are on most days, not simply our best. We could hire for who we are today and develop everyone for who we need to be tomorrow.

What This Book Is About

So, what does all this mean? What is happening? Is work really that universally dissatisfying, or is something else afoot? In moments like this, I always turn to a theory that was introduced to me way back in 1997 by Jodie Foster in the movie *Contact* (yes, I am a bit of a sci-fi buff). That theory was Occam's Razor, and it states that all things being equal, the simplest answer is probably the right one.

As you will see in upcoming chapters and through the stories of the interviewees, much of this mass dissatisfaction is attributable to *fit*. This book works off a simple premise. If talent can find *right fit* companies and roles more often, then less of their creative energy will go to context and coordination cost and more to their craft (what they are brilliant at doing) every day. Thus, they will naturally experience higher energy and engagement, less languishing burnout, will do better work in less time, and hold a stronger sense of meaning and mission. Once this occurs, the company, in return, will regain lost discretionary effort, more capability to learn, higher levels of coordination and collaboration, and higher levels of innovation and performance. Companies will have a more stable climate from which to pivot, transform, and grow. This symbiotic relationship only works if both talent and companies take a step out of the habits we have built and toward a new way of finding fit. If they do, the end result will be healthier, stronger companies filled with content and committed talent. Oh, and remember that pesky $7.8 trillion? That just might be found as well.

For the remainder of the book, each chapter will take on an aspect of *right fit* and attempt to provide mindsets and tools that can help both talent and companies. In Chapter 1, I'll explore the trends that have contributed to this crisis of commitment and the need to reorient everything around fit. Chapter 2 examines the psychology that guides our actions and why they matter in the search for *right fit*. Chapter 3 provides insight into why self-reflection is an important place to start the journey to find *right fit*, while Chapter 4 provides some reflective exercises to help you down that path. Chapter 5 walks talent and leadership through how to assess a potential company and job with *fit* in mind, while Chapter 6 assesses the ways a company works and its alignment to your work preferences. Chapter 7 and Chapter 8 show how to embark on a longer fit journey through inspirational and relational buffers to keep *right fit* intact or make a *wrong fit* experience palatable. In Chapter 9, we explore how companies should rethink their work practices and how they preview themselves to prospective talent, while Chapter 10 examines how companies could reimagine the recruiting and (re)recruiting of talent for *right fit*. Finally, we wrap up all of the bits and pieces in the Conclusion.

To ensure the book has practical application, peppered throughout the text are insights, excursions, and real stories of *right fit* and *wrong fit*:

- **Company & Talent Insights:** Tips, tricks, questions, and takeaways that can help talent find *right fit* and company to create it.
- **Reflective Excursions:** In-depth exercises or activities that will aid talent and companies to reflect more deeply on *right fit* and how to achieve it given their circumstance.
- **A Fit Assessment:** An assessment tool that can help talent assess how well their natural preferences for work match their current company.

- **Real Stories of Fit:** Real stories pulled directly from the interviews, these are narratives that describe how *right fit* or *wrong fit* feels and the outcomes that result from having either.

Who Should Read This Book?

This book is written for anyone who is attempting to build a career and find a place where they can practice their craft—the emerging investment banker straight out of university looking to learn and be mentored, a seasoned HR practitioner who's ready to apply their experience to a job in a new industry, the marketer looking to make a jump into sales, or any number of other knowledge workers who want to further their career and feel like their work is meaningful. The aim is simple—to help all *talent*, the creative minds and capable individuals that fuel our companies, to find *right fit*.

What if you're a manager or leader who is responsible for shaping and designing the company culture and its ways of working? This book is written for you as well. Because *right fit* is fundamentally about the match between the way a company works and the preference of talent, neglecting to mention tools, tricks, tips, and better practices to help leaders and managers would leave the conversation incomplete.

So, I've designed the book to speak to readers who might be wearing one of three hats (Figure 0.3):

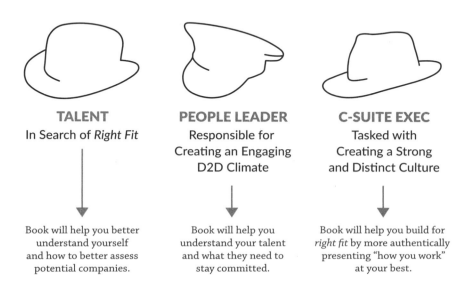

TALENT
In Search of *Right Fit*

Book will help you better
understand yourself
and how to better assess
potential companies.

PEOPLE LEADER
Responsible for
Creating an Engaging
D2D Climate

Book will help you
understand your talent
and what they need to
stay committed.

C-SUITE EXEC
Tasked with
Creating a Strong
and Distinct Culture

Book will help you build for
right fit by more authentically
presenting "how you work"
at your best.

Figure 0.3: The Three Hats

If you're focused on your own career and finding a place to work where your fellow employees value what you value and work how you work, then this book will give you tools to find those companies, make subtle shifts to be successful in those companies, and build buffers to retain fit when you move teams or are undergoing a significant transition.

If you're a people leader who is responsible for creating an inspiring and engaging day-to-day climate, this book will provide you insight into what matters to your talent, direct your attention to places where engagement and commitment might be at risk, and offer some simple strategies to find the right team members and help them be successful.

If you're a founder of a company, an enterprise leader, or the head of HR tasked with creating a strong and distinct culture, this book will help you see the world through the lens of *right and wrong fit* versus *good or bad culture*. It will give you a way to uncover how the company works "at its best" and create touchpoints for your talent that help you to select those who work like you work, re-recruit everyone to a more consistent way of working, and create buffers to keep the talent you want inside the company and fully committed to your purpose.

So, you might read this book today as you search for your first role in your first company. Later, you might pick it up again when you become a team leader, or, better yet, CEO. Regardless of who you are, this book is particularly valuable if you find yourself in one of the following situations (see also Figure 0.4):

- You are currently interviewing for roles at new companies.
- You have recently joined a new company and are trying to figure out how to be successful.
- You have recently moved teams or changed roles inside your current company.
- You are in a role where you are struggling to stay engaged.
- You feel like you can't practice your craft or do your best work.
- You're thinking about leaving a place where you once had *right fit*.
- You're in a *right fit* experience and want to stay there.

A Call to Right Fit

We have all faced *wrong fit* or *hard fit* experiences in our careers (whether it was moving to a new team in our current company or a new role in a different one). Why does this happen? How can talent better assess the company/team they're joining before they join? How can you more quickly identify the real ways of working once you're there? How can you stay where you are and jump out of bed every morning excited to go to work? As leaders of companies, how do you better align who you say you are to how it feels to work at a place every day? How do you rediscover the ways of working that are your company at its best?

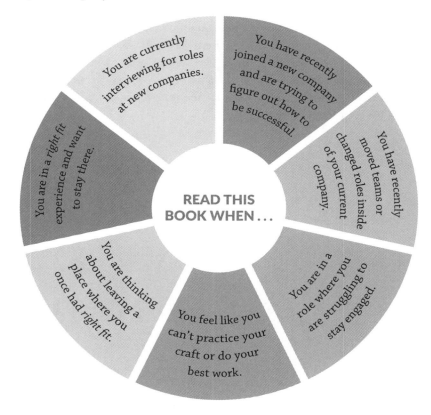

Figure 0.4: Audience for This Book

If you are a leader or executive in any company, the ultimate question is, "Are we clear and consistent about how work gets done, so the right talent will choose us and thrive?"

If you are a talent in a company, the ultimate question is, "Do our ways of working really fit the way I prefer to work?" It's important to take a moment to note here that there will be times in our lives when *right fit* has to take a back seat—when our choice of where we work, the job we take, or the talent we hire is driven by other factors. Sometimes we just need a paycheck, medical insurance, or skilled individuals filling empty seats so we can produce our product or provide our service. That's okay. More than okay, actually—it is essential. And, as long as we understand the trade-offs we make and the strategies to create fit over time, this book can still help more of us be more committed in more moments of our days.

As you'll discover in the upcoming chapters, *fit* and finding *right fit* are game changers, and there is no better time to focus on them than right now. Now is the time to boost engagement, inspiration, well-being, and meaning in the work we do. Now is the time to increase the value of work for ourselves and our organizations. Now is the time to level the playing field and balance the power held in the choice of where we work, how we spend our days, and why we stay. Now is the time to make work feel less like work. Now is the time to find *right fit*.

Let's begin.

PART 1

CONTEXT

+

RIGHT FIT

CHAPTER 1

How the Workplace Has Changed

REAL STORIES OF FIT
A Wrong Fit Story
26, female, consumer goods company

First experiences at work can shape us in ways we cannot even imagine. When they are good, our careers accelerate at hyper speed, and when they go wrong, it can be physically, mentally, and emotionally debilitating. When I asked this interviewee what *wrong fit* felt like, she responded immediately with "terrible." She then went on to offer, "I am not a person who struggles with mental health or depression or anything, but I was genuinely depressed. I slept whenever I wasn't working. I would have panic attacks. I was so genuinely stressed all the time about everything and nothing. So, it [*wrong fit*] took like, all of me, pretty much."

When she described *wrong fit*, she said, "I didn't feel like I was set up to succeed. I didn't feel like they cared to onboard me. I was kind of just left to my own devices to figure stuff out." But, upon even more reflection, the talent said, "I really felt like I was watching or letting things happen at this company that were compromising my own values."

This was a common sentiment across many interviews, where the talent felt like the way the company worked or behaved did not make sense to them in subtle ways that were pervasive but not totally noticeable until the dissonance built up. And, the build-up impacted performance, mental health, and their relationships. This interviewee said, "I couldn't even enjoy time with my family. I just felt bad about everything." The advice from this talent, who was just starting out on her career journey when *wrong fit* hit, is to "trust your gut. I think that we all have feelings about stuff, and they are usually right. But, we need to trust those feelings a bit more than we do, even when we have no tangible information backing them up."

When we fit, we know it. We feel it in our bones. We see it in the quality of our work product. And, we hear it in the energy and excitement that echoes in our offices and meeting rooms. The better the fit, the more value can be created for talent, for companies, and for the world. With those motivating factors in mind, everyone, talent and companies alike, should be striving for *right fit*. So why does it seem like *wrong fit* is more the norm?

In an article published by the *New Yorker* in 2021, Cal Newport shared stories of career downsizing and company jumping due at least in part to a reassessment by knowledge workers of what matters.[1] Around the same time, the Future Forum surveyed over 10,000 knowledge workers and found a prevailing disconnect between company's post-pandemic workplace policies and employee preferences.[2] Articles like these, focusing on the state of the relationship between companies and talent, do not paint a rosy picture. Conflicting wants, needs, and priorities seem to be the critique du jour.

With *wrong fit* dynamics dominating the workplace landscape in our psyches, the big question is how do we find the *right fit*? Before we tackle that, though, we need to first get the lay of the land and how we arrived in this place. In this chapter, we'll discuss the current state of the job market (bad) and how it affects the talent swimming around in it (worse). We'll then explore the seven trends that have helped set the stage for this moment of misalignment, where finding *right fit* has become an epic and arduous journey. Lastly, we'll connect the dots and break down what the trends tell us and the questions we should really be asking.

A Talent Market in Flux

As mentioned in the Introduction, *right fit* is a deep and authentic connection to how a company works day-to-day. Companies searching for talent and talent looking for a place to thrive are both struggling. Finding *right fit* is *hard*. Painfully hard. In one Harris Poll, over 63% of those surveyed reported their job search lasting for as long as six months.[3] Further, according to a survey by the recruiting platform Jobvite, approximately 30% of new joiners leave their job in the first ninety days.[4]

Meanwhile, companies are maneuvering through a talent market that is riddled with complexity from quiet quitting to wavering dedication and engagement to struggles in creating a work environment that is attractive to both their current ranks and future recruits. In a recent study by Braintrust, the average company is hiring for sixty-six knowledge worker jobs with one-half of the roles taking thirty-plus days to hire.[5] That translates to the equivalent of three cumulative years spent recruiting talent that needs to be hired now.

For companies to continue to have impact, they need to be staffed with talent who are capable, committed, and connected to both why the world is better with the company in it and how the company works day-to-day. That symmetry isn't happening fluidly or easily today. In this chapter, we explore the *why* in more depth by examining key trends that have shaped the job market, talent's perception of what a great company is, and companies' imperfect approach to acquiring the future talent they need.

Where Is Everyone?

With the ever-increasing movement of talent due to the Great Resignation, the fear of commiting to companies prone to short-term-focused mass layoffs, and shifting models of work, we can expect that talent will continue to be on the move with greater regularity. As we look at the talent movement in 2022, 77% of talent that resign do so in the first three years, with 45% resigning within one year.[6] The reasons most cited for these moves are vast but fall into a few main categories, including career (opportunities for growth and achievement), job (availability of resources, training, expectations, stress), and work/life balance (schedule, commute, work policies).[7] One thing is abundantly clear: employees are becoming more discerning in terms of the aspirations they have for the places they work and less willing to compromise.

Even if talent decides to stay, in a recent survey of over 2000 US employees who had been in their role for less than six months, researchers from Lattice found that over half of them were actively looking for something new.[8] That figure is astounding, considering conventional "career management" advice argues that talent should stay at a job for at least two years before changing employers.

What does all of this add up to? There is something happening inside organizations that is jarring to talent, putting them in a place where they are questioning their choice—and whatever it is, it is bad enough that many stay actively on the job search even when firmly settled in their company. It might be that everyone is just keeping their plan B at the ready, but it feels bigger than that, like something more pervasive is occurring.

For instance, if we move beyond new joiners, many others are eyeing the door as well. The Bureau of Labor Statistics reported that in March of 2022, total quits (voluntary separations across the US) reached a high of 4.5 million, with especially notable increases occurring for highly tenured employees and women.[9] So, it's not just new joiners that are finding less fit with their companies; many others are questioning their choice to remain where they are. Fascinatingly, even if a worker experiencing *wrong fit* has not left their current job, there is a good chance they will, or if they stay, they will be less productive. In 2020, PwC estimated that 65% of employees were looking for a new job,[10] and Gallup estimated that businesses lost $7.8 trillion of productivity due to actively disengaged employees.[11]

So, the race for commitment and dedication starts with a daunting uphill climb that has left many organizations unsure of how to retain their talent, and it has left many talent uninspired by the shifts being made. More and more talent are actively asking the question, "Does my company work the way I like (need) to work?" And with that question, more companies are left wondering, "Can we build an experience where talent (who works the way we work) will stay?"

Unfortunately, both talent and companies are defaulting to a belief that the days of the twenty-year career at a single company are waning and that movement across companies will be the norm. My belief is that this might be the norm now, but it doesn't have to be our future path. At our core as human beings, we want to be a part of a community and be committed to something bigger than ourselves. We want to belong. Further, we are looking for businesses to be a source of belonging, as shown in the 2023 Edelman Trust Barometer, where businesses are reported to be the most trusted institutions, with expectations for them to help solve our societal issues.[12]

So, what's standing in our way?

The Trends

Most conversations about company culture, engagement, or the future of work begin with the rise of COVID-19 as the primary source of the disruption. However, COVID-19 was not the cause of our current struggles; it was a great accelerator of trends that had been bubbling for some time—trends that are pushing us into this crisis of commitment we find ourselves in. Before we get into how to create *right fit* by choosing companies with more precision or building companies where the *right fit* talent will want to come and stay for their career, we need to understand a bit more about how we got here. There are a few trends that play a part in how both talent and companies currently view the world.

Trend #1: The Rise of the Culture Deck

In 2009, Patti McCord, the then Chief Human Resources Officer (CHRO) of Netflix, created a presentation that powerfully displayed a relatively new and compelling employee experience called the culture deck. It was filled with poetry, powerful visuals, and a promise to employees that was as progressive as it was enticing.[13] Though the deck was likely part reality and part aspiration, when Netflix released it to the world, it set in motion an era of employee experience marketing that widened the gap between how we talked about our companies' ways of working and the actual reality of their day-to-day.

Netflix's original intent of the culture deck was to create a playbook for how the company worked and provide talent a preview of what to expect upon arriving there. In 2013, Sheryl Sandburg referred to Netflix's culture deck as the "most important document to come out of Silicon Valley."[14] At the time, Sheryl, like many, saw it as the obituary of the big, bureaucratic company of old and a call for a new way of working, a new type of company. Not only did it influence the way we thought about work, but it also resulted in a movement toward highlighting an aspirational version of a company experience and creating big, bold, beautiful employee brands that rivaled that of their products. From Netflix's original deck, this practice of poetically describing culture spread across Silicon Valley and into nearly every major company around the world.

TALENT INSIGHT
Make sure you take what's on career websites and in culture decks with a grain of salt. Those assets are largely aspirational.

COMPANY INSIGHT
Beware of overpromising and under-delivering around culture. Your career sites set expectations, and the more the day-to-day veers from them, the less talent will show up for you.

However, these decks, like social media in general, had unintended and largely unseen impacts. These brand campaigns made culture aspirational and the day-to-day climate less and less of a priority. We began talking more about who we aspire to be than focusing on how work was actually getting done. We began to see the rise of recruiters who are expert marketers, CHROs and Chief Talent Officers spending time on the speakers' circuit, and companies whose reality began to veer from the ideal they aspired toward.

I have had the opportunity to work with many founder-led and privately held companies over the course of my career, and I remember discussing this point with an owner who ran a highly engaged, principle-driven company. When I asked them why they don't invest more in telling people how great the company is, they said, "The moment you start talking about the company is the same moment you lose focus on becoming a better one. We do; we don't talk." Unfortunately, with the rise of culture decks, we have become more adept at the talking than the doing.

Trend #2: The Ping Pong Table of Purposeless Perks

Alongside the rise of the culture deck was another phenomenon: the revival of the ping pong table. Now, I grew up with a ping pong table in my home in the Ozark Mountains, and there's no better way to pass time, laugh, compete, release stress, and build a little camaraderie.

However, as the ping pong table found its way into the halls of our offices, something else started to happen. Companies began revamping their perks, places, and bells and whistles to make the employee experience more enticing. Many made their spaces beautiful, carved out snack bars and hip cafés, provided apps for everything from meditation to learning on the go, extended benefits, curated more social gatherings, and aimed to make the workplace more akin to a shopping mall or an amusement park than a place of employment. This movement was an attempt to brighten up the dismal "coma-inducing cubical" landscape of the '90s and entice the next-generation worker to the office, provide them distractions, encourage them to stay at work longer, and hopefully inspire higher levels of creativity and innovation.

> **TALENT INSIGHT**
> Beware of the power of perks. Most extrinsic motivation tools (pay, perks, place) become less important every day you have them. Try to focus more on the work you will do and how it will get done.

> **COMPANY INSIGHT**
> Provide for your talent. Create an experience that is engaging, but use your assets to reinforce your purpose, how you have impact, and what you value. That will net you committed talent who are a genuine community as opposed to talent who are simply consuming your company.

Now, don't get me wrong, there are many arguments to be made that innovative office design and carefully crafted perks (healthy food, gyms, ergonomic desks, informal community space, etc.) can reduce stress and increase productivity. And some, like additional parental leave and tuition reimbursement, make society net better off. However, as more and more campus or office perks emerged, the message became less about purposeful connection to the company, the stakeholder, or societal impact and more about buying talent's commitment and engagement. For all of the money spent in these arenas, employee engagement has stayed constant or dipped over the last decade (see Figure 1.1).[15]

As the cycle to entice talent continued, talent grew to hold a consumer mentality around their companies. They learned to expect more—more perks, more offerings, more excitement. As companies attempted to satiate talent's expectations to be surrounded by perks, many became disconnected from what matters in their company. Even if a company held fast and didn't make widespread changes to their offices, they did scramble to differentiate along any number of perk categories, from pay to benefits to more development to elevated titles or more flexibility. The race to impress talent was on, and clarity about what actually matters was being clouded by more and more stuff.

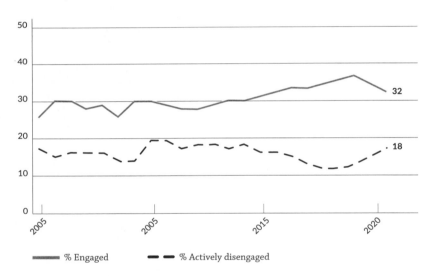

Figure 1.1: US Employee Engagement Trend, Annual Averages
Source: Jim Harter, "U.S. Employee Engagement Needs a Rebound in 2023," Gallup, January 25, 2023. gallup.com/workplace/468233/employee-engagement-needs-rebound-2023.aspx#:~:text=Story%20 Highlights&text=After%20trending%20up%20in%20recent,2020%20to%2034%25%20in%202021.

Trend #3: The Decade of Decedent Growth

According to the Center for Budget and Policy Priorities, 2009 to 2020 marked the longest economic expansion in the last eighty years, totaling 129 months.[16] This time was marked by unprecedented levels of cash, public and private investment, start-up creation, and growth of companies big and small. The S&P 500 was at 919 in March of 2009 and is, as of the writing of this book (even after the recent economic retraction of 2022/2023), at 4,158.[17] This was a time of great innovation, especially in the technology space, but it was also relatively easy to expand, given the favorable economic conditions, including low interest rates and stable consumer spending.

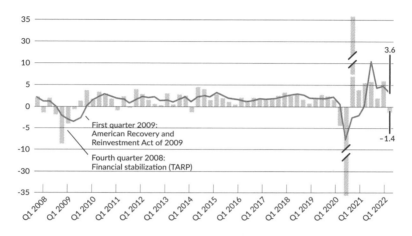

Figure 1.2: A Decade of Growth

Source: Center on Budget and Policy Priorities. "Chart Book: Tracking the Post-Great Recession Economy." Center on Budget and Policy Priorities. Updated May 27, 2022. https://www.cbpp.org/research /economy/tracking-the-post-great-recession-economy.

So, leading companies across industries saw healthy returns year after year that exceeded expectations and allowed them to invest, creating even greater opportunity and broader reach.

However, growth puts pressure on culture. When growth is that consistent over that long of a period, invariably ways of working and leadership habits are formed that don't help in tougher times. Companies learned how to hire at a greater rate of speed but lost the muscle of deep assessment of values and skills. Leadership learned to tell glowing stories of success but lost the ability to help their talent continually grow faster than the company. Businesses learned how to invest in innovation and technology advance-

TALENT INSIGHT

What are the knowledge, skills, and mindsets you need to strengthen to ensure you are ready to lead during more turbulent times?

COMPANY INSIGHT

How can you reorient all of your people to "how the company makes money" and focus more energy on the areas that matter most?

ment but lost much of their ability to drive focused, effective execution in the service of the consumer and the mission. The net impact is that many of the muscles we need in more uncertain and dynamic times are not readily available, as we did not stay vigilant in building companies that are as good at execution as they are at expansive growth. One obvious symptom of a larger problem are the proliferation of meetings during the COVID-19 pandemic and the rash of recent layoffs in tech in late 2022/early 2023 due to "over hiring."

Trend #4: A Crisis of Commitment (Or Lack of It)

In 2021, Pete Davis wrote one of my favorite books of late, called *Dedication: The Case for Commitment in an Age of Infinite Browsing*. In it, he makes the case that with all of the abundance that surrounds us, we have entered into a constant state of infinite browsing where we strive to "keep our options open"[18] over "the option to choose to dedicate ourselves to particular causes and crafts, places and communities, professions and people."[19] He ends the book arguing that dedication is the medicine the world needs and provides us all an invitation to transform the "vacant lot of life into a lush garden . . . place by place, cause by cause, craft by craft, person by person."[20]

This pursuit of dedication struck me as both tilting at windmills and the greatest challenge of our time. The easiest thing to do is to dip a toe into something, try things on but never purchase, put your hand halfway up in the hopes you don't get called, or love something until something better comes along. Heck, I have been that person myself a few times, attracted by what could be or what might be waiting around the bend.

Rarely is the new thing universally better, because life is life and companies are, well, companies. With that said, movements like the Great Resignation are fueled by real dissatisfaction with the way work feels and real hope that there are bigger and better

> **TALENT INSIGHT**
> Reflect on what it would take for you to stay at your company for the next ten years. What would need to be true for you? What stands in the way of you fully committing?

> **COMPANY INSIGHT**
> Employees want to know the company is betting on them long-term and that there are progressive experiences on the horizon. How can you invest more time in the progression of your current talent versus using the blunt instrument of hiring to close capability or skills gaps? How could you embed the potential career path in every job advertisement? Or, how could you create the equivalent of a twenty-year job description?

opportunities awaiting us in the future. In essence, talent is seeing a clear opportunity to improve their situation. According to research conducted in 2021, for many, it worked—but not for all. Among college graduates, only about one-half improved their situation on any of those three factors.[21] So, the grass may not be greener. And, because many were able to work remotely for the first time in their lives and found even more access to more places, I fear infinite browsing will get worse before it gets better.

Trend #5: The Side Hustle Economy

The counterpart to dedication is the idea that variety is the spice of life. If you look at the year just before the COVID-19 pandemic hit, even with a strong economy, 46% of Americans took on a side hustle to cover their monthly budget.[22] Gig economy companies such as Uber, Instacart, DoorDash, Task Rabbit, Upwork, and Fiverr beg people to put their extra time and creative energy into something other than the company they work for—as the companies are neither paying talent enough to survive nor recognizing their diverse skills in a way that pulls them closer to the company as opposed to pushing them further away. As a CLO (Chief Learning Officer) and Chief Talent Officer, the rise of the "side hustle" economy is fascinating and something our largest companies and biggest brands have yet to fully comprehend or embrace as a source of inspiration and innovation.

Back in the day when knowledge workers could survive (or thrive) on the salary they made in their company, idle "work" time was spent thinking about how to be better, help the company do more, or find a solution to a problem that had been nagging your team. That's because, for the most part, a knowledge worker's job covered the costs of our lives, provided us with a sense of purpose, and gave us a certain amount of security. So, in return, we gave more of our "work" time and creative energy to our company. As the reciprocal relationship between talent and the company

> **TALENT INSIGHT**
> Many of us feel constrained in our current roles, like we're being asked to be a narrowed version of ourselves. So, our creative energy flows to other places. What would you need in order to give more of your creative energy (not more time) to your company?

> **COMPANY INSIGHT**
> How could you reimagine the financial opportunities available to your talent? How could you provide more financial security, create opportunities for talent to explore other passions, and make side hustles a net benefit for both the company and talent?

waned, and our 9-to-5 jobs failed to fully meet our financial aspirations, idle "work" time and discretionary effort were pointed to areas that could be accretive to the livelihood of talent. Thus, the side hustle.

With the side hustle economy, dedication has become diluted. Our time, energy, and creative juices are now flowing to other things, other places, and other financial opportunities. One might argue that formal employers are, now more than ever, getting the rest of us, not the best of us.

Trend #6: Being More versus Doing More

With any major traumatic event, either at the individual or societal level, we reevaluate who we are, what we want, and how we are moving through the world. The events over the last few years have allowed words like purpose, meaning, and worth to enter into our workplace vernacular in a way that has never before been seen in business, as reported in *Forbes*.[23] Companies are asking the question, "Why is the world better with us in it?" and talent are asking, "Does what I am doing matter?" These are big, existential questions that are both difficult to answer and impossible to ignore. They are creating a short-term dissonance as we reexamine how we are spending our days and whether the amount of energy we are investing is worth the value being created. As shown in the aforementioned article by *Forbes*, a stronger sense of purpose and meaning is becoming more important as a lever for consumer loyalty and is paying dividends to companies and leaders who embrace its importance. Higher levels of physical health, more consistent company growth, and a sense of work feeling more meaningful are just a few of the benefits noted.[24]

> **TALENT INSIGHT**
> Examine how you are currently spending your days in and out of work. What activities are getting the majority of your time and energy? Are these the activities that provide you a boost, inspire you to be better, or allow you to practice your craft? What if you found 10% more time to be more inspired?

> **COMPANY INSIGHT**
> If you could reduce administrative tasks by 10%–20%, it would free up time and mental capacity to solve bigger problems and create bolder innovations. Time is finite, so point as much of your talent's time to what matters most.

A great example of this is the recent article citing the 95,000 hours of meetings that Shopify has removed from the calendars of their employees to create more time for them to be "makers" and create more meaning for themselves and their company.[25] Another article from 2017 studied the time use of the typical knowledge worker and found that 41% of tasks don't add value, and two-thirds of the day is spent either in desk work (mostly administrative) or managing across the organization.[26] (See Figure 1.2.)

Much of what knowledge workers are doing at work does not have a strong connection to their purpose or to that of their company. The more time we spend on non-value-added tasks or administrative duties that don't have a clear link to our success or that of the company, the more we can feel burdened by them and experience a drop in our energy or engagement over time. Though we are supremely busy and have full lives with many responsibilities and stressors where burnout is ever-increasing, the answer might not be simply to do less. It might be to better connect all the things we do to a higher purpose.

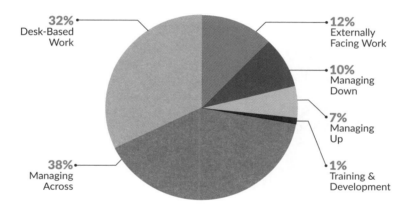

Figure 1.3: Time Spent on Activities at Work
Source: Julian Birkinshaw and Jordan Cohen, "Making Time for Work that Matters," *Harvard Business Review* (September 2013). https://hbr.org/2013/09/make-time-for-the-work-that-matters.

If you examine the greatest craftspeople in any field—athletics, art, business, politics, etc.—they are not bound by a lack of energy; rather, it is the opposite phenomenon. They are obsessed and seemingly cannot rest until they have created, designed, or brought to life something new, different, better, or more meaningful. This is due, at least in part, to the motivational process of inspiration. As I state in an article for *Dialogue Review*, "Derived from the Latin inspirare, 'to breathe in,' inspiration is quite literally the motivational process by which someone absorbs the creative energy or insight of one object or experience and uses it to bring something new, different, better, or more meaningful into the world."[27] When we are inspired, we have a nearly insatiable energy to create. When we see purpose in our daily activities, they feel less daunting and more meaningful.

Trend #7: Peripheral Proximity and Hybrid Working

The last trend encompasses many of the ones above but is important to note. Our definition of proximity and place when it comes to our relationship with our companies is changing. In a 2022 report, McKinsey notes that 25% of workers in advanced economies and about 10% percent of workers in emerging economies could work from home three to five days a week.[28] That is four to five times the pre-pandemic levels.[29] This shift will reduce the need for mass transit, alter the make-up and density of our urban core, and allow talent that has been previously limited to compete for more jobs in more locations.

Additionally, the nature of work within those jobs that require proximity is also shifting. Retail spaces are moving to digital, restaurants are opening ghost kitchens and shipping meals longer distances, and big box retailers are opening smaller formats and creating more autonomy in scheduling/work relationships. The most technologically progressive companies are creating a "work from anywhere" model (Spotify, 3M, and Airbnb) or condensing campuses to fewer, more collaborative spaces.

In a 2022 study, Zippia estimated that 74% of US companies plan to implement a hybrid model moving forward.[30] Interestingly, nearly 60% of construction company Gesler's 2,300 office building projects have started in the last year, telling us companies are still planning to have physical centers, but the utility and flow of them is changing to be more meeting spaces and hot desks versus permanent offices and assigned cubes.[31] And we're still at the beginning of understanding this trend and how our spaces will evolve. I hope they go in the direction of purpose and multi-use spaces that pull in both talent and consumers in cool and unique ways where physical proximity aids the experience. Need to solve a big problem collaboratively? Head to the office. Want to see, hear, and speak with consumers? Jump in your car and go to the office. Want to learn, grow, and develop? Head on in. Want to get to know your coworkers on a deeper level and build trust? Meet up at the office.

Moving Beyond Framing the Problem

As we consider the above trends, a picture starts to emerge for companies and for talent—one where reciprocity, trust, and commitment are under pressure as each party tries to fulfill its needs. This dynamic has left many in a *wrong fit* experience where the world makes a little less sense than it should and where doing good work is as fleeting as the feeling of being in a truly engaged culture. This makes sense when you consider that culture is simply the combination of all of our behaviors, what each of us chooses to do every day, both leaders and their teams. If we fit, we hum, we connect, we create momentum and produce work with grace and ease. It is akin to the feeling you have when you walk out of the door in your favorite pair of shoes or outfit—empowered, energized, confident. When we don't, we get frustrated, burnt out, disengaged, or unproductive.

There is a way through this time that is less about change and more about leaning into the idea that there is someone and somewhere for everyone. Instead of taking a job because we revere a brand or trying to change our cultures, spaces, and ways of working to be inviting to everyone equally, maybe there is another way, helping like-minded people and companies to find each other. Now, this is not to say we should stop working on our culture, refining our day-to-day experience or evolving the way we work to meet the demands of the market. We should always seek to be better, and there are plenty of culture books out there that can help.

In the meantime, I have come to believe that we should accept a bit more fully who we are, right now, both as individuals and companies. There are many wonderful companies out there and they are, in the ways that they work, more distinct than they are duplicative. In honor of that truth, we should look toward how we work to tell us a bit more about what we believe and what is valued.

If you're talent, maybe it's time to start searching for a place you can love day-to-day in balance with searching for a position you can do or a brand you revere. And, if you're a leader in a company, maybe it's time to reevaluate who the company truly is and create an experience that fits those who "love what we love" as opposed to either allowing many cultures to exist under one umbrella or trying to create a place where everyone can be, on average, not unhappy.

The following chapters attempt to help you learn how to do both those things with a bit more intent, by asking talent to see the perspective of companies and companies to better appreciate the hopes and desires talent have when it comes to *right fit*. My hope is that, in doing so, we will all see a boost to engagement, inspiration, well-being, and meaning in our lives and a greater return for our shareholders and customers. After all, they're the ones who allow us to be employed in the first place, right?

So how do we find the *right fit*? The trends leave us with some significant questions that I will list here.

- How can talent and companies alike more authentically convey who they are and how it feels to work with them? What would a more authentic view of culture look like?
- How can companies attract talent based on the power of their brand AND who they are, how they work, and why the world is better with them in it?
- How can companies work smarter by reducing the administrative load on talent and ensuring that more of our moments at work are meaningful?
- How do we create a relationship between talent and companies that focuses on making the twenty-year career possible if not probable?
- How can we get more creative energy from our talent without asking them to sacrifice more of their life?
- How do companies get clearer and more consistent about how they work when they are at their best so talent knows how to show up every day?
- How do companies help more talent find right fit more often with less effort?

We will look to answer these questions throughout the rest of the book.

REAL STORIES OF FIT
A Right Fit Story
38, female, management consulting

I'd bet Voltaire didn't know he would become a prophet for *right fit* when a line from his poem, *La Bégueule*, was translated as "perfect is the enemy of good." You see, *right fit* does not mean perfect fit. It simply means that on more attributes than not, the day-to-day experience we have fits who we are and what we need to practice our craft. This point was a central feature in our interview with a communications expert who is now a management consultant. She describes herself as a corporate newbie, as she only entered the corporate world in 2013. However, after interviewing her, it's apparent that she's no novice. She is a seasoned corporate expert who has spent a significant amount of time considering who she is and what she values.

When thinking about a *right fit* experience, she described it as a combination of "feeling the momentum of moving something forward every day" and "good vibes." The latter point was important to her, as she noted that in a *right fit* experience, she felt like she was working with "cool people in a place where I could spend some time." She was careful not to mistake work feeling good with her being able to bring all of herself to work. "The whole 'bring your full self to work' or whatever is total bullshi—. I have never been my full self anywhere. I want to be able to show up and practice my craft in the unique way that I do it. That is all I need."

She has three factors she considers important in achieving *right fit* but admitted that they "don't have to all be there all the time. Two out of three is fine." One, the work must be work she really cares about. Two, the people she works with must be very intelligent and accountable. Three, the people must also be "cool" and be people she enjoys having a relationship with and learning from. She believes it is almost impossible to find any one company where all of her pillars are met at all times. And for her, this is okay. She understands trade-offs must be made.

CHAPTER 2

Why *Right Fit* Is So Rare

REAL STORIES OF FIT
A Wrong Fit Story
52, female, human resources

When you stop to think about it, life is impossibly short. In our more honest moments, we are all worried about the ticking clock of time. This is especially true at work, as it's the one thing that pulls us out of our life commitments (family, friends, community, passions, etc.) and into a world that is often our greatest source of stress. After a long career at a consumer goods company, this interviewee spoke openly about her *wrong fit* experience, starting the conversation by telling me that she "felt like a boiling frog," as if she was losing her sense of self in "little ways across many days" until she realized she was not a fit for the company and the company did not fit her.

She said she could now admit that she didn't do the work to really understand the nature of the company and the recipe for success. She offered, "It is a bit of an ego thing. I was flattered. They wanted me. It was a bigger role and a VP title. And, because I was the major breadwinner in the family, I couldn't just leave. But, I saw that things were off early and just tried to ignore it." The interviewee went on to talk about how she got more and more determined as she realized *fit* was not there. She thought, "I could change things. I could make it better," but in the end, it was just too hard. What the company needed her to be and become was too far from who she was, so she left and is still working through the trauma she experienced while there.

Her advice to others was spot on. She said, "A career is one of the most 'high-investment' decisions we will make in our lives. The choice has real implications and ripple effects on your partner, kids, friends, and family. Yet, we spend more time mulling over the choice of which air fryer we will buy than what job we will take or company we will join." She advised talent to go beyond the pros and cons list and think about how your life would change if the job went right and if it went wrong. If the stakes are high, then be even more careful.

The average talent will spend 113,880 hours at work during their life-time.[1] That number is the equivalent of thirteen years of our lives, and it represents the second biggest expenditure of time, behind only sleep.[2] When companies or talent question why it might be important to find purpose, satisfaction, or *right fit* in one's chosen career, I give them that sta-tistic. Embedded in it is the important role that companies have in ensuring we, as adults, are healthy and happy and have a general sense of well-being. I always thought in my lifetime we would see a company with the employee brand of "Work here, and you'll walk out healthier." I still believe that will happen, either by proactive choice or because we will all see what I see, that we spend most of our adult lives at work.

How we feel at work is integral to our overall happiness. According to Bronnie Ware, a palliative nurse and best-selling author of the book *The Top Five Regrets of the Dying: A Life Transformed by the Dearly Departing*, the biggest regrets are all focused on disappointing the ideal self, or the person we are when we are happiest or most engaged.[3] Though a person might not feel the pain of letting down their ideal self in the moment, the more time spent in work experiences trying to fit in versus being in a place and a role that has *right fit*, the more apt a person is to feel unfulfilled, disengaged, or uninspired. In every sense possible, our lives and happiness depend on how we feel at work, and as goes our happiness, so does the company's livelihood.

With that in mind, this chapter will attempt to explore the idea of fit a bit more deeply by examining why and how *right fit* is a reciprocal need between the company and talent. First, a bit more color will be provided around how *right fit* and *wrong fit* feels to the talent interviewed in the study for this book. Then, the impact of *wrong fit* on both talent and com-panies will be explored by diving deeper into the current state of work and where there are opportunities to improve it. Finally, the chapter will end with a deep dive into the psychological barriers that make *right fit* difficult to find and retain.

How Fit Actually Feels

During each of the interviews, talent were asked to share how *right fit* or *wrong fit* felt when they were in it. The visceral emotion and colorful descriptions provided were astonishing. Regardless of which experience they described, our interviewees were still holding on to the emotion of it, even if the experience was years or decades in the past. These emotional states stayed with them, either because they longed to have them again (*right fit*) or still feel the pain and regret of a low point in their career (*wrong fit*). Figure 2.1 is a table that sums up some of the most colorful quotes on how fit feels.

SO, WHAT DOES "FIT" MEAN, REALLY . . .

Right Fit	*Wrong Fit*
"I didn´t worry about the clothes he was wearing, that relationships formed faster; I felt more comfortable more days and I laughed early on."	"I felt like I was on a Ferris wheel. The work never ended and didn't really feel like we were going anywhere."
"I could practice my craft. Period."	"It was impacting my relationships, my mental health. I just didn't want to go to work."
"You are putting in the hours, but it doesn´t feel like work."	
	"It was like being punched in the face every day in a different way."
"Felt like being excited to show up for work every day. It felt like home."	
	"Everyone has a secret decoder ring for success, except for me."
"I never had the 'Sunday Blues.'"	

Figure 2.1: *Right Fit* vs. *Wrong Fit* Interview Quote Samples

When the interviewees described *right fit*, they didn't speak about these experiences as times when they were happy, though that was an obvious outcome. They spoke about these experiences from a standpoint of feeling like they were making the best use of their time at work. Further, the interviewees talked a lot about this feeling of comfort or being at home—where they were putting in hours, solving big problems, and being challenged, but it didn't feel hard to get work done. They could practice their craft or do the things they could do really, really well. If we return back to the ideas from *The*

COMPANY INSIGHT
Wondering how to improve your employees' well-being? Well, it isn't another well-being training. Look at your company's work principles, practices, and platforms and ask if the way you work is making your employees healthier. If it isn't, employ some human-centered design to close the gap. To learn more, head over to Chapters 9 and 10.

Five Biggest Regrets of the Dying, our interviewees didn't feel a sense that the time spent was being wasted or a cause for any regret. They weren't disappointing their "ideal self."

If we compare these sentiments to *wrong fit*, the differences are staggering. First, the *wrong fit* experiences were emotionally even more raw, and it almost felt like the interviewees were still processing the impact of their *wrong fit* jobs. There was a profound sense that they had not yet fully resolved the "why" behind them, nor had they made peace with who they were or how they showed up when they were in them. *Wrong fit* experiences were still being sorted through and felt mysterious to most that talked about them. Nearly all of the interviewees commented that when they were in *wrong fit*, they lost confidence, weren't able to practice their craft, and felt more isolated and lonely than they ever had at work. One interviewee stated the feeling this way: "You feel bad. You feel like a prisoner who actually signed up to go to jail."

The State of Talent Today

The impact of *wrong fit* is no small thing. Let's consider again the $7.8 trillion[4] of lost productivity annually across the globe mentioned in the Introduction. My mind races with what those trillions of dollars represent. To put that number in context, it is nearly one-third of the annual GDP of the US,[5] almost twice the market cap of Apple, Google, and Amazon combined,[6] and twelve times the amount spent on college every year in the US.[7] And, this number doesn't account for the follow-on impacts on talent of carrying the regret and disappointment that surrounds *wrong fit* experiences. When I spoke to one of my interviewees, she described having a couple of *wrong fit* experiences in a row, and she wondered aloud, "Is there something wrong with me? Why does this keep happening?"

When talented employees are not allowed, not able, or not willing to do their best work, they cannot thrive at work or outside of it. The most innovative product ideas never make it off the "back of a napkin," technological and manufacturing advances are never fully debugged, branding and merchandising are unfinished and uninspiring, and operational processes remain unrefined and ineffective. The more insidious outcome is the compounding emotional effects of being in this state. According to interviewees, the longer a talent is in a *wrong fit* experience, the more they lose confidence, competence in their craft, and care for the purpose or mission of their company. Their "ideal self" erodes, so much so that many of the interviewees spoke of needing to shed behaviors they developed to survive and to rediscover the ones that made them great in the first place. They were, almost without knowing, speaking to the power of culture to shape our behaviors, our values, and our sense of self.

With $7.8 trillion of lost productivity globally, the number of employees who wake up every morning dreading turning on their computer or heading to work is staggering. They are not reaching their potential, showcasing their talents, or feeling like the time spent away from their families is worth anything more than a barely equitable paycheck. The end result? Nobody is truly winning.

Not only is talent not winning, but they are also barely able to summon the engagement to make it to the starting line. Our organizations are filled with individuals who are burned out, languishing, stressed, disengaged, uninspired, and often on the search for something better. In 2022, Gallup reported that engagement in the US saw its first decline in over a decade, with 32% of full- and part-time employees being engaged while 17% are actively disengaged.[8] Talent struggles in the modern workforce almost regardless of company, industry, region, or country. In January 2021, Adam Grant, a renowned organizational psychologist, coined the term languishing to describe the felt experience of the average employee during the last few years. By his definition, languishing is a "state of stagnation and emptiness."[9] It is not hopelessness, but rather a feeling of aimlessness or joylessness. Though this feeling might have been a shared experience for some, there were many who experienced a much more pervasive and damaging impact of working in their companies during this same timespan, downright misery.

In the 2021 annual Work and Well-Being Survey conducted by the American Psychological Association, 79% of employees had experienced work-related stress in the month before the survey, and nearly three in five employees reported negative impacts from that stress, including lack of interest, motivation, energy, or lack of effort.[10] Further, 36% reported cognitive weariness, 32% reported emotional exhaustion, and an astounding 44% reported physical fatigue—a 38% increase since 2019.[11] Now, some of this is absolutely due to the COVID-19 pandemic and the weight of the times we live in. But as we reach the "new normal," those numbers don't seem to be decreasing, which may signal a more permanent shift in either how we experience work or how our companies design it (or not, for that matter).

Interestingly, the World Health Organization has set a new definition of burnout as "a syndrome resulting from workplace stress that has not been successfully managed."[12] The WHO goes on to characterize burnout by three dimensions: feelings of energy depletion or exhaustion, increased mental distance or negative feelings about one's job, and reduced professional efficacy.[13] If the World Health Organization is leaning in, it is time to take the epidemic of burnout seriously.

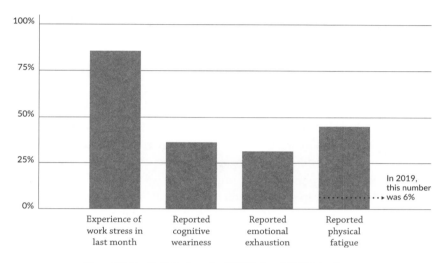

Figure 2.2: Key Statistics from the APA Work and Well-Being Survey
Source: Ashley Abramson, "Burnout and Stress Are Everywhere," *American Psychological Association Monitor* (January 1, 2022). https://www.apa.org/monitor/2022/01/special-burnout-stress.

Broadly, from the talent's standpoint, companies have not yet been able to create environments that allow their talent to survive, let alone thrive. This isn't due to a lack of trying; on average, companies have invested more and more into the environment at work. However, the investments have not paid off. Let's start with the simple fact that the most expensive element of running a business is labor. Depending on how you parse out the cost of labor (hiring, wages, bonuses, benefits, facilities, etc.), the total can add up to over 70% of an operating budget,[14] by far the biggest consistent investment a company makes. Further, during the recent pandemic, one study showed that 88% of companies made significant changes to their benefits packages,[15] while another showed 90% of employers increased their spend in wellness programs.[16]

In some stellar research on earnings calls during 2020, Gartner found that talent investments in the form of benefits spending increased five times versus years prior.[17] Adding further validity to Gartner's findings, Paychex's 2022 survey of CHROs found that, on average, companies have increased benefits by over 22% when compared to pre-pandemic levels.[18]

Talent in the modern company is struggling to find meaning, stay resilient, and remain committed to the companies they have joined—they are looking for something else, something that is less about hygiene factors and external motivators. And, companies have responded by spending more than ever before on their employees and their experience. However, something is missing as companies are struggling to turn those investments into a better, more engaging environment. In other words, they are unable to turn those investments into more and more consistent *right fit* experiences for talent. So, what do we do?

The Psychological Barriers to Fit

We should start by looking at the psychology behind fit. Though companies are investing more and more in their employees, increasing talent's engagement has proved an elusive goal. Likewise, talent desperately wants *right fit*, but those experiences feel impossibly hard to find and retain. This disconnect is caused, in part, by aspects of our own hardwiring that make finding fit more difficult. You see, our brain is a complex system that has impacted evolutionary survival instincts, external influences, and our own internal struggle between what we want and what might be best for us. There are three concepts that are worth exploring in regard to our search for and struggle to find *right fit*: cognitive dissonance, BIRG-ing, and approach/avoidance systems.

Cognitive Dissonance and Fit

A familiar but not well-understood psychological concept called *cognitive dissonance* (the discomfort of making a choice or acting in a manner that is incongruent with one's stated values, opinions, or preferences) helps to explain the gap between what talent wants or expects, what organizations are providing, and the $7.8 trillion of lost productivity that is the result.

On an individual level, cognitive dissonance occurs when our perceptions of ourselves (who we are, what we value, what we are capable of, and how we show up in the world) don't match a decision we made or a way that we show up in a given moment. The

> **TALENT INSIGHT**
>
> If you wonder how finding productivity benefits you, think about having 20%–30% more of your day spent in meaningful work that has you practicing your craft or contributing in ways that fulfill you. Don't know what fulfills you? Check out the Fit Excursions in Chapter 4.

resulting feeling of unease, uncertainty, or regret is the dissonance between what we did or decided in the moment versus what we would do or decide when we are at our best. Cognitive dissonance can help us get more in tune with how our choices reflect our beliefs and values. However, severe cognitive dissonance can motivate us to change our beliefs or choices by settling into an environment that might not be healthy for us. In other words, we will resolve the conflict by shifting what we want or what we believe we deserve. Historically, cognitive dissonance research has focused on the individual, but the emerging concept of *collective cognitive dissonance* argues that if the voiced promise or aspiration (i.e., espoused values and culture for a company) of an organization or group is at odds with the day-to-day reality that is experienced (i.e., the day-to-day environment created), a whole group can feel anxiety, frustration, or fear.[19]

> **TALENT INSIGHT**
> Deep reflection about our choices before we make them is vital to diminishing cognitive dissonance and potential *wrong fit*. A strategy for doing this is to try on the choice. Begin sharing the choice you are planning to make with friends or family and pay attention to how you feel. If there is hesitation, doubt, or anxiety as you share, mine that, as there is likely something not lining up.

Cognitive dissonance is important to fit. Paying attention to it can help us make smarter decisions at the moment of choice and help explain how and why it feels so damaging when we choose poorly. Cognitive dissonance is very much our "spidey sense," a way for us to tell, almost subconsciously, that something we are getting ready to do or choose doesn't line up. Recent studies using MRI scans of the brain have shown that cognitive dissonance activates the part of the brain where our "survival instinct" lies.[20] However, we often ignore this dissonance (more on that in a bit) or, in service of "fitting in," will change our preferences or behaviors to make something that doesn't fit work for us. Like, trying to make a *wrong fit* right.

Thus, we will choose to live with or manage cognitive dissonance because we create it knowingly, like when choosing chocolate cake for dessert over a more healthy alternative. Other times, that dissonance cannot be avoided due to constraints such as forced compliance, a lack of information, gaslighting, or the sunk cost in a decision already made.[21] Regardless of the reason, living with dissonance comes at a cost to our psychological well-being and mental health.[22] With that said, research has shown that if individuals are able to recognize the cognitive dissonance and the feeling is strong enough, a positive motivational state can be created where individuals show a higher intent to seek the behavior change needed to get back into alignment with core beliefs and values.[23] The takeaway is simple: cognitive dissonance may not feel good, but we should sit with it and pay attention to it because at some level it is our own subconscious telling us something isn't in alignment.

Approach and Avoidance Systems

When we make choices in situations where our options are constrained, the information is murky, or the stakes are high, we often will feel that tinge of cognitive dissonance that something is off. That *something* could be low-level misalignment with values or beliefs, or it could be our *avoidance system*, the emotional response system that pays attention to the environment and whose sole purpose is to stop us from doing things that put us in danger, sending us often subtle and usually subconscious signals that we are in danger physically, mentally, emotionally, or some combination.

Interestingly, we don't always catch the cues or trust that nagging feeling in our gut. Sometimes, we enter into dangerous situations, stay in these moments instead of turning away from them, or we make choices that are detrimental to us in the long term. We choose to buy a product we don't need, stay in an unhealthy relationship that doesn't feed us, walk down a dark street at night by ourselves, or join/keep working at companies that don't fulfill us or fit how we work. So, why do we do this?

Well, one explanation is that there is another system that can dominate these moments: the *approach system*—or, the emotional processes that urge us to fulfill our deepest pleasure-based desires. This system plays to the base level of our being, wanting more of what makes us feel good. Sometimes, those "feel good" desires misalign with what we value or what is safe or good for us. This system is joy-seeking, ego-affirming, and out to satiate our wants and extract as much pleasure as possible from our surroundings. Remember the *wrong fit* story at the start of this chapter? The flattery of a bigger title, better pay, or more responsibilities plays to our egos and can activate this system very quickly, causing us to limit our view of the situation or make a choice that might bring pleasure now and pain later. If you have ever had dessert after a big meal and regretted it shortly after, say hello to your approach system.

Let's turn now to how this impacts *right fit*. In many of the top places to work, the power of the brand, the pull of beloved consumer products, the beautiful offices and abundant perks, and the potential wealth creation play directly to the approach system and make it nearly impossible for talent to see, let alone properly assess, *right fit*. So, talent can easily end up accepting jobs with companies that don't value what they value or want to work how they work. Discerning between excitement due to *right fit* versus excitement due to gaining riches and spoils can be subtle. BIRG-ing, the next concept we'll explore, can help explain why.

BIRG-ing and Fit

To better understand our attraction to successful brands and revered products in our decision-making about who to join, talent can look toward a well-studied area of social psychology called *BIRG-ing*,[24] or basking in reflected glory. A team of researchers led by Dr. Robert Cialdini studied this celebrity-and success-based form of indirect impression management, or our propensity to affiliate more readily with entities or individuals who are deemed successful. What they found is that we will use others' success to boost our own self-image (BIRG-ing) by connecting ourselves to their success, or, alternatively, distance ourselves from failure (CORF-ing, cutting off reflected failure).

> **TALENT INSIGHT**
> If you joined a company where you also are a consumer, that can create a powerful connection, but it could also cause you to remain in a job or within a company that doesn't fit your goals or work style. The pull of the consumer brand is powerful, so make sure you pay attention to whether you're there because you like the product or because you actually like working at the company. If you want to explore further, head to the Fit Assessment and Chapter 6.

They researched this phenomenon by assessing students' reactions the day following a win or a loss by their football team. What they found was students tended to describe the game with "we" language and wear their team colors or logo after a win (BIRG-ing) and use "they" or wear unaffiliated clothes the day after the loss (CORF-ing). This research has extended well beyond sports and into areas such as political affiliations, parenting, and the workplace, with the most important point being that we will often be driven to build a strong connection or make a decision due in part to our subconscious impression management or indirect desire to look good.

The research on BIRG-ing shows that we will be drawn to align ourselves with teams, movements, and companies that appear to be successful or revered. So, the more powerful the consumer brand, the employee brand, or the number of "best place to" lists that a company is on, the more likely talent will be enticed to choose them regardless of what it's like to work there. As our interviewees noted, there was often a mismatch between the experience of being hired into the company and what it was like once they arrived, and that mismatch was rarely positive, a subject we will dive into deeply further in the book.

Finding Fit Versus Fitting In

An additional psychological factor can be found in the benign-sounding "fitting in." The end goal of any modern workplace must include creating a space where everyone who works there feels like they belong and can do their best work. We know from extensive research that higher levels of belonging have a significant impact on performance, with Harvard Business Review citing research that showed a 56% increase in performance and a 75% reduction in sick days, equating to a potential annual savings of more than $52M for a 10,000-person company.[25] In that same research, the authors shared an additional insight from EY's Belonging Barometer that over 40% of 1000 people surveyed felt isolated at work.[26] There is a clear upside to creating belonging, much like engagement, but the reality is severely lagging behind the promise.

COMPANY INSIGHT

Having a strong consumer brand can be the ultimate talent attraction mechanism. Just ask the likes of Apple, Google, Nike, Amazon, or Netflix. However, the consumer brand also sets an expectation for how it will feel to actually work for the company. If the day-to-day isn't great, the consumer brand will keep talent there for only so long. Want to learn more about what you can do? Head to Chapters 9 and 10.

Though there's a wide range of explanations for why a person might not feel a sense of belonging, ranging from work-related stress to unconscious bias and inequity, we'll take a page out of Dan Heath's book *Upstream: The Quest to Solve Problems before They Happen* and move on from examining the feeling people have in their workplaces. Instead, we'll take a closer look at how to solve this issue at the decision point to join or not join, to stay or go.[27]

From a talent perspective, fit is not about fitting in. It's not about materially altering one's perception of identity to be liked or seen or revered. Instead, it's about deeply knowing and exploring our own values, norms, and behaviors, then expertly comparing and contrasting them to those of the company before a shared commitment is made. The very definition of fit is "to be the right shape and size for." We try on jeans, test drive cars, and buy most products with a thirty-day satisfaction guarantee. Yet, we join companies based on a very narrow and curated set of interactions, knowing little about whether we fit and on what factors we align or not.

Talent almost never really sees, or peers deeply into, a company before they join it. And, companies rarely get a deep look at talent and how they might show up after the flattery of a job offer or newness of a new position have worn off. For all of our structured interviews, campus visits, and background research through references on Glassdoor, our ability to construct a pure and accurate view of the day-to-day life in a company is barely appreciated, let alone kept at the center of the process. That seems counterintuitive given we will spend an estimated 1932 hours at work annually, which equals the already mentioned 13 full years and two months[28] at our place of employment over our lifetimes. To put the lifetime number in context, we will, on average, spend about 328 total days socializing with friends, 3.7 years eating, and twenty-six years sleeping over that same period.[29]

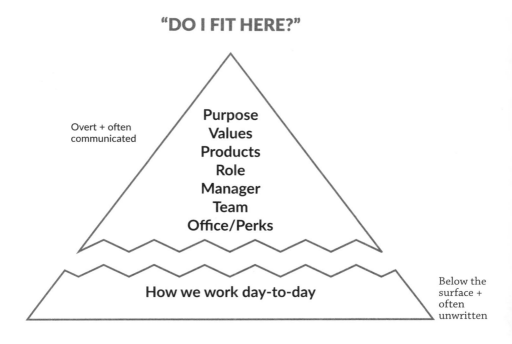

"DO I FIT HERE?"

Overt + often communicated

Purpose
Values
Products
Role
Manager
Team
Office/Perks

How we work day-to-day

Below the surface + often unwritten

Figure 2.3: The Elements of Fit

Fit matters, and working on fit might be the way we make real inroads in belonging, engagement, and the lost productivity in companies today. Social science has long held that once we join a group and feel a sense of connection or the signs that belonging is possible, we begin to value and conform more readily to the group's behaviors and norms. This conformity from a place of belonging is a human need and is rooted in our search for survival and protection and community. We choose to tighten our bonds with a group that holds shared norms, behaviors, rituals and values in return for security, safety, camaraderie, and affiliation. In a sense, we will give up just a little individuality to gain the benefit of being a part of something bigger than us.

When talent begins from a place of *right fit* or alignment with the company, success comes easy, and a person is more likely to seamlessly move and adjust with the needs or expectations of the company over time. However, when we land in a company where there is misalignment or *wrong fit*, we end up using our creative energy to "fit in" and in doing so are, almost daily, writing with our nondominant hand. We might still assimilate to the norms, values, and ways of working of the company, but the toll is additional stress, burnout, feelings of incompetence, and a lack of progression of one's respective craft.

Fit has many elements including purpose, values, craft, capability, manager, team, location of company, job description, and ways of working. But, it is the last item on that list that sits mostly out of sight until after a job begins, even though it accounts for the majority of our day-to-day experience.

So, as talent, how do you find *right fit*?

How do you avoid letting your surface-level desires or impressions of management drive your choices?

How do you avoid spending your thirteen years at work in a way that feels more meaningful than mediocre?

And, as a company, how do you build for *right fit* and get back some of the $7.8 trillion of lost productivity?

How can you use your status as a revered brand or beloved place to work to get the right talent, not talent that simply admires you the most?

The path is simple, and it starts with thinking through the following questions, many of which I'll try to help you answer through the remaining chapters.

Table 2.1: Fit Questions for Talent and Companies

AREA	QUESTION TO BE ANSWERED	TALENT PERSPECTIVE	COMPANY PERSPECTIVE
Interviewing	How do we interview differently to ensure a better fit?	How well does the company's/division's/team's way of working fit my values, beliefs, and skills?	How well does a potential talent fit our current "profile of success"?
Onboarding	How do we onboard to create a deeper dedication?	What do I need to shift, shed, strengthen, or start doing to be invaluable and fully engaged?	What do our new joiners need to see/know/do/feel so they can sustain success over the long term?
Performing	How do we sustain excellence and engagement over time?	Am I of craft or of company? How do I keep true to my reason for being here clear?	How do I better utilize the multiple skills of talent that have figured us out?
Transitioning	How do we maximize the value of a move?	How do I know when it is time to go and where I should head next?	How do we use transitions to re-recruit our talent to the company we are versus the one we were?
Transforming	How can we help create an even better future?	What can I do day-to-day to make my company better?	What can we do day-to-day to create the best place to work on earth?
Avoiding	How do you avoid the pitfalls, potholes, and purgatories of fitting in?	How do I know when joining up was actually me selling out?	How do you care for your employees without carelessly designing your orgs?

REAL STORIES OF FIT
A Right Fit Story
53, male, retail

There is no "perfect fit" company. If you're looking for a perfect fit, it's probably best to go out and create a company from scratch. However, there are companies that make sense more often than they don't. Sometimes, the ways of working are a pleasant surprise, as in the case of this interviewee.

The interviewee described *right fit* eloquently when he said, "You sing in the morning . . . you don't count your hours." Interestingly, his *right fit* experience was not automatic, as he came into the company from an acquisition. He offered, "I was looking at options outside of the new company but was asked to join a leadership seminar with fifteen leaders from the acquiring company, and over the course of the week, I found they had similar values, interesting backgrounds, and a way to work that felt very familiar." He then shared that this alleviated the cognitive dissonance he was feeling because "the culture that had been described to me is maybe not the culture that these leaders are experiencing or creating." In the end, this interviewee spent about five years at the acquired company, acknowledging that the fit was strong.

His hope for future recruitment processes is that everyone is "super transparent in the process." He said, "I don't want a happy candidate; I want to make a satisfied employee. So, if [a company] acquires [employees] based on great marketing, [the employees] will ultimately arrive and be dissatisfied. Maybe it is better to be super clear and super authentic up front."

PART 2

TALENT

+

RIGHT FIT

CHAPTER 3

Beginning the Search for *Right Fit*

REAL STORIES OF FIT
A Wrong Fit Story
45, female, digital retail

"It went terribly wrong on day four." This is how my interviewee started her *wrong fit* story. She said that the interview process in this purpose-driven company allowed her to "meet some great people who told me to turn down my other offer and save lives with us." After her first status meeting with her new boss, she knew in about the first fifteen minutes she had made the wrong choice. "I had relocated my family across the country, was excited about the mission of the company, and then had my first status with my boss . . . and I came face-to-face with how she worked. I knew it wouldn't work for me. I left there sobbing, realizing I made another horrible career move." This experience in *wrong fit* is pretty typical: as talent bumps into their new leaders, managers, and teammates' ways of working, they start to feel like something is off, like the company is somehow different than what they had pieced together during the interview process.

That moment of uncertainty is horribly stressful. Many new joiners made life-changing choices before taking the job, including moving to a new city, foregoing equity at a previous company, or letting go of networks that were strong and track records of success that allowed them to be seen and valued. Thus, the stress of the decision builds very fast, and within a few short weeks or months, talent will describe themselves similarly to how this interviewee described herself. "It felt like every decision I was about to make, I would question myself. I started to have fear-based ideas and so many more questions in my head about whether something I was about to do will go well. Then, you see how decisions are made and they make no sense. . . . I had no sense of belonging at work."

So far, we have discussed the general state of the job market, the relationship between talent and companies, and the trends that have pushed both workers and businesses into *wrong fit* scenarios. In this chapter, we'll take a deep dive into the search for *right fit* from the perspective of talent. First, we'll consider the questions that help talent take stock prior to the search. Then, we'll explore what talent should really assess when weighing a new opportunity against the one they currently have. Along the way, we'll explore the psychology, the pitfalls, and the best practices of finding *right fit*. That said, this chapter is also relevant for the job recruiters and business leaders who struggle to find talent that fits the way the company works. The discussion here will help build a better understanding of the things that truly drive talent, what they look for in their work lives, and the questions that are helpful to answer for them along the way.

Cutting Through the Noise

You have decided it is time to find a new job. You shore up your resume, update your LinkedIn profile, and renew your account with the latest job board or talent marketplace. You start reaching out to your network and maybe even start applying for a few roles that fit your skills and experiences. The clock starts ticking and the pressure mounts. More applications are sent, infinite follow-up emails are written, and then—at just about the time you think you'll never work again—the interviews begin to flow in. Before you know it, you've landed in a new role at a new company and you're super excited. But, did you land at the best company for you? Do the lived values of the company match your own? Does your manager work in a way that works for you? Is this job getting you closer to the life you want to have? For the vast majority of us, the answer to those questions is "I think so? Maybe?" The truth is we likely don't know because the criteria we use to judge fit is often too narrow or defined by what we see on company career pages and read in the job descriptions. In essence, the very nature of the recruiting process shields us from gaining a deep and authentic view of how a given company works day-to-day.

This doesn't have to be the case. There is a way to think about the job search that gives you much better odds of landing in a place where you can not only get a job that you can excel in, but one where you can build a long-lasting career.

Companies don't have to be way stations or stops on a road to somewhere else, nor does our fit in a company have to wax or wane with a change in CEO, our manager, or strategy. However, it often does. This sense of fragility was a consistent thread in my interviews, and it spurred many of my interviewees to constantly be on the lookout for a "Plan B" or a fallback. Companies can be destinations that align to the many stages of our lives, but only if we can see them for what they are, not what they aspire to be—and only if companies cease treating talent as cogs in the wheel and start seeing them as discerning customers who are trying to decide where to apply their brilliance and practice their craft.

COMPANY INSIGHT

There are ways to present the company that will attract the right talent, those who will integrate easily and almost immediately help reduce the productivity loss felt from hiring the most capable person for the job versus the *right fit* talent for the company. If you are dying to know more, flip to Chapter 6.

The need for amazing talent to drive growth is well documented—talent is in short supply and the potential productivity gain from having a *right fit* talent is nearly unlimited. In one study, researchers found that in complex environments, including academic journal publications and entertainment awards, highly competent talent can be up to 800% more productive than the average talent.[1] The researchers were able to prove that there is no standard bell curve when it comes to performance. In fact, there is a curve similar to the 80/20 rule, where the top 20% of talent produce 80% of the value in their respective fields. So, there is little doubt that, from entry-level positions all the way up to the top executive roles in large companies, finding talent matters and talent landing in companies that are a *right fit* is essential to gaining market share, improving productivity, and ensuring that we all have meaningful careers.

In service of finding the best talent in highly competitive markets, some companies have pulled out all the stops—culture decks, stunning career websites, engaging internal recruiting teams, job descriptions that read like poetry, high-touch interactions, and exceptional perks and pay. As a quick test of this movement, think of your favorite consumer brand or a service you use on a regular basis. Go to their website and scroll to the bottom of the landing page. You will almost certainly find a tab for "Career." I encourage you to explore these pages to get a sense of how companies are talking to prospective talent. You will likely find what I found—much of what we see in a job search is crafted and honed with a precision that would rival most big-brand marketing campaigns. It is a sales pitch, an aspirational offer to entice us. However, even for all this effort, when asked whether their companies recruit highly talented people, nearly 82% of Fortune 500 executives said no; further, 93% don't believe they develop the people they do hire quickly and effectively.[2]

Stepping back and zooming out on the recruiting process, it's clear that knowledge workers on the job search are often being shown the shiniest version of the truth, i.e., the company on its best day. And, candidates who are seeking their right-fit employer arrive in their best clothes with their most rehearsed and well-honed answers to interview questions, ready to showcase the greatest potential version of themselves. In this situation, companies and talent are first-date ready. We have swallowed the pill that the only way to win the war on talent or land our dream job is to showcase the aspirational versions of ourselves instead of our true selves. So, nearly all of the assets used by talent and companies are more marketing and *impression management* (the process by which we try to influence the judgment someone has about us by regulating information in social situations) than they are material to finding *right fit*. They are designed to show the most inspiring version of the truth—just enough of an incentive to get either party to say yes. They are certainly not created to show what life is like on a random Tuesday. Maybe the problems start right there.

From both the talent and company perspective, do we do a disservice by presenting the best possible version of ourselves? Well, to answer that, just think about every really awesome first date you have ever gone on. How many of those relationships were over by the third, fourth, or fifth date? How many were over in less than three months? Because the market has been so competitive, recruiting has become something of a mash-up of a dating app, SharkTank, and the best Superbowl ad ever made. Both talent and the company have been seduced and blinded by the ideal aspiration of us on our best day as opposed to doubling down on who we are on a typical Tuesday afternoon.

What if both the candidate and the company focused on something else, something more realistic, less polished, more honest? What if our interactions were less like first dates and more like family reunions? What if talent presented a more holistic professional profile and companies a more realistic experience job preview? If the talent and companies started from this place, we might create a different set of assets that would lead toward new questions, deeper insights, truer assessments, and more likelihood of getting *right fit*.

Figure 3.1 presents a look at what those assets could be. For talent, values, career aspirations, their craft, ideal leader profile, and derailers (or turnoffs) could be the crux of the CV or resume. And, for companies, the employer brands could be designed to convey lived (not aspirational) values, the long-term talent promise, a realistic job preview, a manager profile, and the true "day in the life." If the recruitment conversations focused more on these areas and were held to seek alignment versus assessing technical competence or showcasing extrinsic perks, *right fit* will be more available, better choices would be made by both talent and companies, and increased productivity would naturally come as a result.

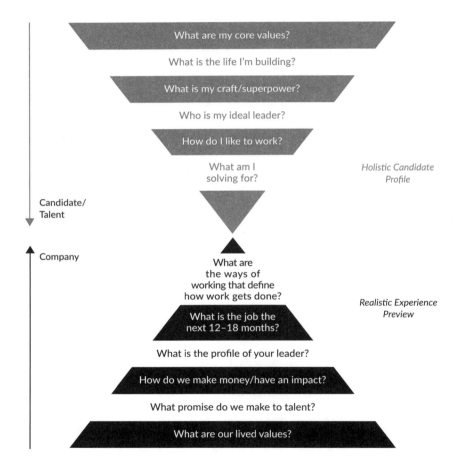

Figure 3.1: The Holistic Journey to Finding *Right Fit*

Let's take a look at where talent should start.

Hey, Talent: Stop, Drop, and Take Stock

When I get a call from a good friend, a past colleague, or a connection from my LinkedIn network, about half the time the person is looking for help out of a stuck place in their job or with their boss. Just last week, a talent that worked for me nearly a decade ago reached out by text, and the final text in the exchange read, "Awesome! Will call you at 10A. Warning . . . I'm going to need a pep talk." He was struggling with the gap between what he hoped would be true during the interview and the reality of what he was facing every day as he did his work.

My advice was fairly straightforward, as this person had been at the company for just over one month coming off a year-long sabbatical from corporate America, the function was brand new, and two new senior leaders had just joined and were making waves (big enough to stir up the water and make everything a little murky). We talked about transitions, what happens when you are building a new department, and that the strain of new upon new would be enough to wear even the best down. We worked on some strategies he could use to reassess the situation and build some buffers (see Chapters 7 and 8 for more on that idea) to keep engagement high. He had his feet back under him for the moment, but I was left pondering what could have been different if we rewound the clock. So, let's do that right now.

> **COMPANY INSIGHT**
> If you're a company leader, it would be easy to gloss over this section. However, what if you could capitalize on these questions in recruiting, interviewing, onboarding, and ongoing coaching to help your talent feel seen, valued, and ultimately that you are on the journey with them? If you want some ideas about how to engage, check out the excursions in Chapter Four. They would be easy additions to your onboarding and coaching.

If I could go all the way back, about two months before my friend was ready to start his search, I would have set him down and asked him to think about eight core questions:

1. What are the values you most consistently hold? (Excursion 1, p. 51)
2. What is the life you are trying to build? (Excursion 2, p. 57)
3. What are your superpowers? What are you best at (versus what do you love to do)? (Excursion 3, p. 61)
4. Are you of craft (or technical skill/expertise), company (the brand/product), or cause (a mission or greater goal)? (Excursion 4, p. 67)

5. Who is your ideal leader? What do you need from them to succeed? (Excursion 5, p. 71)
6. If you were to start a company, what would you do? How would you want it to feel? (Excursion 6, p. 74)
7. Above all else, what matters most to you right now? What are you solving for? (Excursion 7, p. 77)
8. How do you bring all of your answers together into a single leadership story? (Excursion 8, p. 80)

COMPANY INSIGHT

The Excursions are in a purposeful order as they build off of each other. But, if you are pressed for time or inspired to answer one or more of these questions right now, there is a page number for each Excursion in parentheses next to each question.

Now, on the surface, these questions seem fairly straightforward. You've likely thought about them at some point in your career search. However, most of us never go deep enough to gain clarity nor keep our answers front and center as we make our way through the job search. Additionally, we almost never use the answers as our primary filter at the moment of choice.

In the next chapter, I'll examine each of these eight questions in depth (and offer some excursions or reflection exercises) to help talent fully discover what defines and drives them, which are necessary to understand on the road to *right fit*.

REAL STORIES OF FIT
A Right Fit Story
40, male, consumer goods

"*Right fit* is anxiety free." This is how this interviewee described the feeling of having *right fit* at his current company. This lack of anxiety is what we feel when a place and the people in it simply make sense at a base level. For the interviewee, "*right fit* is seamless . . . I get to worry about my work and doing a good job instead of all the other stuff." Two elements stand out at his company that cultivate a sense of *right fit*. First, the company is purpose-driven and has "this self-filtering thing where the people that join are so motivated by the mission that they are willing to make a little bit less money. One of the rewards is that your day is great because everyone is purpose-driven first." Second, the day-to-day environment is "anxiety free, but it doesn't mean it isn't hard. It is just that the ways of working are built with a vibe of 'do your best.' It doesn't have to be perfect. That is very different than other places I have been."

At the heart of this interview is symmetry, where both the purpose and principles of how work gets done and how we treat each other are not just aspirational poetry—they exist in big and small interactions every day. The interviewee noted that "the things I picked up on during the interview process and from people I know were surpassed ten times in the actual experience. The day-to-day is really great." We should all hope for a bit more of what this interviewee has.

CHAPTER 4

Self-Reflection and Fit Excursions

As mentioned in the previous chapter, this chapter will explore eight questions that are foundational to finding *right fit*.

Each reflective question has an exercise (or what I call an excursion) that will help you gain a deeper and richer view of what matters most to you as a talent and a person. You can complete the excursions either in conjunction with the flow of the book content or you can treat them as exercises to do after you finish reading the book.

These excursions will help you think more deeply about who you are, what you value, and what you need to remain engaged and committed to your job, your team, your company, and (most of all) your life. Not all excursions will work for all readers. Use the ones that resonate, that feel important right now. One day, you might pick up this book again and another excursion might just catch your eye. The beauty of all these excursions is that they can (and should) be done every couple of years or whenever you find yourself ready to make a move.

Before diving in, make sure you have something to drink and snack on, a couple of pens, a highlighter, and your favorite journal or some scratch paper. These excursions will require a total of about three hours to complete. But, I can promise that at the end you will find ah-has, blinding flashes of the obvious, new edges, and more motivation to create a career that is in harmony with your life. And, away we go.

▶ EXCURSION #1

Examine your most consistently held values.

A value is a person's principles or standards of behavior, one's judgment of what is important in life. We like to believe we hold many values, and we do. However, a few core values (often three to four) determine most of our life choices, most of the time. Look back over your last few big life decisions you made (choice of university, company move, home move, major purchase, etc.) and think about the values you kept front and center. Are you always worried about cost first (if so, you likely value financial security)? Or, are you primarily worried about location (if so, status or community might be a value)? Knowing what values innately drive our decisions can be one of the surest ways to stay centered during a search for a new job. They'll keep us grounded and focused throughout an often overwhelming process.

Clarifying what we value can help us more consciously do things that are good for us versus do things that we simply desire. Values are a rudder to life well lived. They allow us to live in alignment, find meaning, stay on course, make difficult decisions, and ultimately live free of regret. If every big life decision was guided by what we truly value, then we might see more fit across the board—with those we marry (41% of first marriages end in divorce[1]), the places we live, the friends we keep, the activities we participate in, and the companies we work within.

The interesting thing about values is we often espouse values that don't exactly reflect how we live. This paradox, often called *moral hypocrisy* (breaking from your own moral standard, whether stated publicly or not), has been studied by many researchers, including USC professor Jesse Graham. His research has found that humans do not act (or even necessarily think) in ways that are consistent with the principles they claim to have.[2]

You see, we may argue that we hold many values, in general, but as we behave in the world, we constantly trade those values off against one another. For instance, imagine that you are confronted with a $100 bill left on the ground under your restaurant table. If you value duty, you might turn in the $100 bill assuming that someone will realize they lost it and want it back. If you value serendipity, you might believe that this $100 bill is meant to be yours and so you would pocket it. If you value charity, you might collect it and give it to a cause you care about. So, how do you figure out what matters most?

Excursion: Lived Value Ladder

A lived value ladder is essentially a short list of the values that most often guide you in the biggest decisions you make. To be clear, it is not those values that you either publicly profess to have (but don't necessarily live) or those that you aspire to live (but struggle to do so). Remember, our decisions are either guided by our values (what is good for us) or our desires (what our dopamine receptors or outside influences tell us we want in the moment). The more we can focus on the value match—what is good for us—of a given role, team, or company, the more you can gauge whether the opportunity will sustain you over time.

This exercise is intended to get at the values that are "lived by you" (those that show up in your day-to-day decisions) versus values that may be "important to you" (values you aspire to hold). The hope is that if you focus on the values you live, then you can more easily align to a company or team that holds the same values.

1. Reflect on each of the value pairs in Table 4.1. The values appear in pairs to help drive a forced choice and think about the relative value of one value against another. You'll have an opportunity to add unchosen values later.
2. Use the Lived Value Ladder Template (on page 56) and take the first pair of values (Authenticity and Kindness) and put one each in either the "Chosen" or "Not Chosen" column of the ladder based on how much they show up in your life when you are making decisions.
3. Repeat this for each pair until you have placed every pair.
4. Look over the "Not Chosen Values" column. There are likely a few values from that list that you think are important. Move 3–5 values over to the "Chosen" column.
5. Using only the Chosen Values column, take the ten values that you live by most (again, in decision-making) and drop them in the grid at the bottom of the page.
6. Rank each value between 1 (most important) and 10 (least important).
7. Test your top five values with friends and family to see if they agree. You might add or delete one or two values from your top five as a result.

You now have a list of your most lived values. Remember, your lived values are one of the best filters to use when you are making big life decisions. The more we are able to construct a life that is aligned to our values, the more harmony we will feel in our day-to-day. This is particularly important as we examine *right fit* in our careers, as the alignment of your values to the company or your direct leader creates a stable foundation for you to succeed over time.

Table 4.1: Value Pairs

Authenticity	Kindness	Creativity	Intimacy
Relationships	Ambition	Honesty	Freedom
Financial Security	Self-Control	Curiosity	Peace
Belonging	Self-Expression	Education	Fairness
Community	Environmentalism	Tradition	Unselfishness
Growth	Independence	Balance	Confidence
Loyalty	Wealth	Love	Positivity
Religion/Spirituality	Politeness	Patience	Determination
Happiness	Generosity	Morality	Authority
Responsibility	Equality	Fame	Kindness
Security	Service	Learning	Leadership
Harmony	Dependability	Humor	Meaning
Health/Well-Being	Courage	Beauty	Practicality
Adventure	Cooperation	Optimism	Popularity
Respect	Tolerance	Stability	Trustworthiness
Compassion	Leisure	Recognition	Challenge
Status	Influence	Other_____	Other_____

Worksheet 1: Lived Value Ladder Template

Chosen/Lived	Not Chosen/Not Lived

Top Ten Lived Values

1.

2.

3.

4.

5.

6.

7.

8.

9.

10.

Having clarity about what you value most can aid in all types of life decisions, as it will allow you to better align the choices you make to what you value most in the world. Next time you are facing a big decision (job, relationship, big purchase, community engagement, etc.), lay out the options you have in front of you and refer back to the list. Ask yourself which of the options best aligns to the values you are seeking to live each day. More often than not, a single choice will emerge as "most aligned." If you are still struggling to choose, ask yourself the following questions:

- Are the values I listed really the ones that are driving me? If not, what values matter to me right now? (You might redo this exercise as our values do shift and move over time.)
- What is attractive about the other options? What is drawing me to them? What makes them attractive? (It might be that one or more of the options are activating the joy/excitement area of the brain or the fight/flight area.)
- What will the follow-on impact of each choice be in three months, six months, a year, and five years? Once you see how the choices play out over time, you might see why and how a value-based choice serves you.

Let's use an example to show how this might play out. Let's say that you have two choices of a home to purchase. One choice (Choice A) is within your budget, close to work/friends, and gives you plenty of space for your current life. The other choice (Choice B) is more expensive, a bit further away from your work and friends, and gives you a ton of extra space to grow into. Now, if you are a person who values community, belonging, and financial security, the obvious choice would be choice A. However, if you value beauty, status, and ambition, you might be more apt to choose B. The truth is there is rarely a right or wrong in these decisions; alignment to who you are and what you are designing for right now is what matters most.

▶ EXCURSION 2

What is the life you are trying to build?

Fast forward twenty years into the future. Where are you living? How do you spend your days? Who and what are you surrounded by? What are you most proud of accomplishing? These questions may feel like an impossibly long way away or right around the corner, yet every decision we make right now (and those we've already made, especially those around our career) influences how we will answer them when we get there. What if you answered them right now and reverse-engineered the remaining moments in your life to get you there? Where did you live? What jobs did you have? How did you decide to spend your free time? How did you progress your career?

Think about this as a long-term map to guide your near-term decisions. No matter how old you are or where you are in life, a little future casting goes a long way. Every decision you make either brings you closer to or further away from your longer-term goals. Without an idea of what life will be twenty years from now, it is impossible to craft a sense of where to go next. All too often, our lives are led by near-term, either/or decisions versus seeing them as a step closer to (or away from) something we are trying to build.

Excursion: Future Retrospective

We all know that no matter how much we wish we could, humans can't predict the future, and only hindsight is twenty-twenty. But, if we could look back from an imagined place in the future, maybe we could design a more meaningful life and have a clear possibility for tomorrow that would help us to make better choices today. Those choices include where we live, how we spend our free time, and where we work, and what we do in our careers. If we know the future we want, we can make a series of smaller choices around our careers that serve the longer term. That way, even if the day-to-day is hard, the outcome has a broader and deeper part to play in the life we envision twenty years from now.

Get yourself in a future frame of mind. Imagine you took a time machine twenty years from today and you are living the best possible version of your life: Where are you? What are you doing? Who is there with you? How you do spend your days?

Once you are in that frame of mind, read through the questions in Worksheet 2 and begin every answer with "It is twenty years from today, and . . ." Provide both an honest answer and an aspirational answer. For the honest answer, share what will likely be true if nothing materially changes in life. For the aspirational answer, work from a clean sheet of paper where all possibilities are on the table. Have fun. Be bold. Keep your eye on the timeframe of twenty years out for each answer. If that is too far for you to even think about, you can always shorten the time frame to ten years.

Once you complete the worksheet, use the future you have built and look at where you are today. You cannot change the choices you made yesterday, but every choice from here on can be made to bring you closer to this ideal future. By framing your choices in service of this goal, you may find that *right fit* takes on a different meaning. In other words, this work can serve as a litmus test for any life decision you make. It can help remind you why you are doing what you are doing right now or help you choose between two options out on the horizon. It can also help you plan in the near to mid-term.

As a personal anecdote, when I was twenty-six, I remember being asked by a mentor of mine, "What is the life that you want? What are you building toward?" That question is one that I have held and reviewed with great frequency over the years. I knew I wanted a wife and kids. I wanted to be intellectually challenged. I wanted to be on the beach listening to the waves. And I wanted to be teaching a class as a professor.

I laugh now because, although life did not go exactly to plan, all of those elements *are* a part of my current reality. I have a wife and two stepkids who I adore. I was a chief learning officer and have taught many leadership courses over the years. I still do today. I live near the ocean (seventy-seven miles) but not at the ocean. At least, not yet. However, as my son goes off to college this year, my wife and I are planning a move to a beach community in Southern California.

The funny thing is, it didn't all happen within twenty years, and it didn't all happen in the way I imagined. But as I look back, one thing is very clear: whenever there was a choice to get a step closer to the future I had laid out, I was able to see it and run toward it with much more speed and courage as a result of this work.

Worksheet 2: **Future Retrospective Questions**

Question: It is 20 years from today, and . . .	Honest Answer (If life doesn't materially change)	Aspirational Answer (If you had a blank sheet of paper)
1. Where are you living?		
2. Why do you love this place?		
3. What is your passion? What is your purpose?		
4. Who is your "family"? What qualities do you admire in each of them?		
5. Who is your best friend? What do they provide to you?		
6. What are you doing for your "career" now (whatever that means to you)?		
7. What do you do with your free time now?		
8. What is the legacy you have left?		
9. What obstacles have you overcome?		
10. Who are your coaches/idols? What do you admire about them?		

Question: It is 20 years from today, and . . .	Honest Answer (If life doesn't materially change)	Aspirational Answer (If you had a blank sheet of paper)
11. What are ten words people would use to describe you?		
12. What are three accomplishments that make you most proud?		
13. What was the finest day of your life?		
14. What was the worst day of your life?		
15. What are two of your biggest regrets?		
16. What advice would you give yourself at twenty, thirty, forty, and fifty?		
17. If you could change how you spent your time before now, what would you do more of? Less of?		
18. What was the most important thing you did when you were 20, 30, 40, and 50 to have this life?		
19. What are two things you still want to accomplish?		
20. What is your six-word memoir (describe the life that you want twenty years from today)?		

► EXCURSION 3

What is your superpower? And what are your shadow sides?

Regardless of where you are in your career, each of us has superpowers —things that we naturally do better than most. They can include our technical skills or craft (finance, graphic design, speechwriting), leadership or interpersonal skills (influence, charisma), and even hobbies or side hustles (party planning, gardening, meditation). Some people might have more universal traits like grit, unbridled curiosity, or problem-solving. For others, it might be more about how we motivate a team or group, skills like empathy, coaching, inspiration, recognition, or optimism for the future. It is vital for you to know where and how you are differentiated in order to find your *right fit*. Ask yourself the following questions:

- What gaps do you fill in every company you have joined?
- What area of expertise are you attempting to hone?
- What do people come to you for?
- What activities do you most often volunteer to take on in a team?

These questions get into a space that is almost always overlooked in a job search and is where you almost always add value beyond the narrowed description of a job or position spec. Often, our greatest sense of accomplishment in an organization comes from activities and interactions that fall outside the parameters of the actual role. By seeing our contributions more fully, we can present ourselves and assess opportunities with a more holistic lens.

However, never forget that alongside our superpowers, we all have shadow sides, or ways that we show up that get in the way of our success. Those shadow sides can come in the form of overused strengths or non-productive behaviors that bubble up when we are under stress. In an *Harvard Business Review* article from 2009, Kaplan and Kaiser provided some intriguing research on what happens when you overuse a skill.[3] They tested the impact of an overused strength on both team vitality and productivity. The major takeaway is pretty straightforward: an overused leadership strength can easily become a liability over time. In the article, the authors point to lopsided leadership—the idea that in leaning too heavily on one strength you risk diminishing the opportunity to develop or lean into another quality. Over time, leaning on an overused strength can both limit our own growth (we are not rounding out our approach and broadening our available tools) and that of the team. The authors are essentially pointing to the long-felt limitations of anyone being seen as the proverbial "one trick pony."

Further proof of the downside of overused strengths or preferences comes through research into how our personality shifts under stress. When we are under pressure, we will initially move toward our preferred style of operating—meaning we will utilize our greatest strengths or superpowers to move through the moment. However, if we are under stress for an extended period of time, we will exhaust our reserves of energy and often flip into our least dominant and least practiced preferences, what Myers Briggs researchers call "the grip."[4] While in the grip, we will show up as an unfamiliar and unproductive version of ourselves. We will show our shadow sides. This flip in our personality and way of operating will feel foreign to us, be relatively unproductive compared to our approach at our best, and will often create more harm than good. It's important to both know your strengths and your shadow sides when you are under stress.

Excursion: Superpower and Shadow Sides

Knowing your strengths and your shadow sides will help you think about *right fit* in terms of whether you are able to (1) help the company, given your superpowers and the gaps they might have, and (2) whether the stressors in the company could result in your superpowers becoming shadow sides. Remember, the more the company works differently from how you like to work, the more likely you will spend your days under stress and will see your strengths become shadows.

Take a moment to think over your career and all of the feedback you have received (assessments, coaching, performance reviews, etc.). What have you been known for? Why do people seek you out or bring you in?

In step one of this excursion, you will uncover your superpowers in three categories (skills/expertise, leadership qualities, and intangibles). For each of the answers, you will be asked to capture what separates you from others with this superpower (What is your zone of genius?). For instance, gardening might be a superpower and your zone of genius might be "saving plants from the brink of death." Or, if you are a world-class problem solver, your zone of genius might be "getting to know the consumer in need at a deep level."

In step two, you will think about how you act when you're under stress and what shadow sides might appear in you. When under stress, do you tend to be aloof or distant? Do you tend to be irritable? Do you have trouble finishing tasks? Do you find that you are argumentative? You will be asked to choose three situations when you were under stress and then pull out what shadow sides appeared.

In step three, you will stand back from how you show up and reflect on the events, situations, and behaviors that cause you stress at work. Reflect back on your most stressful moments at work and think about what was going on around you. Were you on a tight deadline? Were you being micromanaged by an overly interested manager? Were you being asked to lead a lot of meetings with senior leaders? Were you working long hours? We all have different triggers for our stress and the more we understand them, the easier it is to minimize their impact. You will be asked to identify those triggers and to identify the three to four activities that help reduce your stress so you can arm yourself against your shadow sides coming to the surface.

EXCURSION 3

Worksheet 3: **Superpowers and Shadow Sides Excursion Template**

STEP 1: Reflect on your past experiences. What do people come to you for? Why are you sought out? Where do you shine?

Think about your superpowers in three categories and capture 1–2 superpowers in each (remember, these are towering strengths or differentiators).

Technical Skills/Expertise: What are the core technical skills or areas of expertise that you have finely honed?	1.
	2.
Leadership/Interpersonal Skills: What do you bring to a group or team that helps them succeed?	1.
	2.
Intangibles or Hobbies: What are skills or hobbies that might not show up on a resume but are where you shine?	1.
	2.

STEP 2: Reflect back on three times in your life when you have been under extreme stress for an extended period. Capture the three situations below and then capture 3–5 ways that you showed up in an unproductive manner (your shadow sides).

Stressful Situations

Where were you?

What was happening?

What were 1–2 shadow sides (unproductive behaviors) that showed up? Did any of your superpowers become overused strengths?

Where were you?

What was happening?

What were 1–2 shadow sides (unproductive behaviors) that showed up? Did any of your superpowers become overused strengths?

Where were you?

What was happening?

What were 1–2 shadow sides (unproductive behaviors) that showed up? Did any of your superpowers become overused strengths?

STEP 3: What causes you to become stressed at work? What are the triggers of your stress? Knowing this will help you think about the right environment and how you can maximize your strengths. Jot down some thoughts below.

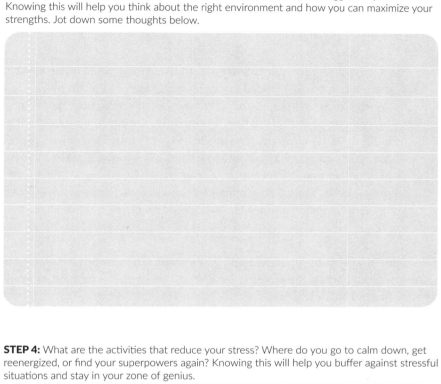

STEP 4: What are the activities that reduce your stress? Where do you go to calm down, get reenergized, or find your superpowers again? Knowing this will help you buffer against stressful situations and stay in your zone of genius.

Though deeper self-awareness is a benefit, the real value add of an exercise like this is in using the superpowers and shadow sides in your assessment of your current environment and any future one you might be a part of.

Use this knowledge to:

- Find environments that allow you to showcase your superpowers, places where you are allowed to do those things that you do well.
- Be on the lookout for stressors. Do your best to recognize them early on so you can limit their impact by resolving the situation expediently or building energy and support needed to get through them with grace.
- Share your superpowers and shadow sides. We often get asked in what situations we excel (superpowers) and what situations we find challenging (shadow sides). The more clear and authentic you are, the more your team members and leaders can create an environment where you excel.

Now that you have completed the exercise, find a colleague that you know well and trust. Run the list by them to see if they can validate your strengths and shadow sides

▶ EXCURSION 4

Are you of company, craft, or cause?

This question is one that I see plague many careers because we are never as clear as we should be about the answer, hoping above all hopes that we can be all three at the same time.

- **Company** is about loving the place that you work so much that you would do anything to see it succeed (being the most committed employee at Company X).
- **Craft** is about doing what you are good at and growing in it over time (becoming the best in the world at Y).
- **Cause** is ensuring that whatever you do or whomever you work for, you are furthering some greater aim, injustice, or issue plaguing the world (being the one who helps the world with Z).

If you are "of craft," you need to find a place where you can hone your skill, your art. If you are "of company," you should take a diverse set of roles and become enmeshed in the company. If you are "of cause," you need to go wherever you are needed and do whatever it takes to see the injustice eradicated or problem solved. Getting clear about what your career is about will help you think about where to be and where to go.

Excursion: Company, Craft, or Cause

More often than not, we search for the next job or bump in pay and title without taking three steps back, opening our eyes really wide, and asking the question, "Why do I do what I do?" The truth is we try, but the advice is to "follow our passion" or "find your true north," and it's not all that helpful. Why? Well, it's at least partially due to the old adage that it's hard to have your cake and eat it too. We can work for a brand that we love, build a deep expertise in a field (or craft), or work on the cause that matters most to us in the world. However, having all three is the career unicorn, as chasing either company, craft, or cause means that you will invariably compromise the other two over time. So, the better road is to ask yourself which is the primary driver of your choices at work *now*. Do you love the product or brand so much that you can't fathom working anywhere else? Are you so obsessed with a certain craft, area of expertise, or job that you can't imagine doing anything else? Or, is there a problem out there in the world that you are committed with all your heart to solving before you die? Don't know? Well, how about we find out.

In step one, you'll head to your LinkedIn profile or pull out your resume or CV and look over your work experiences to date. Try to remember why you joined each company, what the job was, what about it you loved and what you were looking to learn or develop. Fill in your answers in the worksheet below.

Next, take a look at the framework and try to answer the questions in each circle as they relate to your experiences to date. One of the three answers to each question should be more aligned to how you have thought about your career than the others. If you are stuck between more than one answer for a given question, circle them both or all three. At the end of the exercise, add up the number of answers in each column and you should see whether you are of company, craft, or cause.

Once you've completed the excursion worksheets on the following pages, you'll have more clarity about the driving force behind your career. With that information in hand, it will be important to do a few things.

First, examine your current experience or role. How well does it align to the focus of your career? You want to ensure your current experience is helping you move towards your career goal. Next, think about what your next move might be in service of your goals.

Here are a few questions to consider:

- If you are of **company**, what areas of the company have you not yet explored? Where in the company is your network least well established? What functions within the company have you not yet worked in or partnered with?
- If you are of **craft**, what areas within your domain of expertise are you lightest? What roles adjacent to your current one have you not yet had? What core tools or processes have you not had the opportunity to work with firsthand?
- If you are of **cause**, who are the leading "changemakers" or organizations that you have not yet had exposure to? What knowledge, skills, or abilities are becoming important to your issue or injustice that you have yet to gain? In what locations or cities is the majority of the action taking place (often there is a center of gravity for a movement and you want to be near it)?

Worksheet 4: **Company, Craft, or Cause Worksheet**

STEP 1: Pull up your LinkedIn profile or pull out your CV and review your major transitions since high school. Then, reflect on and answer the questions about each transition.

	Why did you choose to take on this role or experience?	What were you hoping to learn or gain while there?	What motivated you to leave or move?
College			
Grad School			
Internship			
Job 1			
Job 2			
Job 3			

STEP 2: Given your answers to the questions above, look at the descriptors of a career in each category and circle which of these is primary or should be primary for you.

	COMPANY	CRAFT	CAUSE
What type of employer do I typically work for?	I am a consumer of the product or an advocate of the brand.	The company is invested in the skill or expertise that I have or am building.	The company cares about the issues and injustices in the world that I care about.
What do you like most about your current role?	I am helping my company achieve its purpose and satisfy our consumers.	I am doing work that is helping me hone my area of expertise or passion.	I am working on the issues and injustices I care most about solving in the world.
What has been most true in my past experiences?	I have worked at just a few companies where I have held a variety of roles.	I have worked at multiple companies often in the same or similar roles.	I have worked in roles and at companies focused on the injustice in the world I most want to solve.
What statement best describes my professional network?	It is mostly professional connections in the companies where I have previously worked.	It is mostly peers and colleagues from my chosen profession and area of expertise.	It is mostly individuals who are working on the same issues or injustices that I am working on.
What statement best describes my next career move?	I will take a new role in my current company wherever they need me to go.	I will take a new role in this company or another that will allow me to gain experience in my chosen profession or area of expertise.	I will go where I can make the biggest impact on the issue or injustice I care most about.
When asked what I do for work, which statement best reflects my typical answer?	I work for [insert company here].	I am a [insert your profession or area of expertise here].	I am committed to [insert your issue or injustice here].
Who are my professional idols or inspirations?	Senior leaders in the company where I work.	Thought leaders in my area of expertise or profession.	"Changemakers" in the issues and injustices I care most about.
	Number circled____	Number circled____	Number circled____
CAREER ADVICE	Take many different roles at the company so you know the ins and outs of the company and have a big network. Stay put because you love the product and brand you represent.	See as many different systems as you can so you can pick up all the better practices. Work under a variety of thought leaders. Don't stay in a single company or move to roles outside your expertise.	Go to where you have the biggest opportunity to solve the issue or injustice. Stay open to new companies, new roles, and new locations.

▶ EXCURSION 5

Who brings out the best in you? What do you need in a leader?

What has to be true for you to reach your potential? One thing for sure is that our leaders matter. We join companies and leave managers (or stay because of them). It is clear from my interviews with talent that a great manager/team leader or a string of them can be the greatest accelerator of a career. We heard stories of individuals remaining at a company because of the manager they worked with or moving within the company (or even to another company) to remain working for or working alongside a given leader. And, there is not a "one size fits all" manager. Some of us need strength, resolve, and a clear set of expectations. Others need empathy, care, and room to make mistakes.

There are universal qualities of great managers, no doubt. But, there isn't one good way to lead. It all comes down to you having the manager YOU need, the *right fit* manager. As you embark on the next excursion, think about the following questions: Who have been your favorite managers? What made them the right manager for you? Has what you looked for in a manager changed over time?

Excursion: Your *Right Fit* Leader

Though Gallup tells us that over 70% of our engagement is due to our manager,[5] most of us don't think hard enough about the kind of manager or team leader that allows us to be our best. It does, partially, come down to how they work and whether that matches how we work. But, it also is due to their style and approach to how they build a relationship with us as their employee, as a team member, and as a person. Good chemistry with a manager is so important and so rare that many successful talent and leadership experts advocate for following a great manager.[6] Thus, if we can construct an "ideal leader profile" for our perfect manager or team leader, we can use that to assess any future opportunity.

Reflect back on the three best managers or team leaders you have had over the course of your career. In the worksheets provided on the following pages, write down their names, when you worked with them, and for how long. Then, use these "muses" to create an "ideal leader profile" by filling in the categories below. Be as specific and as "behavioral" (what you saw them do) as you can. The more detail, the better.

Worksheet 5: My *Right Fit* Leader Worksheet

STEP 1: Capture the names of your three best managers/team leaders.

	Name of leader	Place you worked with them	Duration of relationship
1.			
2.			
3.			

STEP 2: Using the three leaders you wrote down in Step 1 as your muses, reflect on and capture your answers to the following questions.

Leader's values: What values did you see them model (through priorities, decisions, time/attention, etc.) every day in their work with you? (You can return to the values listed in previous excursions.)

Leadership style: What principles and practices did they use to engage you, communicate with you, coach you?

Teaming approach: What did they do that really rallied the team?

Approach to recognition and development: How did they recognize your contributions and develop your skills and abilities?

Personality and personal attributes: How would you describe them as a person? How did they walk through life?

STEP 3: Formulate your answers into a single profile (done in a "Mad Libs" style to make it a bit more fun and pithier).

RIGHT FIT Leader Mad Lib

Moving forward, I would like my ideal manager/leader to value

_____ and _____. I would like them to

lead by _____

_____. When they are bringing the team

together, they will consistently _____

and _____. They will show appreciation by

_____ and will develop my skills

through _____.

Overall, they're an important role model for me because in both

work and life they stand for _____.

EXCURSION 5

Great managers or team leaders might not be the sole predictor of career success and workplace happiness, but they are a great accelerator. Now that you are clearer about your *right fit* manager, you can use this information in a number of important ways.

First, you can assess how close your current manager is to your *right fit*. If there are areas where they are not measuring up, use positive reinforcement and feedback to shape their behavior (remember, great managers are made not born—they are made by the teams they lead).

Second, as you look for new roles at new companies, ensure that you are assessing the hiring manager on these values, skills, and qualities. If you don't see them in overt ways during the interview, it is best to assume they don't exist.

Last, use this formula when you lead people. Often the things that we look for in our managers represent raw skills or approaches we will be gifted at ourselves. Leadership is modeled, and we gain our skills as managers from our managers.

► EXCURSION 6

If you started a company, what would you do? How would you want it to feel to work there?

Across my interviews, talent in *wrong fit* experiences often commented that they wished their company did a few things differently. In essence, they were describing what life would be like if they had a hand in creating their company, if they could construct their ideal way of working. This insight spurred these questions: What if you had the opportunity to create a company from scratch? What would the company do? How would it operate? How would you want it to feel to work there? What work principles or practices would you put in place to make it better than your experiences to date?

Excursion: Ideal Company

Back in 2015, Rob Goffee and Gareth Jones wrote a book on organizational culture that started with one of the best questions ever asked: "Imagine you have been asked to design the best company on earth . . . What would that company be like?"[7]

Instead of focusing on universal truths, like day-to-day work is meaningful, I can be myself, etc., we want to use Goffee and Jones's question to get at how *your* idea of the best company would feel day-to-day. Thinking about your ideal company, if you could create it from scratch, might help you know what type of companies you should work for to have a better chance at *right fit*.

Imagine this scenario: You have just been handed $20 million from a venture capital firm that bets on great leaders over cool ideas. In return for the $20 million, they simply ask you to pull together five of your most trusted colleagues and create a growth company.

Using the Worksheet on page 76, answer the following questions:

- What is the industry?
- What are the company's values?
- What is the purpose?
- How is the office designed?

- How will the company do work (e.g., work principles, practices, and platforms)?
- How will you gather and socialize?

After you've filled out the worksheet, take a look at your answers to the questions and make sure you have been as detailed and specific as possible. The more information you include, the clearer of a picture you create and the more beneficial it will be moving forward.

Now that you have designed your ideal company, it is important to step back from it and pull out information that could help you think about the ideal company for you.

Consider the following questions:

- What industry motivates you?
- How do you want work to be done?
- What are the values and qualities of the people you most want to work beside?
- What type of purpose motivates you?
- How do you like to gather, socialize, and come together to collaborate?
- What work platforms do you like most?

Now the hard part (it is where we once again look in the mirror at your current situation). Using the ideal company that you just mapped out, take a look at your current experience and how it fits with your ideal. Try answering the following questions:

- How well does your current experience align to your ideal?
- Where is there symmetry?
- Where are there differences?
- Does this help you explain why you feel energized or drained?
- Does it help you think about what you might look for in your next experience?

We will likely never find our ideal, and that is not the point. The point is to line up as many of the factors as you can for as long as possible, and then recognize where you might be making a compromise. Even knowing where there is a mismatch can help us accept where we are and how it might feel to do work every day. It can also help us respect more deeply what we do have.

Worksheet 6: **Your Ideal Company**

INDUSTRY (What Market Does Your Company Play In?)	
CORE VALUES (What Are Your Company's Core Drivers?)	
PURPOSE/PRODUCT (What Is Your Offering & Reason for Existing?)	
OFFICE LAYOUT (What Is Your Office Designed To Do?)	
WORK PRINCIPLES (What Are Your Company Norms & Non-Negotiables?)	
WORK PRACTICES (How Does Work Get Done Day-to-Day?)	
WORK PLATFORMS (What Technology Do You Use to Do Work?)	
SOCIALIZATION (How/Why Does Your Company Come Together?)	

▶ EXCURSION 7

What matters to you most right now?

Our careers are both about long-term progression and short-term needs. And, every job opportunity needs to be thought about in a larger context. Where are you in life? What challenges do you face right now? What do you need to feel less stress, worry, and anxiety? What would you like to be true in six to twelve months? These are the questions you ask and answer to put your career choice in the context of what life throws at you. When our work is integrated into our life, we excel. When it doesn't, everything is just harder. Sometimes we need to take a role simply to get through a moment in time in life. That's okay. Our careers can be central to our life in some moments and they can be enablers of our life in others. Be honest about what you are solving for and get specific about what you need most.

Excursion: What matters most for you right now.

In a perfect world, we would have the privilege to take the ideal job at our *right fit* company without any consideration of pay, location, or day-to-day demands. However, the world is far from perfect and often our career has to be a means to an end versus an end in and of itself. Sometimes, we need to make a different choice because of where we are right now and what matters to us more than anything else. Maybe you will have two kids in college and you need to choose the job that provides the most financial security. Maybe your partner has a great opportunity in another city and you need to find a new job in a new town. Maybe you have a side hustle that is proving to have legs and you need a job at a company that has a clear and consistent schedule or flexibility to come and go as you need. We can get in the trap of treating jobs as if they exist in parallel to life, but they don't. We should search for harmony between life and work. This exercise is intended to help you get there.

Start by reviewing the list of six major life categories below and write down notes about your current reality in each category. Next, capture where you want to be with each category in twelve to eighteen months (i.e., what you want to be the same or different). Finally, looking at the gap between where you are and where you want to be in life in eighteen months. How could your career choices help you? What would you need to do the same or different? How does this change how you think about your career choice?

Worksheet 7: **What Matters Right Now**

	STEP 1: Where are you right now? What is happening in this area? Where is there stress?	**STEP 2:** Where do you want to be twelve to eighteen months from now? What will be the same or different?
Financial security		
Family		
Friends/ community		
Health (physical/ emotional)		
Spiritual		
Personal passions/ hobbies		

Final Reflections

What stood out to you most about what matters right now? What is the biggest shift twelve to eighteen months from now? How does this work (above) serve your Future Retrospective (Excursion 2)?

Now that you've completed this excursion, think about what might be a few near-term steps you could take to find more alignment. The secret is to not jump ship immediately in the hopes of landing somewhere better. It is truly about assessing where you are today and what you are solving for and taking steps over time to bring more alignment. Careers (and life) are a marathon, not a sprint. They fall under the category of things that benefit from progress toward a goal every day versus seismic shifts in hopes of winning the career (or life) lottery.

► EXCURSION 8

What is your talent story?

If words make the world, stories make the world more beautiful. Story-telling is an increasingly important part of business, as noted by Jeremy Grenny in the piece he wrote for *Harvard Business Review* titled "Great Storytelling Connects Employees to Their Work."[8] The article makes the case for why and how storytelling is an essential tool for leaders of modern organizations. He makes this point eloquently when he shares

> People's feelings about their work are only partly about the work itself. They are equally, if not more so, about how they frame their work. Do they see what they're doing as a mind-less ritual? Do they see it as empty compliance? Or do they see it as sacred duty? If you change the frame you change the feeling. And nothing changes frames faster than a story.[9]

At the heart of finding *right fit* is changing the frame of how you see yourself, the company you are currently in, and any company or team you might decide to join in the future. If we can create and share a different story about ourselves, who we are, what we value, and the life we hope to build, then we can very much change the decisions we make about our current job or any job we might take in the future. So, before we move forward with the next part of the book, which will focus on how to better assess a company during an interview or once you are working there, we want to bring all of the excursions together. To do so, you will write *The Story of You*. This story is not intended to be your bestselling autobiography, but rather a cohesive story of you, what you want, and what you will bring to any company you join.

Excursion: The Story of You

Lay out all of your responses to Excursions 1–7 on the desk or table in front of you and use those reflections to craft your story by completing each story prompt with your answer. Then, think of a time when you saw that answer in action (when you exemplified the quality or made a decision that aligned to your answer). Last, create your story. The story should be both pithy and poetic. It should be something you could use as the summary at the top of your CV or in an interview when you get asked to "tell me a little more about yourself." You might need to run through a few drafts to get this fully complete.

Worksheet 8: **The Story of You**

	Story Prompt	Your Answer	Example Anecdote
Your Values	At my core, I am a person who values…		
Craft, Company, Cause	The driving force behind my career is…		
Your Future Retrospective	Over the course of my life, I hope to…		
Super-powers	I uniquely contribute to my company by…		
Shadow Sides	When I get stressed, I will often…		
Ideal Leader	To get the best from me, I need a leader who will…		
Ideal Company	I am looking for a company that…		
What Matters Most	When I think about the next year, my primary concern is…		

Conclusion to Part 2

Through Part 2 of this book and the associated excursions, you gained a deeper and richer sense of who you are, what drives you, where your career fits into your life, and what you need out of your next experience (or the current one) to create a stronger sense of harmony (or, symmetry between the life you have and the life you are building toward.) This self-reflection step is vital to finding *right fit* and was repeatedly brought up by my interviewees as something they wish they had spent more time on before hopping into the job search. So, if you have completed these excursions, you're ahead of most.

Now that you have a better sense of who you are, what drives you, the life you're building, what matter most right now, and your leadership story, the next step is to learn how to do a deeper and more holistic assessment of the company you are in, are interviewing with, or just recently joined. The aim of the next part of the book is to help you answer the question, "How does the company really work and does its way of working match with my own preferences?"

Let's dive back in.

PART 3

INTERVIEWING AND ONBOARDING

+

RIGHT FIT

CHAPTER 5

Don't Judge a Company by Its Career Page

REAL STORIES OF FIT
A Wrong Fit Story
32, male, not-for-profit leader

When my next interviewee began the job interview process for his current company, he knew almost immediately this place was different. Though there were many aspects that attracted him, two stood out in terms of helping him determine fit: "a video that the company produced on the role that gave him and other candidates a more human look at what it felt like to do the job . . . and . . . they had me do an exercise that was a real issue they were trying to solve for the company. It happened to be something I had done before, and it was fun to share my experiences." This learning orientation remained a part of the experience through interviewing and since he joined, especially around the ways of working. He described the company's approach as "building the ways of working as we work . . . the expectation is that we bring the mindset of trying and learning in every situation."

This interviewee compared the symmetry in the ways of working at his *right fit* company to his other experiences, where "navigating the differences in manager support and how that varied from team to team, function to function, has always been hard. It felt like a Ferris wheel where the work never ended, but it never felt like we were going anywhere."

His advice to others looking for *right fit* was compelling. "If you find yourself not able to go to sleep or have trouble getting excited in the morning, it is probably time to start looking for a better opportunity."

TALENT INSIGHT
Insomnia and restless sleep is becoming an epidemic, at least in the United States. Though trouble sleeping might indicate dissatisfaction with your job, it could also be the onslaught of information, stimulation, always-on technology, and constant dopamine hits. Learning to rest, really rest, is a vital skill for the future. This includes sleep, vacation, and bringing intention into moments big and small. Rest is not nice to have, it is a key ingredient of high performance, a lever for growth, and an amplifier of happiness.

In 2020, a senior director from a large consumer brand, after nearly fifteen years of working at the company, decided it was time to look at something new. She got a call from a well-renowned firm right away. From the first moment of the process, she was hooked—the recruiter was captivating, the interviewers were smart people who seemed to care about what she cared about, the mission of the company was breathtaking, and the pay and perks were potentially life changing. Without hesitating, she leapt.

If you fast forward about ten months, she was among the millions of actively disengaged employees whose day-to-day reality didn't at all match up to the promises made through the recruiting process. She expected to have a world-class manager, but instead received someone who barely had the time to meet with her. She was promised the chance to build innovative products, but quickly learned that by innovative, they really meant a newer version of what they already had. She was promised a team but was not allowed to hire. She was supposed to be surrounded by great thinkers who would help her do more, but instead she found a highly competitive and entrenched team.

She was devastated and left confused about how she made such a big mistake with her career.

This talent is not alone and that experience is not unique. She bought what was sold to her. The assessment is only as good as the information it is based upon. If we think about choosing a company as a decision akin to buying a product, we can turn to a body of research on consumer choice to understand a bit more about how and why this experience occurs.

Using the foundation of a deeper sense of self created through the excursions in the previous chapter, this chapter seeks to aid talent to assess a potential experience with a bit more depth. The chapter begins with a deep dive into the psychology of choice (i.e., buying decisions) and how to avoid the pitfalls. Then, it moves into the sources of information that a talent should lean on when attempting to learn more about a company. The chapter concludes with a set of questions that an interviewee could use in a recruiting process to get a better sense of how it will feel to be a part of the company day-to-day.

If you're reading from a company perspective, this chapter will help you reflect on your current recruiting and interviewing processes and the space you provide to the interviewer to make an informed decision or not.

The Reason Behind the Decisions We Regret

We have all looked back at high-stakes decisions we made in our careers and our lives and wondered how we ended up making a misstep, ignored pertinent information, or failed to listen to ourselves or others who were telling us to go in a different direction. In a previous chapter, we discussed the impact of cognitive dissonance, avoidance and approach systems, and BIRG-ing on why we might be susceptible to opportunities that might not suit us. Now, we want to take on the moment of decision itself and how our minds might limit our ability to see or pay attention to the right information.

A compelling body of research around product decisions, concludes that in the interest of closure (making a decision), a buyer will be more likely to limit the search for disconfirming information (information that would cause them not to buy) when the information provided initially is consistent.[1] In other words, when the early signals we get about a product or a place are positive and hold true, we will likely stop our search for new information or comparisons to other options. This phenomenon is called "motivated reasoning," or the tendency of buyers to move faster toward a decision when early signals help to form a clear sense of value for money.

A further examination of buyer decisions helps us understand how our choices might be a result of misinformation or our own willingness to fill in the gaps on information that might be vital to a *right fit* decision. Research around missing information found that buyers are more likely to interpret missing attribute information in a way that supports the purchase of the option that is superior on common attributes between choices.[2] Another way to think about this idea is that when a product appears superior on shared traits or attributes (aspects that are comparable across products in a single category), we will fill in the gaps on missing information in a manner that supports that superiority on less common or more difficult to ascertain elements.

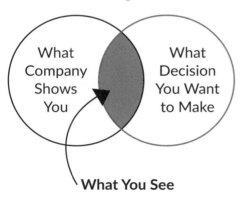

What You See

Figure 5.1: A Visual Depiction of Confirmation Bias

Last, in research around *confirmation bias* (the tendency to interpret new evidence as confirmation of one's existing beliefs or theories; see

Figure 5.1), pioneered research showing that potentially confirmatory evidence tends to be taken at face value while potentially disconfirmatory evidence is subjected to critical and skeptical scrutiny.[3] In other words, if we are motivated to make a decision between two choices, we will trust information that leads us toward that choice versus away from it.

Though confirmation bias is one of the most cited by our interviewees as they reflected on their decisions to choose *wrong fit* companies, there are over eighteen cognitive biases that get in the way of us making rational decisions. They are categorized and listed in the visual below and can be helpful to review before making any big decisions to see if you might be falling victim to one of them. Other biases of note in *right fit/wrong fit* decisions include bandwagon effect, availability heuristic, anchoring, and belief bias. (See the full list in Figure 5.2)

SOCIAL

Bandwagon: Uptaking of beliefs and ideas increase the more it has been adopted by others.

Blindspot: Viewing oneself as less biased than others.

Courtesy: Giving opinions/conclusions that are viewed as more socially acceptable in order to avoid causing offense/controversy.

Reactive Devaluation: Devaluing ideas because it originated from an adversary/opponent.

Stereotyping: Assuming a person has characteristics because they are a member of a group.

FAILURE TO ESTIMATE

Availability Heuristic: Overestimating the importance/likelihood of events given the greater availability of information.

Belief Bias: Basing the strength of an argument on the believability/plausibility of the conclusion.

Clustering Illusion: Erroneously overestimating the importance of small clusters of patterns in large data.

Confirmation Bias: Focusing on information that only confirms existing preconceptions

Gamblers Fallacy: Believing that future probabilities are altered by past events, when in fact they are unchanged.

Risk Compensation: Taking bigger risks or being more careful when perceived safety or risks increases.

COGNITIVE BIAS

SHORT-TERM VISION

Anchoring Effect: Relying too much on the initial piece of information offered when making decisions.

Illusion of Validity: Overestimating our ability to make accurate predictions, especially when data appears to tell a coherent "story."

Status Quo Bias: Preferring the current state of affairs over change

FINANCIAL

Hyperbolic Discounting: Preferring a smaller, sooner payoff over a larger, later reward.

Ostrich Effect: Avoiding negative financial information by pretending it doesn't exist.

Post Purchase Rationalization: Tendency to retroactively ascribe positive attributes to an option one has selected.

Endowment Effect: Tendency for people to ascribe more value to things merely becuase they already own/have them.

Figure 5.2: Types of Cognitive Bias
Source: https://www.visualcapitalist.com/wp-content/uploads/2018/03/18-cognitive-bias-examples.html

How Choosing an Experience Is Like Buying a House

If we apply this body of summary research to a search for a *right fit* company, it helps us better understand why many of us end up in places that feel like we landed on Mars when we were shooting for the moon. If we're motivated (i.e., excited) to make a decision about a new company or experience or there is a superior choice on the common attributes (more beloved consumer brand, more perks, better office spaces, more compelling career site, better pay, etc.), we will tend to either fill in the gaps of missing information about the company or role or we will ignore disconfirming information entirely (i.e., write it off as a blip or anomaly). Thus, we often will land in the company we "wanted" to choose, only to find that our expectations start to veer pretty quickly from our reality. This experience was backed up by my interviewees, who often admitted that, upon reflection, there were obvious signals that they simply ignored or explained away.

Now, though social science can explain some of our faulty choices and why we end up sprinting toward dead ends and *wrong fit* companies, we have some significant help along the way. When you think about the information available to you about a company, most of it is a "mostly true version of the truth." What do I mean by that? Simply that the information provided intentionally paints a broad stroke but doesn't give enough information to really see the cracks, blemishes, and wrinkles that every person and every company has. It is the employer-brand version of Snapchat filters or the Facetune App, both of which give an aspirational and augmented version of the truth.

Buying a home is a similar experience. When you go to one of the many home-buying websites and you click on a property, you see the address on a map (that doesn't show you the quality of the other homes or the landscape surrounding them), well-coiffed photos of the spaces (taken at full bloom on the sunniest day at an angle that makes every room look big and well lit), and basic stats on the number of rooms and the basic size (but rarely anything about the flow of traffic or the proximity of spaces). It is the perfect house—on paper. Then, you go to the house, walk through the door, straight into a weird wall, a tiny entryway, banged-up wood floors, or a smell that is a cross between sweat, fried food, and possibly cat litter. And, you turn around and walk out. Sound familiar?

Here's the thing: we rarely, if ever, get to truly "walk through" our company before we purchase, given that we are often on-site for a few hours and in a very contained environment, and that means all we have are the pretty photos. So, how do we peek our head in to upend the confirmation bias that comes from well-coiffed information? A thorough assessment of any company or function starts with widening the sources of information you use, narrowing in on the most important questions to answer, and then forming a "realistic company profile" that allows you to stand back and take a hard look at the opportunity.

Opening the Aperture on Our Company Research

Through the interviews with talent for this book, I learned that many trust the information they see/gather on companies, meaning they take it at face value during the search process and mostly use it as the foundation for their choice to join or not to join. However, upon reflection, very few of the talent felt the information provided during recruitment gave them a realistic preview of the company. The talent I interviewed generally used these sources to make their decision:

- Job description
- Company career website
- Culture deck
- The recruiter's pitch
- The interviews
- Past or current employees in your network
- Public employee review site (i.e., Glassdoor)

Interestingly, if we were to map these sources based on whether the information is produced by the company or by an objective entity external to the company (internal versus external) and whether the information is based on objective data or is subjective opinion of one or many (objective versus subjective), we find that most of the sources used fall into a single category: internally produced by the company and relatively subjective. If we combine this internal information with our tendency to BIRG and potentially make biased decisions, the deck is stacked against talent from the start

COMPANY INSIGHT
Though most leaders would hope to give a realistic preview to prospective talent, the likelihood is that many of the created assets are aspirational or misaligned, meaning that they don't create a cohesive and consistent perspective. One thought is to throw them all up on a wall and ask yourself, "What message are we sending to prospective talent? How well does that message represent the reality of what it feels like to be here day-to-day?" If you want to look a little deeper, check out Chapter 9.

in finding true *right fit*. Thus, it is not all that surprising that a misalignment often exists.

If talent were to think more broadly about the sources of information available to them, they might also include the following:

- Annual report/quarterly earnings calls
- ESG (environmental, social, and governance) reports
- LinkedIn profiles of the company's top executives
- Best-of lists (most admired companies, best place to work, etc.)
- News articles/podcasts by leaders
- YouTube videos of leaders presenting at conferences/alumni events/business schools

Once you have all of the information gathered, read it with purpose—examine it in a way that helps you uncover whether this company aligns with what you stand for. My suggestion would be to create six buckets:

- Company purpose/mission
- Products/customers
- Values/beliefs
- Ways of working
- Reputation of function/team
- Leadership/management approach

In each category, you should focus on your personal alignment with the information gained based on your reflections during the Chapter 4 Excursions. Are you energized by why the world is better with this company in it? Do you use the products/services (or would you, if you had reason to)? Is the culture and how the company works attractive to you? Does your function/team/leader have a good reputation?

As you seek to answer these fundamental questions, I encourage you to try not to break four rules:

- **Rule 1:** If the information appears in less than three sources, ignore it or continue to look for proof of it.
- **Rule 2:** If the information is only found through internal company materials, look for external examples of it.
- **Rule 3:** If the information is only from subjective sources, look for data to support (or refute) it.

- **Rule 4:** If something feels off in your gut as you reflect on it, continue to dive deeper into it. Don't ignore it.

Objective

- Annual report
- Earnings calls
- News articles/Podcasts
- Videos of leaders presenting
- Best company lists
- LinkedIn profiles of top execs
- Company review websites

Internal ——————————————————————— **External**

- Interviews
- Job description
- Recruiter pitch
- Past employees
- Career website
- Culture deck
- Traditional sources

Subjective

Figure 5.3: Traditional and Additional Sources to Use in Company Research

Be the Interviewee and the Interviewer

Even if you have all the information in the world about the company, it does little for you unless you know what you're looking for or what questions you should ask during the recruiting process. The initial research helps, but most of us walk into a recruitment with a single question that we are trying to answer: "How can I position myself as the best candidate for the job?" Though the sentiment is laudable, the very nature of the question can lead us astray. If we see a recruitment process as a competition where we need to stand out, it might drive some unin-

> **TALENT INSIGHT**
> Remember, all you have access to is curated information, so use this to see if *right fit* is *possible*, not to decide if definitively it is there or not. There is more digging to be done in Chapter Six.

tended consequences where we end up "acting" versus "being." In other words, we may be predisposed to show up how we believe the company wants to see us as opposed to authentically who we are at our best in the work setting.

Numerous studies have shown that candidates employ extensive impression management techniques such as fake humility, ingratiation, and self-promotion in the interview process in hopes of conveying that they are the best candidates.[4] In doing so, we are biasing the assessment of cultural fit by the interviewers as they will inherently base their view of us off these interactions. Additionally, our own ability to assess the company and our fit within it will be limited, as our finite focus will go to managing our impression via cues in the immediate environment versus measuring our fit via subtle signals of how the company works or who the interviewers are when they are not trying to woo you.

So, what strategies can you use to both allow a bit more of your true self to show through in an interview and focus on the signals that will help you assess your fit? Start by having a core set of questions that you need to answer before deciding whether the job, the company, the manager, or the team is a good fit. These questions go beyond the normal hygiene questions (pay, vacation, benefits, job responsibilities, path to growth, etc.) and move into better understanding the ways of working day-to-day in the company.

Question 1: What is the profile of the person who succeeds here?

The day-to-day climate of a company is simply the aggregate of the behaviors allowed. Another way to think about this is that culture is created by how we collectively choose to behave. The beauty of this question is that it moves beyond someone describing what the company values through platitudes and poetry and asks them to provide a deeper and richer view into how the company defines success. If you want to get really deep, ask the interviewer to tell you about a real person in the company. Who are they? What department do they work within? What are the primary values the person

TALENT INSIGHT

If you are an early career talent, you might be thinking that you shouldn't ask questions like the one's in this section, that you might sound overconfident or judgmental. Put that fear aside. You deserve to know the place you are joining, and these questions make you sound mature, deep, and thoughtful, not judgmental. And, if the recruiter or hiring manager reacts negatively to them, well, it might not be the place you want to join.

holds? How do those values show up? What are their strengths? What are their weaknesses? What would their performance review say in summary?

As part of their company brand campaign, your interviewers will often answer this question with the leadership competency "greatest hits": bias for action, great collaborator, smart, value-driven, curious, growth mindset, agile, innovative, inclusive, etc. My encouragement would be to probe: How did this person showcase a bias for action? What was their approach to collaboration? How did they show they were curious? What makes them more innovative than the average employee? What would their fellow teammates say about them?

Question 2: How does the company get work done?

There are some fundamentals of how work gets done that drive whether we succeed (or not) in a company, and these ways of working are different from company to company and often (unfortunately) from team to team. We rarely get a view into these ways of working during interviewing, and, even worse, we are forced to bump into these practices slowly during our first ninety days in our attempts to uncover "the secret decoder ring to success."

You see, every company has a specific way it likes to work—the principles that work is based on, the practices that they ask talent to employ day-to-day, and work platforms (or technology) that enable work to happen. Similarly, we each have our own learned preferences in these categories as well. There are some key questions that can help us better understand how we work or suss out how the company we are joining might work. These will be explored in depth in Chapter 6 as we help talent to gain insight into these ways of working more quickly in their onboarding as it is difficult to get a true feel for these elements given the nature of our current interview processes. However, always pay attention to signals of them as the recruitment process is that "way of working" in action. The questions are:

- How does the company make decisions (top-down, consensus, individually, etc.)?
- How are problems solved (data analysis, human-centered design, scrums, etc.)?
- How are ideas socialized (two-page memo, white paper, walking deck, informal storytelling, etc.)?
- How is conflict resolved (person accountable decides, superiors break ties, disagree and commit, etc.)?

- How is feedback given (third-person/hearsay, first-person/in the flow of work, via technology, it isn't [smirk], etc.)?
- How are relationships built (beginning of meeting, at the bar after work, in the cafeteria, through working together, etc.)?
- How are employees recognized (through performance systems, via internal comms, during townhalls/large meetings, through recognition systems, etc.)?
- How does information flow (top down, to everyone all at once, to a select few, through formal channels, through informal channels)?
- How are people developed (through experience, through coaching, through formal programs, etc.)?

Question 3: What is the company's relationship to time?

This is probably one of the hardest questions to discern a clear answer to and one of the most important to your sense of livelihood over time. At the heart of the question is the rhythm and flow of work. My wife often comments about the companies I work for that they "have no boundaries," as my colleagues would often call or email or "ping" me during all hours. Part of this is due to the global nature of my work, but part of it is simply due to the organizations' relationships to time. The last few companies have put a premium on being available over being considerate about working hours.

Further, the relationship with time shows up in calendars. Do they believe productivity equals a full calendar of meetings? Do they believe that your work should get done in the moments between meetings, or do they block out focused time? Is unlimited vacation really unlimited, or is it just masking the belief that we shouldn't take time off at all? Is balance something that's built into the flow of work (e.g., how projects are scheduled) or something that they train you on how to do (thus taking more time from your work or your life—ironic, I know)? Do you need to be at the office or in a meeting to be deemed productive?

Question 4: What is the reputation of the function/team you are joining?

It's easy to assume that you are joining a team that is on the rise. I mean, why else would the company bring in outside talent? Well, the truth of the matter is that most outside hiring is either due to a capability gap (the capability is not visible, resident, or able to be built quickly inside the current team) or due to a shift in the approach of the team/function (due to lackluster performance, a vision that is no longer fit for service, or, you guessed it, reputational issues.) Knowing where the team stands currently will help you better understand what the job will entail beyond simply accomplishing the tasks in the job description.

Question 5: What are your day-to-day duties?

What will the first three deliverables be once onboarding is complete? The job description is likely one of the most helpful recruiting tools for companies but the least helpful piece of data for potential talent. You see, the job description was created to help the organization understand where the role will fit into the larger company, what the purpose of the person/team/function is, and the base-level skills that any prospective candidate must have. What it doesn't do is tell you much at all about the day-to-day job you will be doing, as the job description is typically a general overview of all the possible activities and responsibilities a job could encompass over time.

What talent really needs to know is what they'll be doing day-to-day inside this larger job description. It is akin to describing what it means to be an Olympic athlete versus showcasing the day-to-day experience of a Winter Olympics biathlon cross-country skier. While the former might speak generally to rigorous training, the latter would describe grueling training sessions of five to six hours in the frigid cold every day, weight training in the mornings or evenings to increase the strength of their legs and arms, and a meticulous regiment of eating, sleeping, stretching, and practicing breathing techniques. The first description sounds beautiful, and the second . . . well, it's a good fit for a few resilient souls (certainly not yours truly).

Question 6: How does the leader get productivity out of their team?

Piles of research have shown that most of the variance in satisfaction[5] of an employee can be accounted for by their manager or leader. Interestingly, a recent study by Artz et al.[6] found that technical competence mattered above all else. If your boss is seen as competent, employees will be happier, and that happiness will result in exponential increases in performance. The opposite is true as well (and, seemingly more prevalent): a person's boss can have a negative impact on happiness and job satisfaction. A study by McKinsey found that over 75% of employees surveyed said their boss is their biggest source of stress at work.[7] So, being judicious about your boss, understanding what they value, and uncovering their technical competence will matter much more than campuses, perks, or coworkers.

Question 7: Where do people go once they leave this job/team/ leader?

This is one of my personal favorite questions as it's a way to see if this job/ team/leader is a launching pad or a dead end. In leadership development circles, it is often contended that the most underrated skill as a leader is being a "star maker," or a person who has a reputation for accelerating people's careers. They are our unsung heroes, as they might stay put in their position but elevate everyone around them, either within the company or into other companies. This question will help you better understand the path of people. Do they stay on this team for a long time, do they move to bigger jobs within the function, or do they go on to be utility players who do many things inside the company?

Question 8: What happens here that didn't happen at the other companies you worked at previously?

This question is all about artifacts and intent. It's about whether the culture espoused has been solidified enough to turn into longstanding and unique practices. At Mars Inc., for instance, the Make the Difference Awards have been going on for nearly twenty years. They are part recognition, part story-telling, and part engagement. In the end, they are a consistent commitment to the five principles and the belief that everyone in Mars should be looking to catch others doing "something great." It speaks to how important innovation, continuous improvement, engagement, celebration, and associates are to the company. Understanding what is unique gives you a chance to see where and how the culture is differentiated.

Question 9: What are the nonnegotiables at the company?

It's important to know the boundaries of what is allowed and how consistent they are across interviews. Most companies allow many different ways of working to enter their system as they grow, so the nonnegotiables become inconsistent and often impossible to discern across functions and teams. The more distinct and consistent the nonnegotiables are, the more you can trust that your experience will hold true to what's being described—that is, nonnegotiables are shared across the company as opposed to residing in a single team or function. If your interviewers have a hard time answering the question, this is likely due to the fact that the nonnegotiables aren't clear or explicit.

Conclusion

Though this set of questions will not guarantee that you end up in your *right fit* experience, they will arm you with ways to move the interview away from the "company brand" and toward the reality of the company experience. I think you'll find these nine questions will create richness in the conversation and depth to the insights gained, and they will elicit a positive response from your interviewers, who will be impressed with your line of questioning. In the end, these questions will lead you toward a more informative and engaging recruiting experience.

For recruiters and leaders who are looking for talent, consider the level of overall breadth and depth of the discovery work recommended for talent throughout this chapter. Any "talent first" company should be ready to pull back the employee-brand curtain and share honestly and openly what it's like to work inside the company. Share it all with pride! Ways of working aren't inherently good or bad—they're simply a part of our secret sauce. If talent comes to the table with the degree of self-reflection and honesty the exploration in this chapter recommends, then the recruiters and leaders should be prepared to meet them there.

Now that we explored how talent prepares for the recruitment process, let's fast forward to day one on the job and how you can show up like an archaeologist or an anthropologist as opposed to an actor or a lemming.

REAL STORIES OF FIT
A Right Fit Story
45, male, healthcare

The heart of *right fit* is all about alignment or harmony between the practices of the company and the sensibilities of any talent. What works for one person does not work for the next, and how one company succeeds is vastly different from another. That's part of the beauty of business: there are many roads to the same end. This interviewee summed this point up when he talked about how *right fit* felt. He said, "For me, there's two elements. There's the head, or how, logically, things have to make sense. The way decisions are made, what bureaucracy exists or doesn't, or how work flows from team to team. Then, there's the heart, or how you are treated by your peers and your leaders or how the system helps [or not] you personally to talk about the things you need to talk about."

What made this interview so interesting was the detailed examples of the *right fit* company and how those elements connected to this interviewee's background and personal history. For instance, he said, "I grew up in a frugal house, and this company was run that way. I really felt like I was spending money for the company the way I would spend my own money. And, I loved that the president traveled coach, because that is how everyone did it."

Though this interviewee has had a successful career, he admitted to having a few *wrong fit* experiences, and he offered that he wasn't necessarily clear in those moments what he was solving for. "Be really clear what your intentions are and what you are solving for and then ask as many questions as possible to see if this place can help you get there. Then, ask yourself what the worst-case scenario is if you say yes, as you need to have supreme confidence in the decision you are making and why."

CHAPTER 6

Figuring Out If You Really Fit

REAL STORIES OF FIT
A Wrong Fit Story
45, female, retail

From a company perspective, a large part of creating *right fit* for talent comes down to having a way of working that is intentional and ensuring that the new hire has a preference for those ways of working. When neither intention nor alignment to talent is there, work gets hard in a hurry. And, it often doesn't boil down to one person. One interviewee shared, "[*wrong fit*] often comes down to reading the leader incorrectly and ending up in a system that is a struggle. It's happened to me a few times where I've met my manager and misjudged who they were day-to-day."

The interviewee offered a unique and powerful alternative view to the central importance of a direct manager on the engagement. She said, "We always say like 80% of engagement is impacted by your direct line manager, right? I don't think it's just one person who impacts *right* or *wrong fit*, I think it is a group of leaders, it's a collective." For this interviewee, *wrong fit* feels like "being out of whack and finding it super hard to fill buckets (your own or others)."

This point gets to the heart of how powerful, shared, and consistent (or intentional) ways of working can be and how much damage misalignment can create. I love thinking about leadership and management as collective acts, not the result of a single person's behavior but of our combined intention (or lack of it).

Remember, at the start of the book, we defined "fit" as a "deep and authentic connection to how a company works day-to-day." As we move from day zero and into the first few months on the job, we should separate searching for *right fit* from attempts at fitting in. The former is about how to assess the match between the ways of working in the company and your personal preferences to give yourself the best chance at success. The latter is about immediately morphing to fit in, a strategy that is fraught with danger. Remember our deep dive into the psychology of fit and fitting in back in Chapter 2? It's time to put those thoughts into action.

To find *right fit*, you should spend your first ninety days focused on understanding the reality of how the company truly works day-to-day and assessing that against your preferences. In other words, the first three months are when you, as the talent coming in, can determine if you found *right fit* or if you'll spend your days fitting in and searching for the "secret decoder ring" of success.

In this chapter, you'll pick up tips and tricks to assess for fit. If you recently joined a new team or company, this chapter will help you determine the extent to which the company, function, or team works in a way that feels natural to you and clarify the areas where you'll need to do a little fitting in— flexing or shifting from your preferred

> **TALENT INSIGHT**
> Pay close attention to your first handful of days at a new company or on a new team. This is the moment when we are often at our most excited and least confident. It is easy to slip into habits that don't fit you, your preferred way of working, or your life. Remember to "start as you intend to continue."

> **COMPANY INSIGHT**
> New talent is highly impressionable. They will move, morph, and maneuver to please you and their new company/team. Make sure they are surrounded by the "models of your culture" early and often. Surround them with the people who best represent who you are and how you work, even if that means they don't go directly to their home team on Day 1.

way of working to make work, well, work. If you currently have *right fit*, this chapter will help you understand a bit more about what makes work feel easy or effortless so you can continue to be at your best. Lastly, if you're a leader, manager, recruiter, or HR professional, this chapter can help you see your organization in a new light, uncover places where your aspirations might not match the reality, or rediscover some ways of working that had become diluted due to growth. Before we get to all that, though, let's spend a little time on the career-stalling process of fitting in.

The Subtle and Insidious Danger of Fitting In

In contrast to *onboarding to assess fit*, fitting in is about using the first ninety days to quickly shift away from your natural preference in an early attempt to be included or feel a sense of belonging. This is a normal reaction to starting a new job. We enter a new place and we're nervous; we want to make a big splash right at the start. So, we tend to immediately mimic the behaviors and ways of working to become part of the team and feel a sense of belonging. Though that approach will certainly ingratiate you to your new company, spending your onboarding time attempting to fit in will likely take a toll on you by decreasing your engagement, heightening your stress, and yielding less fulfillment over time.

Remember how it felt to write with your nondominant hand at the beginning of the book? That's the feeling of *fitting in*. You can do it—humans are amazingly adaptable when our survival is tested. And, you will get better at the company's ways of working over time. However, it will take you quite a while, and no matter how well you master them, those new approaches will likely never be as easy as the ones you naturally gravitate to or have built over an extended period of time.

Based on my interviews in researching this book, even with continued success in fitting into environments (environments that are *wrong fit* for the interviewee), those initial feelings of disengagement, stress, lower confidence, and a lack of fulfillment tended to get worse, not better, due to the constant demands of impressing management or "acting" our way through our work puts on us. In that sense, fitting in takes continued effort and is often externally focused, meaning we shed our natural ways of being in the world to be effective inside of a certain team, group, or company. Brene Brown described this idea very simply when she wrote, "fitting in is being accepted for being like everyone else."[1]

In many of the interviews around fit, I found this phenomenon often playing out in the *wrong fit* experiences. As talent sees that they do not fit, they will make attempts at fitting in (or assimilating into the ways of operating within the company or team) by pushing harder or working longer hours. On the other hand, when *right fit* is there, something else happens entirely. One interviewee shared that when looking back to her *right fit* experience, which happened to be earlier in her career, she realized that what she missed most from that time was that "on a day-to-day basis, I didn't have the mental overhead of how to do a thing. . . . I could practice my craft." This company assessed for fit to ways of working or operating and made those ways of working clear through what the interviewee called "school," where they actually learned how to do work at the company. At the end of the interview, this interviewee offered that when the ways of working aren't clear or aren't shared, you end up "chasing someone else's formula" or "building a new way to work yourself," and that is exhausting, demotivating, and ultimately doomed.

So, why do many of us resort to fitting in as our primary approach to onboarding and feeling belonging? It's at least partially due to the way the company presents itself.

Dating Apps and Onboarding

The best analogy I have for onboarding is, it's like a dating app. Now, I must admit I've never had to use a dating app, since I found my life partner before they were a thing. But many of my friends have, and they often describe this "buyer's remorse" experience where the online dating profile doesn't fairly represent the person who sat across from them on their first date. In an article by the *Washington Post*, it was estimated that over 80% of people lie about information in their dating profiles.[2] Most of these lies are small and, though they may be obvious upon meeting, they don't negatively impact individuals' experiences. Interestingly, about 50% of people say their matches don't meet expectations, and only about 16% of those who use dating apps have relationships that last longer than three years.[3]

According to my dating friends, the dissonance between "the aspirational version" of the person and the "day-to-day version" often result in shock, disappointment, frustration, and even a quick scan for the closest emergency exit. Hearing these stories, I've always wondered whether my friends' reactions would have been different if they'd met these same potential mates randomly on the street or in a coffee shop. Would they have found a connection? Is the issue more about the expectation than the reality? Is this the same issue we face in terms of fit with our chosen company? If so, what do we do about it?

As I reflect back on my own transitions across the companies I chose to join, it struck me that I was often expending great amounts of energy over extended periods figuring out how the system worked, how work got done,

> **TALENT INSIGHT**
>
> If you are in your early career, you may not be super clear just yet on how you like to work. Nonetheless, this section can help you. It can put you in the position to see and try out different ways of working. By knowing there are many options to how work gets done, you might find more opportunities to test them and learn a bit more about yourself.

and what success looked like. I remember it feeling like trying to walk through a maze in total darkness. I made it through, but had to bump into the boundaries again and again and again. It became a test of survival more than a quest for excellence.

It left me wondering: Why don't companies give their employees a map? Tell them how work gets done, warts and all? Show them the tangible ways to succeed? Create a "dating profile" that is less airbrushed and more honest? The truth is, it's because most companies rarely fully understand or know how to articulate how work actually gets done, leaving it up to individual leaders to determine it for their teams and individual talent to figure it out over time. Even more damaging can be the "recruiting carrot" we often give leaders and managers to "come here and you can shape it or build it yourself." Instead of providing leaders carte blanche around how their function or team will work, we need to provide freedom within a framework—points of consistency across teams and clear degrees of freedom within them. One interviewee, a CEO of a large consumer goods company, stated it best: "Frankly, we don't talk about how we work enough—how we do things day-to-day. We should be much more rigorous, more transparent about them. This is in my influence."

The Three Versions of a Company

Part of the reason talent finds themselves in the dark maze of "fitting in" is that companies are subconsciously creating three different versions of themselves as talent comes into the organization, leaving talent confused about where they landed. This is, again, not purposefully done, but stems from three different motivations or outcomes for each of the early touchpoints with talent.

First, we have "the company we would be if we were at our best." This is the most ideal version of the company, the one that is bright and shiny and filled with potential. This is the version of the company most recruited talent gets presented to them. Why this version of the company? Because the company is trying to motivate you to make a choice, to buy their brand and their product—to buy *them*.

Second, there's the version of the company that is shown to talent on their first day. This is typically done through orientation—benefits, introductions of the most revered leaders in videos or live on stage, visuals of how the company operates and the products that are produced, and interactions with some of the systems and processes that will be a part of the new employee's life. Again, this version of the company is curated and carefully produced—an experience akin to being toured through a museum versus finding your way down a bustling city street. This is a more truthful version, but typically steers clear of the sacred cows, dead horse, odd quirks, idiosyncratic artifacts, and unspoken norms that are a core part of day-to-day life.

The third and last version of the company is "how it is for most people, every day." This is the version that comes out, often over time, through stories and interactions, experiences, and emerging routines.

Interestingly, the more these versions vary, the harder the experience is for talent to find their way to a *right fit* experience. This is due to the dissonance between the first two versions of the company and our ongoing experience of the third. The first two versions of the company set the expectation for the third, and when they don't match, talent struggles.

One way for companies to avoid the pitfall of failed expectations and truly find talent with the *right fit* would be for the company to be brutally honest about themselves and their ways of working and to reveal their quirks and peccadilloes on the first meetup. Find ways to make the company's real ways of working the key selling point for attracting talent as opposed to being hidden or Photoshopped to appear more attractive. Without that kind of change, companies set potential talent up for disappointment.

> **COMPANY INSIGHT**
> Impression management is not only an individual phenomenon. What do companies gain from presenting a scrubbed or idealized version of themselves? Not very much. And, when the version from recruiting doesn't match the reality, you just create questions and worries and stress. Why not just be honest? There is plenty of talent who will like who you are. Remember, there is someone for everyone. Maybe use the Fit Assessment at the end of this chapter to assess both how you present yourself to prospective talent and how you actually get work done. If there's a big gap, fix it.

Treating the First 100 Days as a Test Drive

The curated nature of a stellar recruiting process sets an unreasonable expectation for the company experience that's made clear in the uninspiring orientation days or clunky onboarding process that follows. As talent continues to progress in their careers, their expectations get increasingly higher for the experience while the gap between expectation and reality seems to only grow wider.

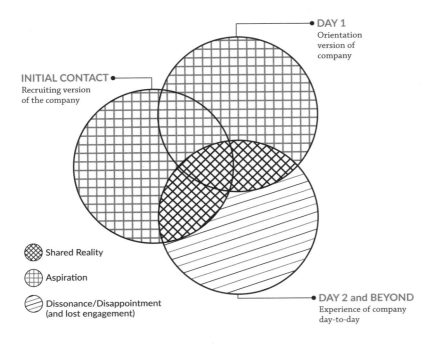

Figure 6.1: The Three Versions of the Company and Their Impact on Talent

There is compelling anecdotal evidence from my interviews that *right fit*, like writing with your dominant hand, allows talent to be more productive, more engaged, feel a stronger sense of belonging, and build skills (craft) faster. Time and time again, interviewers told me that in their *right fit* experiences, and I'm paraphrasing a quote from Dean Carter (the ex-CHRO of Patagonia) here, the company was "putting more into their life than they were taking out."[4] In other words, there was a steady upward trajectory to the engagement curve over the first few months. In *wrong fit* experiences, that journey looks more like an EKG readout (Figure 6.2) that falls off over time.

The EKG readout is a fairly normal occurrence as talent often spends their early days "bumping into the company," meaning that what they thought would be true wasn't. So, they experience some friction or dissonance, put in additional effort to resolve it, shift their level of expectation for the future, and then determine how this new information fits in with what they have learned to date. Thus, instead of seeing an uptick in commitment, energy, or productivity, they move up-and-down at a fairly steady clip and in doing so are losing any commitment, energy, or productivity that they had banked based on their early interactions. In other words, they're left with more knowledge of what to expect but less energy over time.

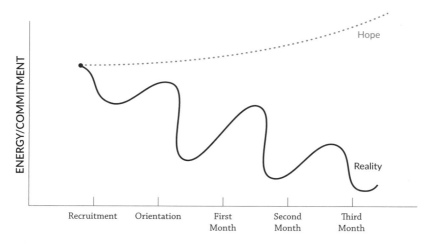

Figure 6.2: EKG Reading of Time to Fit

However, there are some simple strategies that talent can put in play in the first handful of days that will help to shift the mindset from "questioning the decision to join" to "understanding the day-to-day so you can be a success." This isn't to say you shouldn't reexamine the decision you made. These strategies will help you view the onboarding process as your chance to collect more information and see the company for what it is versus what you believe it should be or what your recruiter told you it would be. To do this, it is important to see onboarding in a new way—less about you assimilating to the company and more about you determining right or *wrong fit*.

Now, before I provide some strategies for you to suss out how the company works, it is important to provide some ground rules for your ninety days in assessing for fit. The ground rules are as follows:

1. **Avoid snap judgments about your fit.** Take the full ninety days to assess where you are, how the company works, and the expectations

that are being set for you. What you see in the first handful of days might look and feel different by day ninety.

2. **Keep a journal, a note on your phone, or a running Google doc.** Return to it at the end of each day. Use it to capture what happened, what that says about how the company works, and how you felt. Reflection in a time of transition is the ultimate tool for learning and growth.

3. **Review what you have learned at day ten, day thirty, day sixty, and day ninety.** Note patterns and themes that come up for you. I'll provide you a framework for the review at the end of the book, but for now, know that these deep dives are vital. And, sharing these reflections with your manager or mentor has the added benefit of making you look like an onboarding rock star.

4. **Let the facts lead you to your conclusion, not the other way around.** Our initial interactions, first impressions, and awkward or clumsy collisions with the company culture can often make us wonder if a place is for us or not. Remember, initial moments are important, but some organizations are big and complex, so let the patterns form over time. This practice of "gathering with distance" is what great designers and journalists do. They use insights to frame conclusions as opposed to the other way around.

5. **Focus your assessment on the ways the company works.** Though values and products and perks and pay are important, they will disappear in the day-to-day and your engagement/commitment will be built on how it feels to be a part of the place. It's harder to access the ways of working, but once you have a frame (keep reading), you will see them much more clearly.

6. **Create buffers to sustain *right fit*.** The assessment is just the start. Once you have committed, you still have work to do to ensure you keep *right fit* intact as you progress in your career and the company continues to grow/transform. We will discuss buffers in the next chapter.

7. **Make a decision to commit, or not.** One of the trends I shared early on was "infinite browsing" from Pete Davis. We stay in this constant state of partial commitment—one foot in and one foot out. It's safer, allows us to not suffer from FOMO, and keeps us feeling unique and different from the masses. It also stops us from doing the hard work to be a deep and consistent part of something bigger than ourselves. In the end, make a choice. You owe it to yourself and your company.

The last ground rule, "Make decision to commit or not," is probably the most important and the most difficult to enact without a framework for what to look for as you move through this new and exciting place that you have chosen to make a central feature in your life—to the tune of eight to ten hours a day for the next handful of years. I say this only to underscore why *right fit* is so important. It would be far better to know how well it fits for you early so you can either work more overtly toward fitting in (if this is the place you need to stay) or find another place to call home that will keep your energy, engagement, and commitment high.

So, where do you start? Regardless of whether you're sitting with your manager, your direct team, your peers, your internal customers, or a computer screen or classroom during training, you should watch for signals about how the company works.

Uncovering the Way a Company Really Works

Every great investigative journalist has a core question or issue they pursue, and they become almost maniacal, yet highly strategic and patient, about answering it. Your job is to be your own investigative journalist pursuing the question of "how well do I fit how my company likes to work?"

This is probably a good time to mention that if you're reading this section and haven't changed jobs or moved companies recently, this is still a journey you should take, as the chances are you might have never looked hard at fit. A deep dive into the questions below could help you better understand how you fit and whether there are some ways of working that are outside your natural preferences and could impact your level of commitment or engagement. In the interviews, this section of questions provided even those that had *right fit* insight on why some days feel harder than others. Even more importantly, it gave those in *wrong fit* experiences some comfort that they're competent and skilled even though they might not be performing as well as they would like. It helped them move from blaming themselves for being ineffective to simply seeing a mismatch between their ways of working and that of the company.

So, whether you're in onboarding to a new team or company or "reboarding" to a company you've been at for a while, here are the questions to use to help you along your way. These questions are a small set of indicators that will help you understand a bit more about how the experience will feel and whether or not your natural or learned ways of working align with that of the company. Remember, the less you fit, the more time, energy, cognitive load, and emotional regulation you will spend fitting in. The questions are:

- How does the company make decisions?
- How do they solve problems/manage projects?
- How are ideas socialized?
- How do colleagues collaborate or do collective work?
- How does the company assess performance?
- How do they give feedback?
- How do they resolve conflict or break ties?
- How do they develop their people?
- How do they celebrate/recognize people?
- How does information flow?
- How do they socialize/gather?
- What is their relationship with time?
- How do they view rest and recovery?
- How do they build relationships?

How does the company make decisions? How do you like to make decisions?

This fundamental question is about where decisions lie and how choices and trade-offs will get made over time. With this question, you're trying to understand the level of empowerment that exists in the company and where work needs to flow in order to get approved or have resources put toward it. The two ends of this continuum are empowered decision-making versus centralized decision-making. Another popular way to frame this continuum is bottom-up (employees close to the work make decisions about their work) versus top-down (decisions are handed down from management and passed through the chain of command). However, that doesn't account for the nuance in this question, as it isn't just about the *how* of decision-making; it's also about the extent to which tradeoffs are being made and whether decisions are faithfully upheld or revisited with frequency. So, as you assess the way your company makes decisions, ask these questions:

- Are decisions made by consensus or by individual leaders?
- Are decisions top-down or bottom-up?
- Is talent empowered to act, or are there checks and balances?
- Is everything a priority, or are there a few meaningful priorities?
- Is a decision set in stone or reevaluated periodically?
- Are decisions driven by the consumer or by the desires of leaders?

So, how do you best observe the decision-making process to understand how it happens in your company? Here are a few helpful hints about where to dig and what to look for:

- Ask yourself if there is a clearly defined strategy that people can make decisions in alignment with.
- Look at the biggest decisions within the company and trace them from where the work happens to who ultimately made the call or approved the resources.
- Listen to the language used around big decisions. Are you being asked to present your ideas to the team above you? Do others in your team refer to "what is best for the consumer" or "what the VP or director want"?
- Is there a sense that decisions are always being revisited or that once we decide, we move? You can pay attention to the longevity of strategy. How long have people or teams been committed to different projects/initiatives? What is the timeline for review?
- Is the focus for a single quarter or year clear? Are you given a ton of projects or just a few? Do teams work hard until they finish a project and then disband or are there a lot of people doing a lot of different things?

How does the company solve problems? How do you solve problems?

Every company has a preferred problem-solving method or approach—ways we move from an identified pain point to a new, better, different, or more meaningful solution. There are many problem-solving methods (Agile, Design Thinking, scientific hypotheses testing, group debate, hackathons, etc.) and countless tools/techniques (five whys, brainstorming, SWOT, Pareto, how might we, six hats, journey mapping, etc.). And, you will likely find that most of the methods and the tools exist in the company you are joining. Thus, the question isn't whether these are used, but which ones are most often employed across most teams—and, even more importantly, what "justification" tends to win the day. That is, what information is most valuable when determining the best solution? To uncover the company's problem-solving approach, examine how teams around you move from pain point to product. Here are a few key questions to ask and answer:

- Is hard data or qualitative insights used to frame problems?
- Do teams come together to share opinions or do sensemaking/interpretation?
- Do we decide and go or test and learn?
- Do we more often talk about consumer needs or company desires?
- Are standard and consistent problem-solving tools used (ex: Miro, Design Thinking, Agile, etc.)?
- Do we tend toward minimum viable products (MVPs) or perfect solutions?

In every company I have ever worked at, there are different ways to solve problems. In the best of those companies, the approach used is well aligned to the size, shape, and complexity of the issue at hand or is created in alignment with the values and affinities of the company. For instance, if a company holds a "consumer decides" value, then problem-solving approaches rooted in design thinking or user experience are probably best. In organizations where "data rules," then a Six Sigma, test-and-learn approach will likely make the most sense.

How are ideas socialized? How do you like to share ideas?

At the core of this question is really two related but separate practices—storytelling and influence. Every organization has a way they like to evaluate the efficacy of a proposed initiative or get others to move from compliance to commitment. Some companies respond kindly to beautiful decks, compelling narrative arcs, and poetic language. These organizations tend to be highly optimistic and brand/marketing focused and use storytelling to sell products. Other companies are logical and believe there is a correct, objective answer to every question. In these companies, data, scientific methods, and the test-and-learn process are prevalent. Here, you will see full sentences and intensely detailed ideas, usually in a white paper or lengthy slideshow with charts and tables and appendices with more data. Many others want to see sharpness of thinking and edited, well-constructed elevator speeches. In companies like this, the "hard-working two-pager" or "design brief" prevail.

Now, each of these approaches is valid and useful and sufficient to take the next step, but not all work for all companies or all people. It's important to know where the team or the company stand on the following aspects of communicating ideas. Use these questions in your assessment:

- Is the preferred pitch medium a deck or a white paper?
- Do we tend to communicate ideas in full sentences or pithy one-liners?
- Do we primarily focus our attention on stakeholder or consumer/user impacts?
- Do we justify ideas through anecdotal evidence or deep research?
- Do leaders engage better with quantitative or qualitative data?

How does the company collaborate/do collective work? How do you like to do work?

No matter the work that is being done (problem-solving, project/initiative design, decision-making, strategy formation, etc.), there is a prevailing way that the company likes to do work and specific tools they use while they do so. This might be one of the most fundamental attributes of a *right fit* experience, as it's the area you'll encounter most, with every meeting you attend and within each team that you join.

It's also in this arena where ways of working tend to diverge as individual team leaders optimize for known ways and approaches in lieu of having a standard way to work together as a team. Does the company meet to do work (that is, very little gets done if you aren't sitting next to or talking with someone else)? Does the company work asynchronously (meaning that work moves all the time through shared documents and offline communication channels)? Does the company believe in divide-and-conquer or that 2+2=5 (in other words, is most of the work done as individuals or in teams)? Is working something that takes place between the convenient hours of nine to five or can it occur whenever and wherever there is effort and interest to move it forward? Here are a few questions to consider:

- Is most work done asynchronously or synchronously?
- Do we meet to do work or to distribute work?
- Once tasks are assigned, do we divide and conquer or work in small groups?
- Is work done mostly in quick sprints or in small increments over time?

- Is work always on, or do we separate meeting and work times?
- How often do we meet?
- How consistent are the platforms and tools used for team-based work?

To best answer these questions, pay close attention to three bits of information early on—the meeting culture (how many, how often, and how big of a group); the primary tools used to communicate, to create, and to store information; and the cadence of work (does most of the work happen in sprints, one to two hours a week over a long period, or is the preferred method to kick off together and divide a conquer separately?). The best way to understand the affinities of the company and the rhythm of work is to:

- Shadow or join a workgroup, project, or initiative early so you can get a firsthand sense.
- Review a peer's weekly calendar and pay attention to the flow of work, meetings, and meeting preferences.
- Speak with a trusted friend to better understand the meeting culture, tools, and rhythm of work.

How does the company assess performance? How do you define success?

Fundamental to the experience of any talent within a company is the measures of success. Are you being measured on output, outcomes, strength of relationships, time in your seat (or hours billed), or some combination of these factors? Often, the communicated metrics upon arrival are not fully aligned to the metrics that are most linked to compensation, reward, recognition, or promotion. Companies generally pay (shorthand for reward, recognize, and promote) employees for one of four things—performance, demonstrated expertise, lived values/behaviors, and long-term commitment. It's important to gain clarity early about the philosophy of performance and compensation (in reality) by getting a sense of where the company/team stands on the following questions:

- Does the company pay for performance or for expertise?
- Are performance reviews annual or ongoing?
- What is most important to performance: quantity or quality of work?
- Is performance based on individual or team effort/accomplishments?

- Do people get promoted because of their performance, demonstrated expertise, lived values/behaviors, long-term commitment, or some combination?

It is important to also examine your own beliefs about performance. How do you like to be evaluated? What do you want to be paid or rewarded for doing? Do you prefer to be in charge of your own destiny or do you like to be rewarded as a team? One of my favorite ways to do this is to look back at the classes you most enjoyed in school. What were your favorite classes? What did you get graded on? Did you work alone or in groups? If we are not clear about how we like to be evaluated, we can find the processes of setting goals, receiving feedback, undergoing a performance evaluation, and being recognized for our work to be either highly motivating or highly disengaging.

How does the company provide feedback? How do you like to receive feedback?

One of the primary goals of joining any company (beyond pay and benefits) is to ensure you are spending your days honing your craft and growing faster than the company you work in. Yet, open, honest, and consistent feedback is a rarity, and even when it is given it doesn't necessarily help us grow or develop. Why is that?

Well, it's mostly a mystery, but Marcus Buckingham and Ashley Goodall offer some interesting insights in a 2019 *Harvard Business Review* article.[5] They argue that feedback in organizations today not only doesn't help talent thrive in the future but also can actually hinder future performance. They underscore what psychometricians have shown repeatedly, that humans are unreliable raters due to both their inability to hold an objective and stable definition of an abstract construct (like business acumen or collaboration), and as a result, they will invariably apply their own experience of what great might look like for them.

In other words, we are fairly self-centered and idiosyncratic in our measurement, and thus our assessment of performance is ultimately random and potentially damaging. In the end, the authors offer that if we want excellence, we should reinforce excellence and expose our talent to others' excellence.

Even so, there are many who believe in, ask for, and appreciate feedback about their edges and their opportunities. How many times have we received feedback, ignored all of the positives, and went straight to the places we could improve? From our educational system, we are trained to focus on the areas where we could be better. In one study from 2014, Jack Zenger found that of over two thousand respondents, 52% said that negative feedback was more helpful than positive feedback.[6] The respondents also believed positive feedback was mostly fluff and that if they were given more "corrective feedback," they would have been more successful. The point? Again, there are different strokes for different folks, but receiving the wrong type of feedback for your profile can turn a positive moment of greater possibility into a path to disengagement. So, make sure to pay attention to how feedback is constructed.

Here are a few questions to help:

- Is feedback given regularly or at prescribed moments?
- Is feedback anonymous/third-person or given directly?
- Does feedback focus on mostly successes or opportunities?
- Is feedback given for development or evaluation?
- Is feedback housed in a system or done informally or "in the flow"?

How do you decide what's most important? How does the company resolve conflict or break ties?

Amazon symbolically put the consumer at the center of conversation by keeping an empty chair in honor of them at every meeting.[7] Patagonia famously embedded their purpose into their legal charter, enabling them to "do good while building a good business."[8] And, Mars uses their Five Principles as a test for the decisions that leaders face day-to-day about what's right for the business and the consumer.[9] In each of these cases, these companies had a very clear way to manage conflict and break ties by laddering up to something that is bigger than the moment an individual, group, or team might find themselves in.

It's also true that each of us has a primary way to manage conflict. Some of us look to the consumers or customers we serve and seek to do right by them. Others seek out more perspectives and look for a pattern of thought to help us. Some others lean on their value systems or principles for what is right or wrong. And, there are even a few of us that like the great debate or hackathon, where the will of the collective drives our next move. In any case, you can ask some questions to better understand how conflict is managed or ties are broken:

- Is the consumer front and center in our decisions?
- Is our purpose used to break ties and resolve conflicts?

- Are our values or principles utilized to make decisions or to justify our actions?
- Do we seek out more information or data when there is disagreement?
- Do we tend to look toward the most senior person in the room to make the call when the team/group can't find their way to agreement?
- Do we build full commitment before you go, or are we satisfied with "disagree and commit" (not everyone is aligned, but we're willing to go forward)?

These are all viable ways to manage conflict or break ties, and generally, one of these approaches will be most prevalent. If you're curious, it is often good to comb through the following:

1. Annual reports: Do they primarily highlight the purpose, the consumer, the values, or the perspectives of leaders?
2. Intranet articles: Are most of the articles about the company living its purpose? Customers using the products? Or, how our values helped us to do the right thing?
3. Town hall speeches/all-hands meetings: Do most leaders reference consumer stories, purpose stories, values/principles stories, or personal/hero stories?

How does the company develop its talent? How do you personally like to be developed?

One of the most popular development taglines of the last couple decades has been "we develop our talent through experience." At first, this sounds great, but the reality is somewhat less enticing. What companies are actually saying is that if you come here and you do good work, more good work will come your way. The work will be more complex and the challenges will be harder to solve. If you solve them, you will learn and grow and become a better leader.

Well, that isn't exactly true. Seminal research from the Center for Creative Leadership and alumni like Morgan McCall tells us that there's a distinct difference between those leaders who continue to grow versus those who plateau at a certain level (the trajectory that we often refer to as "hero to zero," or someone who rises fast and then is let go because they can no longer succeed in the bigger and more visible role).[10] That difference is that the former group takes key events that we all face (hardship, turnarounds, new teams, lateral moves, difficult relationships, etc.) and turns them into "lessons of experience" that alter, at a fundamental level, who they are and how they will lead in the future. The other group has a singular way to do things that has been a success, and they mine it until they can no longer be successful. Turning key events into lessons of experience takes constant self-awareness, feedback, coaching, reflection, and testing out new behaviors—things that most companies fail to invest in at the level needed to truly help their people grow. So, to assess whether a company is mature in its talent development strategies, ask these questions:

- Does the company believe talent develops through experience or through formal training?
- How is coaching used, for growth/development or for performance?
- Are careers about upward promotion or collecting experiences?
- Do development programs impart new skills or embed culture/purpose?
- Who owns my career, the company or me?

How does information flow? How do you like to receive information?

Anyone who has worked in an organization understands that information travels in a variety of ways—most are not linear or how you think information should travel. However, we rarely stop to ask why information travels along those paths. The flow of information can tell you a great deal about an organization, its culture, and where decisions get made.

According to Gallup, only about 13% of employees believe their organization's leaders communicate effectively.[11] So, the content and style of communication within a company will likely leave something to be desired from an employee standpoint. Even so, the why and how of communication can tell us a lot about what and who matters in the company.

In regards to what matters to a given company, Gallup[12] offers that most organizations communicate for six distinct reasons—to define, inspire, and align; to inform; to teach; to drive action; to make decisions; or to collaborate. Read as many of the company communications as you can—notes from top leaders, annual reports, earnings transcripts, intranet articles, video interviews, articles that quote executives, anything you can get your hands on. In those communications are distinct clues about both how the company is looking for you to show up and what information matters most. Is this a company that looks for input, tells you what matters most, offers lessons of experience to help you learn, or attempts to build energy and excitement around the future? Is the organization data-driven, built on optimism and positivity, visually compelling, or operationally minded?

Is this a company where information is given to everyone all at once, shared by a small number of executives to the masses, or cascaded to teams through their leaders? Are these formal, one-way interactions or more fluid, two-way interactions?

How does the company socialize/gather? How do you like to socialize?

The rise of Silicon Valley, with its city-like campuses and beautiful gathering places, altered the landscape of the modern company from a place we go to work to a place we go to live. Having spent time at many of these companies, including Google, I've found that there is both an awe at the abundance they offer to employees—from food to gyms to massages to dry cleaning—and there is also an inherent sadness that these "campuses" are created to keep people at their company, encourage community to be built there as opposed to our urban core or our once bustling neighborhoods. If you are twenty-two and just out of school, this feels like an extension of life in college. If you are a forty-year-old mother or father of four, it can feel like you are in a constant state of FOMO.

Further adding to the breakdown of community is the corporate offsite, or the idea that we need to leave our worksite to do real, heads-down work for our company. I have always struggled with these meetings, as they invariably left me wondering if there wasn't some ironic and poignant lack of operational rigor that had leadership teams thinking we had to leave our place of employment to be productive for our place of employment. If we're stealing weekends and taking evenings, shouldn't we get those back? If this is a quasi-celebration or reward for a team that has worked hard, then shouldn't we reduce the time spent in dark and windowless conference rooms and maximize the time in the location? Shouldn't we be looking up and out at the world to grow as opposed to looking down and at each other to get stuff done? If we want to understand the phenomena of quiet quitting, look no further. When "perks" aren't really perks but are rather a thinly veiled way to get work out of employees beyond the forty-hour work week, talent becomes jaded and burnt out.

Now, I know this is a fairly cynical view of these privileged perks and that companies offer these offsites to drive cohesion, build commitment, and celebrate hard work. It is also clear that regardless of the company or the era, there has always been a need to socialize, to develop deeper relationships, to build rapport, and to let off steam away from the office, together. I get that. It's important to understand these customs as they will give you a sense of what is required from you and what matters to your company. Here are a few questions to get you started:

- Does the company expect me to be at the office beyond nine to five?
- Does the company invite family to events, or do we separate home and work?
- What do my coworkers do together? Do they drink? Do they travel? Do they drink and travel? Do they learn? Do they exercise? Do they get inspired? Do they get to know the consumer?
- Does the company celebrate? How? Where? What milestones do they recognize?
- Does the company get work done in meetings, in-between meetings, or at offsites?

What is the company's relationship with time? What is your relationship with time?

Coming out of the dizzying roller coaster ride that was the COVID-19 pandemic, I have been struck at how much my relationship with time has changed, maybe forever. In many moments time stood still, moved at a glacial speed, and a day felt like a month and a month felt like a lifetime. Those were the in-between moments, the eventless weekends, the holidays and three-day weekends without any change of scenery or cast. And, then inside a single work day, time flew, hours disappeared under the glow of Teams, meets, Zooms, and livestreams.

Many years ago, I read a book called *Einstein's Dreams* by Alan Lightman that was this cool and vertigo-producing fictional set of stories dreamed by Albert Einstein that tested the limits of time, relativity, and physics, providing a glimpse into what the world might look like if time was constructed differently.[13] That book changed my view on time. It is malleable, and each company has their own relationship with time. Some companies never have enough time—meaning the normal day is too short to accomplish it all. Other companies have too much time, almost like there is no urgency or need to move at a pace faster than walking speed. Some companies see time as fluid, where you work hard and then you play hard. Some companies move fast and race against time. Others take all the time they can to make a decision or commit to work. Reflect on these questions as you think about your company's relationship with time:

- Do people in this company have too much or not enough time?
- Is there a constant buzz of activity or peaks and valleys?
- Is time during the day used to have meetings or get work done?
- What are the typical working hours—nine to five or always on?
- When I'm on vacation, am I still available or unreachable?
- Are meetings set back-to-back, or are they scheduled with breaks between?

How does the company view rest and recovery? How do you view rest and recovery?

If you have ever watched an elite athlete prepare for an intense sporting event (or have done so yourself), they will tell you that high performance is achieved by managing high output and performance with diligent rest and recovery. Quick sidebar: I'm an avid weightlifter myself and have learned a great deal from my trainer about "download weeks," or weeks when you lower your output to allow your muscles to start to find homeostasis so you can make another eight- or ten-week push. In other words, you're doing enough to keep your body at a certain level as opposed to too little that your muscles weaken. These weeks are different from rest days, which are intended to allow healing and recovery in the middle of high-intensity work.

Given the state of organizations today and punctuated movements against burnout (see the Great Resignation and quiet quitting headlines of 2021–22), I wonder if we're on the brink of a new way of thinking about rest, recovery, and download weeks versus our current mindset of vacation, no-meeting Fridays, and well-being training. It seems that we still have much to learn from elite athletes, artists, and other masters of craft who understand rest and recovery is performance, download weeks are about maintaining excellence while recovering energy, rest weeks are about building muscle by reducing any and all stress on the system, and time spent out in the world is about inspiration.

So many people have weighed in on the debate about working from home versus working from the office, and to me, it's always felt like an incomplete conversation. It isn't about where you work, it is about how you perform, recover, manage your energy, and find a flow. It isn't like we don't have tools for this (if you could see my right index finger, you would see a matte black Oura ring). The technology exists—we just don't fully understand how to make it work at scale. Trusting employees to manage their rest and recovery feels like a recipe for people spending weeks at the beach on the company's dime, and staying in the current system feels archaic and tactless. I don't have the answer here, but I know we need one and think about it daily. Regardless, you should look at how your company thinks about rest and recovery by exploring the following questions:

- Is PTO unlimited or fixed (finite)?
- Would most describe their day as "I am busy" or "I am fulfilled/challenged"?
- Is well-being a core value or a training course?
- At the end of a project, do we start the next one or take time to recover/reflect/reset?
- Do leaders take vacation quietly, or are they vocal about taking breaks?
- Are breaks, lunches, and other types of restful moments between meetings encouraged?

Right Fit Isn't Ever Perfect

It is now painfully obvious that there are numerous dimensions you can use to assess your company's daily work. And, after reading this chapter you are probably much more informed about what to look for and discouraged that you'll never find a *right fit* company as no place will be a perfect match. You're right, and that's okay.

What you should examine is how often a company aligns with your preferences and beliefs about how work gets done. The more the company fits your preferences or you fit theirs, the easier the transition will likely be and the more fluid and energizing day-to-day work will feel. This also allows you to put an appropriate amount of energy adapting to the ways the company works a bit differently than you. You can lean into these areas with a growth mindset, psychological agility, and excitement because you have firm ground beneath you and places of familiarity that feel like, well, writing with your dominant hand.

The mistake most talent make in transitions is that we don't assess the gap in the fit and the different expectations early enough. As a result, the stress and tension of endlessly trying

> **COMPANY INSIGHT**
> If you are an executive leader of a company or a founder, it is important to model the culture that you aspire to have, especially when it comes to your relationship with time. Your relationship with time becomes everyone else's, and how you decide to work sets the floor (minimum expectation) not the ceiling (the most extreme example). Being intentional in your relationship with time has ripple effects throughout the company.

to fit in causes us to go from being confident in our craft and optimistic that we can contribute to feeling like an exhausted outsider who never got the secret decoder ring on how to succeed.

Part of the issue we face is that many of us have never explored the question "How do I like to work?" Like good soldiers, we simply join our companies and work like they ask us to work. However, if their way doesn't align with our natural ways of operating, we can feel slow, clumsy, uncertain, and over time can lose our sense of confidence. In the upcoming assessment, we'll look at ways of working to determine how well you fit with your current situation, regardless of whether you're thinking about leaving your current company, have just joined a new company, or are trying to assess a new opportunity for fit. This last one is a little harder, as you probably don't have all the answers about how the potential company works, but it's worthwhile even if it only gives you a bit more assurance that fit is there.

> **COMPANY INSIGHT**
> Be a partner with new talent in their *right fit* journey. You can do this by acknowledging the importance of *right fit* during onboarding as well as providing opportunities for talent to assess their fit over the first hundred days. When talent explores self-evaluation and their fit with the company, everyone benefits by removing the clutter of uncertainty.

The *Right Fit* Assessment

To help you better assess how you work and how well you fit your current company (regardless of whether you are new or have been there for a while), I have created an assessment of how work gets done. It will help you answer two fundamental questions: How do you like to work? And how well do you fit your current company's ways of working?

Remember, you will never find a perfect fit, but alignment to how a company works and how you naturally work can be the foundation for a meaningful, fun, and engaging experience.

Once you understand how you fit in your current company, if you find that it's not a fit and you end up looking at a company that might be the place for you, you can also use the below as a way to assess early fit . . . as long as you have enough information on the potential company to constructively answer the questions.

Step 1: Look at each of the continuums below and rate yourself accordingly based on your preferred style of working by circling the corresponding number. -3 to -1 means that you prefer the way of working on the left. 0 means you prefer both the left and right equally. 1 to 3 means you prefer the way of working on the right. If you could work the way you wanted to, how would you want each of these elements to happen?

Step 2: Complete the assessment again, except this time rate how your current company/team works day-to-day by putting an "x" over the corresponding number. Remember, this could be the company you've been at for a while, a prospective company you're interviewing with, or the company you recently joined. Ideally, you would use this assessment in all three of those moments, but you should absolutely use it at the end of your first ninety days at a job.

Step 3: Count the relative gap between your number and the company's number and mark it on the sheet. For instance, if you rated yourself a −3 and the company a 1, the relative gap would be 4. Place an asterisk by the areas where there is a difference of three or more points between your preference and your company's way of working. If you are seeing numerous places where you differ from your company, that might give you a sense of whether this is a *right fit* or *wrong fit* experience.

Step 4: Review the full assessment, paying particular attention to the number of places where there is *right fit* (company/you work in similar ways) and where there are wide gaps (three points or more) between you and your company. You might choose to count up how many areas you align on and how many have a gap, so you can see your total score out of 55 elements of work.

Then, reflect on the following questions:

- What did I learn about how I prefer to work? What surprised me?
- How well do my preferred ways of working match my company? Where are the biggest gaps?
- If there is, generally, a strong match, why would I consider leaving or looking for new roles?
- If there are significant gaps or differences, how has that impacted my engagement or stress? What do I need to do to be successful in the long term (to fit in)?

THE FIT ASSESSMENT

How You (and Your Company) Like to Work

For each item, circle the number that represents your preference and then place an "x" on the number (or circle the number with a different colored pen) that represents your company's way of working. Write the gap number in the space provided. If the gap is three or more, place an asterisk next to that item. When complete, add up your total number of asterisks (*wrong fit*) and no asterisks (*right fit*). This will show you the overall gap between the fit of you and your company.

How do I make decisions?

Reach consensus	-3 -2 -1 0 1 2 3 Gap_____	Chosen by individual leader
Respect top-down decisions	-3 -2 -1 0 1 2 3 Gap_____	Respect bottom-up decisions
Empowered to decide	-3 -2 -1 0 1 2 3 Gap_____	Seek approval to decide
Everything is a priority	-3 -2 -1 0 1 2 3 Gap_____	A few things are priorities
Decisions are followed	-3 -2 -1 0 1 2 3 Gap_____	Decisions are revisited
The customer drives decisions	-3 -2 -1 0 1 2 3 Gap_____	Leaders drive decisions

How do I like to solve problems?

Use insights/ideas from subject matter experts	-3 -2 -1 0 1 2 3 Gap_____	Use data from reliable sources
Solve individually with input	-3 -2 -1 0 1 2 3 Gap_____	Solve collaboratively as a team
Work in a test-and-learn environment	-3 -2 -1 0 1 2 3 Gap_____	Work in an "80% done and go" environment
Problem is defined by leaders	-3 -2 -1 0 1 2 3 Gap_____	Problem is defined by consumers
Use standard tools	-3 -2 -1 0 1 2 3 Gap_____	Use individually preferred tools
Solution needs to be perfect	-3 -2 -1 0 1 2 3 Gap_____	Solution needs to be good enough (MVP)

How do I like to communicate ideas?

White paper	-3 -2 -1 0 1 2 3 Gap_____	Deck/slides
Full sentences	-3 -2 -1 0 1 2 3 Gap_____	Pithy statements/ cool visuals
Stakeholder-centered framing	-3 -2 -1 0 1 2 3 Gap_____	Consumer-centered framing
Anecdotal evidence/ external	-3 -2 -1 0 1 2 3 Gap_____	Deep research/ internal
What is true/ not true	-3 -2 -1 0 1 2 3 Gap_____	What is possible/ could be

Numbers/data	-3 -2 -1 0 1 2 3	Stories/user muses
	Gap_____	

How do I like to collaborate/cocreate?

Synchronously	-3 -2 -1 0 1 2 3	Asynchronously
	Gap_____	
Meet to do work	-3 -2 -1 0 1 2 3	Meet to distribute work
	Gap_____	
Divide and conquer individually	-3 -2 -1 0 1 2 3	Work in small groups/teams
	Gap_____	
Work in sprints	-3 -2 -1 0 1 2 3	Work in small increments over time
	Gap_____	
Work in a scrum	-3 -2 -1 0 1 2 3	Separate meeting and working times
	Gap_____	
Meet as little as possible	-3 -2 -1 0 1 2 3	Meet as much as needed
	Gap_____	
Use standard project tools	-3 -2 -1 0 1 2 3	Use project tools we like most
	Gap_____	

How do I like my performance to be assessed?

Rewarded for higher performance	-3 -2 -1 0 1 2 3	Rewarded for deeper expertise/learning
	Gap_____	
Annual performance reviews	-3 -2 -1 0 1 2 3	Performance reviews are ongoing
	Gap_____	

Rewarded based on quantity of work	-3 -2 -1 0 1 2 3 Gap_____	Rewarded based on quality of work
Performance metrics are individual	-3 -2 -1 0 1 2 3 Gap_____	Performance metrics are collective
Promotions are role and scope based	-3 -2 -1 0 1 2 3 Gap_____	Promotions are sustained impact based

How do I like to receive feedback?

Feedback is given regularly	-3 -2 -1 0 1 2 3 Gap_____	Feedback is given at set intervals
Feedback comes anonymously	-3 -2 -1 0 1 2 3 Gap_____	Feedback is given directly
Feedback focuses on strengths	-3 -2 -1 0 1 2 3 Gap_____	Feedback focuses on opportunities
Feedback is truly developmental	-3 -2 -1 0 1 2 3 Gap_____	Feedback is evaluative/ comparative
Feedback is formal/ system based	-3 -2 -1 0 1 2 3 Gap_____	Feedback is informal/ in the flow of work

How do I like to resolve conflict or break ties?

I ask my consumers	-3 -2 -1 0 1 2 3 Gap_____	I argue or debate with peers
I look to company purpose/values	-3 -2 -1 0 1 2 3 Gap_____	I look to the leader in the room

I seek out more information/data	-3 -2 -1 0 1 2 3 Gap_____	I seek out a coalition with other team members
By vote	-3 -2 -1 0 1 2 3 Gap_____	I provide input and let the team leader decide
I debate until I have full commitment	-3 -2 -1 0 1 2 3 Gap_____	I disagree and commit

How do I like to be developed?

Through experience/ coaching	-3 -2 -1 0 1 2 3 Gap_____	Through formal learning/development
Coaching is for growth/learning	-3 -2 -1 0 1 2 3 Gap_____	Coaching is for performance
Careers are about moving up	-3 -2 -1 0 1 2 3 Gap_____	Careers are about collecting experience
Development is to impart skills	-3 -2 -1 0 1 2 3 Gap_____	Development is to connect to culture
I own my career	-3 -2 -1 0 1 2 3 Gap_____	Company determines my path

How do I think about time?

I always have enough time	-3 -2 -1 0 1 2 3 Gap_____	I never have enough time
I like a "constant buzz"	-3 -2 -1 0 1 2 3 Gap_____	I like moments of rest/recharge

I use working time to meet	-3 -2 -1 0 1 2 3 Gap_____	I use working time to do stuff
I keep a set schedule most days	-3 -2 -1 0 1 2 3 Gap_____	I vary my schedule to my projects
I like to work 9 to 5, five days a week	-3 -2 -1 0 1 2 3 Gap_____	I like to work when you need to

How do I view rest and recovery?

PTO should be unlimited	-3 -2 -1 0 1 2 3 Gap_____	PTO should be fixed/earned
On vacation, but available	-3 -2 -1 0 1 2 3 Gap_____	On vacation, out of reach
"I am busy most days"	-3 -2 -1 0 1 2 3 Gap_____	"I am fulfilled/challenged most days"
Well-being/health is a core value	-3 -2 -1 0 1 2 3 Gap_____	Well-being/health is a nice to have
A end of project, I start a new one	-3 -2 -1 0 1 2 3 Gap_____	At end of project, I take time to recover

Totals

Total asterisks (wrong fit)	(Total: 55 questions)	Total no asterisk (right fit)

MY RIGHT FIT/WRONG FIT ASSESSMENT

REAL STORIES OF FIT
A Right Fit Story
44, female, healthcare

The first few months at any new job or experience are naturally filled with uncertainty. This interviewee shared that when you transition, the world is new, you are relatively untested, and there is "a degree of reticence and wondering if they will trust me. Can I prove myself?" Due to the relatively broken interview process, her strategy in these first months "is really about me sussing out how well we both did about figuring out whether this is a good match. It's like we got married quickly and are now asking the question of whether we are okay living together."

The "sussing out" process is important, as it means that you're putting efforts into understanding how well you and the company did in the interview process versus jumping straight into judgment over whether something works or didn't immediately. When I asked this interviewee what she looks for to tell whether *right fit* is emerging, she said, "the first word that comes to mind is it feels easy. Even though the work's not easy, it feels like it is going to be fine. We'll figure it out." For her, *right fit* is more boundaryless, less compartmentalized: "When I'm in a *wrong fit* experience, I'm protective of everything outside the box . . . if I'm on vacation, don't dare email me. With *right fit*, the boundaries are very fluid. It's not like work has taken over my life, but rather like it is an extension. I think maybe integrated is the word."

Her advice for individuals who are in the "sussing out period" or in a *wrong fit* experience is to be careful not to "split yourself into how you succeed at work and who you are as a fundamental person." The longer you do that, the bigger the schism becomes. This interviewee said that eventually, "my creative energy was waning, and I wondered if I was becoming a different person entirely." Her solution was to find people who kept her sane and grounded through those times so she could stay mindful of the split. Eventually she had to accept that "I am not a bad person because I can't succeed here. I am not a bad person for not fitting in."

PART 4

BUFFERS

+

RIGHT FIT

CHAPTER 7

Inspirational Buffers and Enhancing Fit Over Time

REAL STORIES OF FIT
A Wrong Fit Story
35, male, technology

Wrong fit can occur inside a company that you have worked in for a number of years even if you don't change jobs, and it can feel like it happens overnight. This was the experience of one interviewee who found a deep attachment to the company due to the people and the purpose, until the latter disappeared. "I stopped doing all the citizenship behaviors inside of the team. I no longer stayed past my allotted eight hours of work or took on additional duties on the team . . . the team's purpose was being compromised for an arbitrary number."

The loss of a connection to purpose eroded this interviewee's sense of attachment very quickly. He said, "If I am honest with myself, the reason I joined the team was because of an extreme belief in what that team was doing. I was able to justify these long work hours or menial work." Then, in a very short period of time, "basically everything that I thought I joined for was essentially obliterated." Once the purpose and connection to the consumer eroded, a number of workplace problems among the team started to appear. He ended up leaving the team within four months and only made it that long because of a promise of a new leader, which never materialized.

Over the course of my interviews researching this book, a few things became abundantly clear about fit. First, not all *right fit* experiences start off that way. They can be bumpy at the beginning as we settle in or can be made more difficult due to a problematic team member, mismatched expectations about the job, or even a less-than-stellar direct manager. Second, *right fit* experiences are tenuous, meaning they can (and often do) erode over time. Just because you have a great fit now doesn't guarantee that it will remain that way. Retaining fit takes work as you progress up and through a company because your role will change, team membership will shift, and the organization will grow and alter its ways of working. Lastly, *wrong fit* experiences can in fact be turned into something manageable, though rarely are they sustainable for an extended period, as there are often too many obstacles to overcome and the toll on talent and their careers, as noted by many of my interviewees, can be significant. With that said, *wrong fit* experiences can be constructed in a way that allows you to be productive without feeling pummeled.

The good news is that, in each of these cases, you can do things to increase the likelihood that *hard fit* experiences (that is, experiences that aren't right or wrong so much as just difficult) start to feel right, *right fit* experiences last a long time, and *wrong fit* experiences don't stall your career or significantly undermine your confidence, well-being, or mental health (you would be shocked, or maybe not, at the number of times great talent found themselves in a difficult moment due to a lack of fit).

With that in mind, the next two chapters will primarily address buffers to fit, or actions that individual talent or company can take to improve the overall experience over time. The buffers will be broken up into two categories: inspirational and relational. In this chapter, inspirational buffers, or those that connect us to something bigger and more meaningful than our current circumstances, will be explored. Relational buffers, or those that center around the people who we interact with within the work context, will be the focus of Chapter 8. These buffers came directly out of my interviews and are based on strategies that talent used to sustain *right fit* or move a step closer to it.

> **TALENT INSIGHT**
>
> With every major transition (new team/new company), transformation, re-org/layoff, or change in leadership, take the moment to reevaluate where you are, what you value, and what you are solving for right now. Sometimes *right fit* slowly and subtly erodes. Better to catch any shifts early and work to buffer against them.

Do we want to put a ring on it?

Prior to jumping into what you can do to buffer *wrong fit* experiences or ballast *right fit* ones, it's important to explore why and how fit fluctuates in other areas of our lives. The easiest place to look is one of the most complex relationships—a marriage or civil union. Marriage is the ultimate expression of commitment and a prime example of how tenuous fit can be over time. We enter into marriage taking vows in front of the law, the church, our family, and/or friends, committing our life to another human. We are essentially saying that I am with you, no matter what. And, we believe that on the day vows are exchanged and often think that vows are all we need. However, those of us who have been in longstanding unions know better (mine is currently going on fourteen years).

The statistics on marriage in the US show that it has about a 50% success rate[1] with 20% of marriages ending within five years.[2] Interestingly, we have become accustomed to marrying (on average) much later, and the later you marry, the less likely you are to divorce. A leading researcher in the field, Dr. Helen Fisher, hypothesizes that this is due to "slow love," or the idea that people have about ten years of practicing sex and love before they wed.[3] We are more prepared and more knowledgeable about what we can give and want out of a marriage, and therefore seem to make better choices. Does this sound familiar to work in any way?

In a 2013 study of divorces, the most common reasons for divorce to occur were a lack of commitment to the partnership, infidelity, conflict or excessive arguing, and domestic abuse.[4] Bettina Hindin, a matrimonial lawyer practicing for over thirty years, summed up failed marriages as being due to "people coming into the marriage with unrealistic expectations of how it is going to be, how they're going to live, and everyday issues like money, children, jobs. It just doesn't happen how you planned."[5]

Interestingly, Fisher notes from her research that "love" is actually a drive, and it is generated in a tiny little factory near the base of the brain called the ventral tegmental area, where dopamine is made.[6] When you are in love, dopamine is sent to many regions of the brain, giving you focus, motivation, optimism, and craving. And, it can turn on and off like a switch. However, falling out of love doesn't mean a marriage is over. Fisher goes on to offer that there are two other systems at play in a relationship as well: sex drive and deep attachment.[7]

So, how is all of this marriage stuff important to understanding *right fit* at work? Well, there are a few lessons we can take away. First, our career, like marriage, is one of the biggest commitments we will make as shown by the thirteen years of life we will spend at work.[8] So, it would be smart to put more consideration and time into those choices. Second, similar to falling for someone you might marry, an initial sense of fit with a company is triggered by the "falling in love" region of the brain, which creates a dopamine response that might "light us up" in a way that our current situation might not. It is the possibility of something new, not necessarily something better. You see, in the former situation (assuming it is *right fit*), we are likely experiencing what Fisher called "deep attachment" as opposed to intense "love."[9] The physical feeling we have in "attachment" is inherently less dopamine and more oxytocin—the hormone responsible for calming the amygdala and our fight-or-flight response. Where dopamine produces energetic excitement, oxytocin is more like a big, neurological hug—more comforting than energy producing. So, given that attachment is really about comfort and safety, when we feel like we're "falling in love" with a job, we might be feeling something that isn't fit as much as fascination.

Second, this idea of successful marriages moving from falling in love to deep attachments presents a super cool possibility for organizations. If we can build deep attachment (aka belonging or commitment), that might just be the silver bullet to stave off future iterations of the Great Resignation or "quiet quitting." Deep attachment or commitment can keep a relationship healthy as long as we constantly examine it, strengthen it, and help each other become aware of its power to sustain happiness. Lastly, the research into divorce underscores the expectation gap that exists at work. A strained relationship can be created due to nothing more than the difference in one's idea of how it will feel to work at a place versus what it is actually like.

Whether you've landed in a *wrong fit* or *right fit* experience, it is important to move from the fascination mindset, where you're focused on a shiny new thing (driven by dopamine), and start building deep attachment in as many spaces, places, people, and practices as possible (driven by oxytocin). Love is fickle. Companies and people change. But, deep attachment is enduring and can sustain us through the highs and lows of any employment experience.

Buffering against *Wrong Fit*, Protecting *Right Fit*, and Enhancing *Hard Fit*

Just as relationships have buffers that can help us sustain ourselves in times of high stress or hardship (things like a full savings account, caring family, a strong community, positive role models, etc.), so does fit at work.

Buffers are vital tools in sustaining *right fit* if you have it and managing *wrong fit* when you don't. These buffers are not static, nor are they more or less available based on level or tenure. Most, if not all, can either be assessed for prior to taking on a new job or moving to a new company or built early on in the experience. However, in some circumstances, you have to make a leap of faith that these buffers are available to you. There are many buffers, but the ones most often cited through my interviews were the following:

- Inspirational buffers
  - *An authentic connection to purpose or cause*
  - *Meaningful work*
  - *Growth opportunities (formal or informal)*
  - *A connection to a consumer in need*
  - *A legitimate relationship with time*
- Relational buffers
  - *A supportive leader/manager*
  - *Meaningful mentors*
  - *Workplace BFFs or doppelgangers*
  - *"Life outside of work is magic"*

You may notice that many of the "perks and prizes" that are often regaled in "best places to work" surveys and company career websites are missing from this list—pay, benefits, beautiful campuses, meals, massage Thursdays, free apps, product discounts, etc. Well, that is purposeful. It's not that these aspects of work aren't important (just ask me about my mortgage and the two kids I'm trying to get into and through college), it's just that they tend to be short-term motivators or hygiene factors—the former of which is related more to the dopamine hit of "falling in love" while the latter is table stakes (if these elements aren't aligned to your station in life, you would be unlikely to even consider taking the job or moving to the company).

A quick, highly geeky example of how weak the relationship is between these extrinsic motivators and satisfaction comes from a meta-analysis (yep, I said it) of 120 years of research over ninety-two studies. Tim Judge and col-

> **COMPANY INSIGHT**
> Extrinsic motivators are often the easiest to build and offer to our talent. However, the impact is short lived, as the motivators quickly become part of the backdrop of our lives at work, meaning their impact diminishes over time. Intrinsic motivators are the opposite: they build over time. Think about how you can strengthen the intrinsic motivators as you read through the buffers and Chapters 9 and 10.

leagues found that the correlation of pay to satisfaction is very weak (and r=0.14) which amounts to less than a 2% overlap, meaning your pay doesn't determine your job satisfaction.[10] Further, an examination across cultures shows that the relationship is pretty much the same everywhere.[11] Even more disturbing is that pay and other incentives can actually have a negative impact on satisfaction, as Edward Deci and colleagues learned over a synthesis of 128 controlled experiments. They found that "strategies that focus primarily on the use of extrinsic rewards do, indeed, run a serious risk of diminishing rather than promoting intrinsic motivation."[12]

These studies and many, many others (thank you, Gallup and Dan Pink) tell us clearly and without a shadow of a doubt that the more intrinsically motivated we are—that is, the more inner drive we have—the more satisfaction we will derive from our jobs. In other words, if we want deep attachment, focus on these buffers and not on pay, perks, proximity, or campuses. With that in mind, let's dive into the inspirational buffers and how to create them for yourself or provide them to others.

Inspirational Buffers

Inspirational buffers help connect ourselves to something bigger than our current situation.

Connecting to Purpose or Cause

Purpose is "the new black" of corporate conversations. Leading up to and through the pandemic, purpose became an increasingly uttered word in executive team conversations and major business news outlets. As a matter of fact, according to Google Trends, the word purpose hit its peak popularity in both Google Search and news between September of 2021 and March of 2022.[13] Not surprisingly, the rise in interest around purpose coincided with the peak popularity of other terms, including the great resignation,[14] hybrid working,[15] languishing,[16] and side hustles.[17] When you step back from these trends, it is clear that leaders and corporations were searching for a way to rebuild commitment, get employees back in the office, and remind their talent (and their consumers) why the world is better with them in it.

Now, it is easy to question whether the rise in purpose is simply marketing or a true shift in the way we construct, create, and redesign our organizations. Either way, an authentic connection to purpose (a company's answer to the question "why is the world better with us in it?") is a consummate buffer to fit as it allows us to put stressors, frustrations, setbacks, and hardships in the context of something that ultimately feels important or consequential. In a 2020 PwC study with over five hundred listed and private companies, they found that over 54% have defined a clear and relevant purpose, but only 13% publicly disclose how purpose is embedded in their cultural and operating models[18]—showcasing how difficult many have found embedding purpose into the heart of the organization to be. Thus, talent, customers, and stakeholders have a hard time connecting to the purpose in their everyday interactions with the company. This so-called purpose gap is widening as branding around purpose without meaningful impact or is being seen as inauthentic or disingenuous and likely will erode value over time.

Obviously, there is a lot of work that companies need to do to ensure their reason for being flows through the operations of the business and the many touch points they have with their talent. Further, they must create the space for that same talent to explore their own sense of purpose. In his book *Deep Purpose: The Heart and Soul of High-Performing Companies*, Ranjay Gulati argues that "companies must clear space for individuality alongside conformity."[19] In other words, in order for talent to serve their company's purpose, they need to be clear about and be supported in living their own sense of purpose.

Until this occurs more regularly, we must all seek out connections to purpose that exist but may not always be in our direct line of sight. If you're looking to retain *right fit* or manage a *wrong fit* experience, try to connect to the company purpose at least once a week.

Here are some ideas:

- Use the product or the service as a consumer in an authentic way.
- Seek consumer stories that resonate on internal or external channels.
- Listen to the earnings calls for inspirational stories of impact.
- Read the company's sustainability or ESG report.
- Shadow someone from the sales organization during client calls or visits.
- Attend or watch the recordings of town halls, all-hands meetings, etc.

Increase Meaningful Work, Decrease Busy Work

One of the most-often cited opportunities to improve your day-to-day at work is to increase the meaningfulness of work. There are two roads to accomplishing this—one is about the nature of the work itself (how much do the core elements of your work align to your passions and interests, provide you the opportunity to learn new skills, or connect to a cause you care about), and the other is about how time is spent (how much time is spent in high-value activities versus low-value activities.) Now, you might be saying, "don't these two elements of work overlap?" The short answer is no, not at all. You see, you can assess your work on two totally independent vectors— how meaningful the work is to you and how much value a body of work will bring to a consumer you serve.

Let's take a practical example. Assume you're a high school history teacher who decided to quit your full-time job and substitute teach for a while. One day, you are called into your local high school to cover class for the English teacher, who is out on vacation. Your teaching credentials allow you to teach English, but it's not your passion, so these eight hours are less meaningful to you than your time spent teaching history, as they don't align to your passions or career interests. However, you believe teaching is important and any hours with a student is a chance to have an impact, so you feel motivated.

Now, assume you're still that history teacher and you are asked to substitute for a high school history class, but you're supposed to spend the day reading from the textbook and proctoring a pop quiz on the material. So, you are in the space that you care about, but the work itself is not high-impact (reading text aloud and proctoring a quiz). It's meaningful to you, but the tasks have relatively low value. The sweet spot is to spend as much of your time in work that is both meaningful to you and high impact to your consumers.

As the Figure 7.1 shows, when you have either meaningful work or high-impact work, you will see commitment. But, to gain true attachment, you need both meaning and impact. In

> **COMPANY INSIGHT**
> One of the most untapped areas of productivity and engagement is for a company to better understand how time is being used at work. Between the statistic that 41% of activities at work don't add value,[20] the importance talent places on meaningful work, and the amazing work technology we have available, there is an opportunity to make more of the day meaningful to more people. If just 10% of our time added more value, imagine the difference. What if that number was 30%?

almost every *right fit* experience, talent that I interviewed commented that the work they were doing both felt important and was in an area where they had a passion or demonstrated expertise.

In an article titled "The Importance of Meaningful Work," Christopher Michaelson commented on the concept of meaningful work and the research he had been conducting in his classrooms for many years.[21] In each of his classes, he asks his students to respond to the following questions:

- What do you expect your job will be a year from now? (pragmatic answer)
- What kind of job contributes the most to the general well-being? (altruistic answer)
- If you could do anything ten years from now, what would it be? (ideal answer)

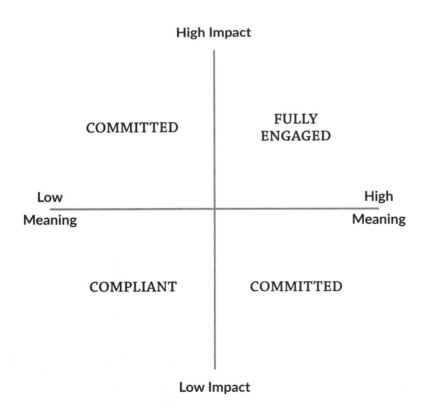

Figure 7.1: Meaningful Work Grid

Interestingly, in 2009 he found very little correlation of answers for each question to the others both in the individuals' responses and across the entire population. Thus, students were, on the whole, saying that though they see how all three objectives matter (having a job, having a job that contributes to societal well-being, and having a job they will enjoy most), very few of them expected to have all three in their career.

Now, if you fast forward, what people expect from their job has changed radically. In a 2021 Gartner study of 3,315 employees who were asked if their attitudes have changed post-pandemic, nearly 55% of respondents said that it has caused them to want to contribute more to society and made them question the purpose of their day-to-day job.[22] Additionally, in that same year an IBM study found that the second most cited reason for changing jobs was because they were searching for more purposeful and meaningful work.[23] Further, McKinsey reported 89% of employees wanted more purpose in their lives and 70% of those same respondents said that their sense of purpose is largely defined by work. The takeaway is that employees are looking for more out of their day-to-day at work.[24]

Employees today are much more aware of the part work should and will play in their lives and are motivated to have a job that contributes to society and that gives back to them personally. Whereas Michaelson showed us that our expectations for what kind of job we will have don't always match what job we should have or want to have, Gartner shows us that there is a stronger pull for employees to search for more meaningful jobs or jobs that integrate into their lives. To find those opportunities, talent will need to be more prepared and more discerning, while companies will need to build mechanisms for recruiting and retention that allow meaning and integration into life to build over time.

If we examine the impact of work (busy work versus high-impact work), we see a similar trend. In 2021, Asana, a SAAS (software-as-a-service) productivity tool, published a survey of more than 10,600 global workers. In

COMPANY INSIGHT

One of the most popular and least understood items in employee engagement surveys is the question about whether "I have the materials and resources needed to do my job." This item is rarely scored well, but our orientation to it is often misguided, as we believe the issue to be people or money-related. If we move upstream, both of those issues are a symptom of a larger issue around the ineffective use of time. Often, when we feel like we can't get everything done, we really need more money and more people, not more tools. Maybe trying to do less or doing the same amount more effectively is a good place to start. If this intrigues you, check out Chapter 10.

this survey, Asana found that people spent about 58% of their day doing "work about work" (communicating about work, searching for information, switching between apps, managing shifting priorities, or chasing status updates). Employees cited that they waste about five hours a week, or six total working weeks a year, because of what they term "busy work" (duplicate tasks and pointless meetings). Not surprisingly, 33% of those same workers felt their attention span is shorter than it was a year ago, meaning that even when they are in a high-value meeting, they are likely distracted or trying to do multiple things. And lastly, about 40% of people and 53% of Gen Z workers say they don't have a clear start or finish time to their workday, resulting in workers saying they experienced burnout 2.3 times in the last year.[25]

So, talent are left with an opportunity to look for ways to increase the amount of "high-impact" work they do within the day. And, if they do that, they'll likely see increases in attention span, lower rates of burnout, and less "wasted time." Interestingly, this issue of time prioritization is not new. President Dwight Eisenhower reflected on the tension when he said "What is important is seldom urgent and what is urgent is seldom important."[26] This quote resulted in the creation of the Eisenhower Matrix, a tool many of us are familiar with and could use a return to in these times. The matrix allows you to separate tasks or work based on how important something is and how urgent it is. (See Figure 7.2.)

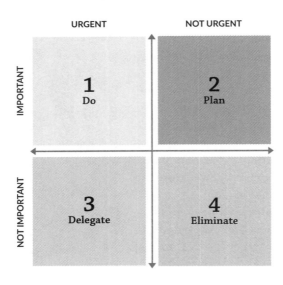

Figure 7.2: The Eisenhower Matrix

Now that it is clear that meaningful work is both about the nature of the work and the amount of time in a day that is spent on it, it should be clear that you can shift some of what you are doing to be more meaningful work. And, there is no perfect world. Everyone, in every job, will have low-value tasks, work that is not a match to their passions or career interests, and "busy work" that is just the price of, well, doing business. The question is not "How can I get rid of the meaningless stuff?" It's "How can I put more of my day toward more meaningful activities?"

- **Do a time study of your work over the last month.** Look at how your time was used, how much of it was structured, where there are nonvalue activities that you could remove or reduce, and where time is seemingly disappearing (meaning it isn't clear where it goes or why). No matter your level, you have some control over your calendar and what you say yes or no to doing.
- **Get super clear about your passions, career interests, and super-powers.** How many coworkers know the full version of your capability and passion to these questions? If you're like most of us, very few. Well, share them. Tell people what you're good at and interested in. Look for opportunities to bring those skills to bear. I promise, once people know you're passionate and interested in something, nine times out of ten, they'll give you an opportunity to do it.
- **Look for ways to bring more of your passion and career interests into your core activities.** In other words, redesign the work you have to create the space for it to be more meaningful. Inside every project/initiative, there is an opportunity to design the way work gets done. Think about what you are doing today. Think about how you could do that if you brought [x] skill/passion/career interest into it.
- **Say "no" more. Raise your hand more.** I have been in corporate America for twenty-five-plus years and the one lesson I know for sure is that every company will use you and your skills however you let them. I have rarely been ridiculed for saying no and rarely not been given a chance to contribute when I raised my hand. Opportunity is there. Take it. But, always say no to a few things before you say yes to something new.

If You are Learning and Growing, Hard Things Are Just a Bit Easier

If you are wondering how learning and growth contribute to a fuller life, just ask Nola Ochs.[27] Nola Ochs was a lot of things—a farmer in rural Kansas, a devoted wife, a mother to four sons, a survivor of dust storms and hard times, and a great-grandmother to fifteen great-grandkids. Maybe the most extraordinary thing she was, though, was a lifelong learner. You see, Nola Ochs was the Guinness World Record holder as the world's oldest college graduate when she earned her general studies degree with an emphasis in history, graduating alongside her granddaughter, Alexandra Ochs, who was twenty-one years old.

As if this wasn't enough, Nola kept on learning, and soon after graduation and a stint as a storyteller for Carnival Cruise Lines, she took on her master's and received her degree at the young age of ninety-eight years old. At her hundredth birthday, she was still taking college courses and was a graduate teaching assistant. Nola is quoted as saying "the yearning for study was always there. I loved to learn . . . It gave me such a feeling of satisfaction."[28]

Nola was absolutely on to something. Multiple research studies have shown that learning can increase the size of your brain,[29] improve your self-confidence,[30] help you become more curious,[31] curb anxiety and depression,[32] and propel you to greater levels of success.[33] So, if you can find your way to a learning orientation during a *wrong fit* or *hard fit* experience, you can gain important lessons of experience that will aid you as your career progresses. Not convinced? McKinsey offers some compelling insights from a study of 1,800 companies globally examining performance.[34] They found that the best companies (highest financial performance) focus both on challenging performance targets and the growth of their internal talent in unison.

> **COMPANY INSIGHT**
> Companies that promote and make time for their talent to engage in learning opportunities and who promote continuous learning as a cultural cornerstone regularly outperform competitors in the marketplace. This isn't about more training programs; it's about how to ensure your talent is growing faster than the company. Check out Chapter 10 for ideas.

The Center for Creative Leadership (CCL) focused thirty years of research on a singular question: "How does talent learn, grow, and change over the course of their career?"[35] Through this research, titled Lessons of Experience, CCL uncovered some fundamental principles that can guide talent in unlocking their potential over time. First, they were able to identify five clusters of events that offer learning opportunities:

- Challenging assignments (increasing scope of role, first supervisory role, turnarounds, etc.)

- Developmental relationships (role models, mentors, teachers, managers, difficult people, etc.)
- Hardships or adverse situations (crisis, scandals, discrimination/injustice, mistakes, career setbacks, etc.)
- Coursework and training (e-learning, training, coaching, books, etc.)
- Personal experiences (graduations, birth of a child, living in a new country, etc.)

Figure 7.3: Top Ways Leaders Learn over Their Career

Though the categorization of events that offer potential learning to talent is helpful, the research produced some other particularly relevant insights:

First, the majority of developmental experiences came from a combination of challenging assignments and developmental relationships, while coursework and training were less frequently cited as foundational.

Second, experience in these sorts of events does not automatically lead to learning. Learning takes work. Talent who continue to progress in their careers use key events and turn them into lessons of experience that shift behavior, change habits, and alter their approach in the future. This can only happen through reflection, relating the experience to context, making connections to previous events, and moving beyond awareness to practicing new behaviors or approaches until a more optimal one is found.

Third, the diversity of the experiences matters. The more types of key events an executive has faced, the more they are able to extend the arena of possibilities where they can operate, gain new skills, and shift their way of thinking and being in the world.

Lastly, and maybe most pertinent to this chapter, hardships represent a very particular type of learning opportunity, as they offer a leader the unique opportunity to learn during and at the close of a tough time.

When you don't have fit in your organization or you are finding it hard to retain the fit you once had, you have an opportunity to lean into a hardship, and by doing that, you can learn some unique and powerful lessons:[36]

COMPANY INSIGHT

We often undervalue the learning opportunity in transitions (onboarding, lateral moves, promotions, demotions, geographic moves, etc.), but they are the moments when talent is most reflective and most open. Companies would be smart to overinvest in key transitions as a way to ensure talent grows over time. See Chapter 10 for more on this idea.

- **Compassion and sensitivity:** Humility is often the bedfellow of hardship. In these moments, we learn that we aren't perfect, invincible, or immune to difficult situations. By going through hardship, we often become more attuned to others' suffering and are more understanding when they are facing difficult times.
- **Self-knowledge and perspective:** When you face a real hardship, you come face to face with who you really are—your limitations, true values, patterns of thought, and even skills that you didn't know you had. Hardships often bring out the most raw version of ourselves.
- **The limits of control:** Hardships provide us a chance to separate what we really control from what we don't. We can become much clearer about where we can impact our own lives and the lives of others and where we might need to let go a little more.
- **Flexibility:** When we come through a hardship, we have greater resilience, strength, and durability to tackle the world. When we can clear out the emotion, we can find a more stable ground. And, it doesn't have to be when the hardship ends, but can be when we have small wins or moments of thriving in chaos.

So, now that you can see how learning can happen from key events, including hardships, you are probably wondering how to make the shift—

how to move from being a victim of circumstance to seeing the moment as a powerful opportunity to learn. Here are a few tips:

Acknowledge you are in an adverse situation or hardship. Learning doesn't happen when we are under stress or in a fight-or-flight situation. In order to learn, we must work to see the situation as something we are a part of, not something that is happening to us. When we see ourselves in the situation as opposed to being impacted by the situation, it gives us the opportunity to eventually shape and use the situation.

Choose your preferred way to reflect. In order for learning to begin, we need a way to capture what we are seeing, thinking, feeling, and hoping for out of the situation. Some people like to journal, while others like to use conversation with trusted friends or prompts of a coach. Just make sure that you get out of your head and create a way to capture all that is happening. Here are a few questions you can use every day:

- *How do I feel in the morning? During the day? When I return from work?*
- *What do I spend my quiet time thinking about?*
- *What happened during the day that gave me energy? What took it away?*
- *What was I hoping to get out of the day? What stood in the way?*
- *What is one new approach I am going to take tomorrow?*

Treat every day as a prototype. Once you have reflected a bit on the situation you're in and have started to see it as an opportunity to learn, it's time to treat every day like a prototype, a laboratory to try out new ideas, take new approaches, bring in new mindsets, and reset your expectations of others. You may be in a really tough spot at work, and you might need to leave to resolve it. Before you go, it's worth trying out some new behaviors, since you have nothing to lose. Prototypes are small, planned experiments that we use to seek answers about whether a product or service will provide value. In one of my early jobs, I remember calling a mentor and telling them "I wasn't happy and didn't feel like the place held the same values I hold." His response was simple. He said, "Stay. If you can be successful with people who don't see the world how you see it, then you can be a world-class consultant." I stayed, prototyped, learned a ton, and then went on to do better work as a result. Jeanne Liedtka, the author of

Designing for Growth, sums up this idea of prototypes as "basic, low-cost artifacts that can capture the essence of the user experience."[37] She suggests testing small attributes in a quick and super rough way so you can gain lessons, alter the approach, and try again. Try out one new way of leading in one situation. Reflect on it. Revamp the approach and try again.

Activate an objective sounding board. We need someone who can give us real feedback about whether we're making progress, not someone who simply listens and supports where we are and how we feel. Both supports and sounding boards are important, but the latter role is different. A sounding board can help you look for forward momentum, new insights, and distance from the situation.

A Consumer in Need Is a Clear Path to Commitment

When we struggle to find our feet inside the company we joined or feel our commitment to a place we have been for a while fade, we tend to focus on the internal factors that surround our day—a demotivating manager, a project that doesn't fully utilize our skills, competitive or uninviting team members, or unfamiliar ways of working. Given everything we have shared about fit thus far (and the rise in quiet quitting, languishing, and burnout), that focus on your day-to-day is vital. However, when we're in a moment of hardship, that focus can feed our cynicism and accelerate our path to disengagement.

To keep confidence, inspiration, and energy high, one of the greatest (and most often ignored) buffers is to find a consumer in need—a consumer that you relate to who needs help in a space where you can be helpful.

The research on how employee engagement impacts consumer engagement is vast.[38] We know that as the level of disengaged employees drops, a consumer's likelihood to recommend the company increases. Further, companies with highly engaged employees have twice the customer loyalty, twice the annual net income, higher safety scores, fewer quality incidents, and three times the net promoter score (NPS) of companies that are lagging on engagement.[39] However, there has been little or no research into how a stronger connection to consumers impacts employee engagement.

Here's what we do know. We know that there are common factors that impact employee engagement, including workplace culture, communication, managerial styles, leadership, and company reputation.[40] Embedded in these factors is a hidden red thread, the consumer. The more we connect to our consumers, their hopes, their aspirations, their challenges, and the ways we are helping them to live better lives, the more we will be committed—especially in the face of challenges or hardships. If you can find your way to the consumer on a more regular basis, you can tap into hidden energy.

If you're in HR, find the most stressed-out employee. If you're in finance, find the general manager who is struggling to pull the levers of their P&L. If you're in UX design or IT, find a potential buyer who is struggling to move through your website. Or, simply bring the consumer into your project by practicing design thinking (shameless plug for Jeanne Liedtka's *Designing for Growth* as a place to start). The consumer can be found in stories, in our neighborhoods, through our current projects, or via our best friend at work. Increase your connection to your consumer and you will see many (not all) of the contextual barriers disappear. This is because when you have a consumer front and center, you naturally want to provide them the best possible experience. So, here's what can you do:

- **In any project or initiative, ask yourself a simple question—** Would the consumer pay an extra five cents on the dollar for this work? If not, what would it take for them to do so?
- **Go through your corporate intranet, annual reports, and leadership town halls** and spend five minutes a day finding one story, case study, or example of how the company is helping the consumer you serve. The more stories you find, the more you will feel pride for and commitment to the consumer.
- **Put the consumer at the center of your work projects.** We often design for the consumer without pulling the consumer into the design. Design thinking gives us a way to build empathy for the consumer, understand who they are, what they need, and why they are struggling. You'll not only see higher levels of motivation to push through with the project but will also gain insights that will allow the project to be a success.
- **Look outside your current *hard fit* experience and find new ways and new spaces to help the consumer.** There are very few teams that wouldn't take help if offered. And, many consumers outside your company need help. Actually many organizations have platforms to allow talent to take on short-term, learning experiences. Find an experience (inside your company or in a volunteer capacity) that puts you closer to the consumer, and spend three to five hours a week in that space.

Spending More Time Won't Result in Better Fit

Back in 2013, Julian Birkinshaw and Jordan Cohen[41] presented some fascinating research on talent's relationship with time. They found that there are actually more hours in a day than we realize. It isn't about making the day longer though; it is about making better use of the time we have. They found that knowledge workers spend a great deal of their time—an average of 41%—on discretionary activities that are neither personally fulfilling nor central to the success of the company. In their interviews of over forty-five leaders in thirty-nine companies, they found that even the best devoted large amounts of time to tedious activities that don't add value, such as administrative desk work and managing across the business. Interestingly, leaders chose to attend meetings they felt were unnecessary because they didn't want to let the meeting host down or miss the chance to socialize. Another reason for these tasks being in our day-to-day is that organizations have pushed administrative, low-value tasks back to their teams to reduce cost. The work still has to get done, but it's now being accomplished by higher-paid individuals.

Often in my interviews, I heard that when talent found themselves in a *wrong fit* or *hard fit* experience, they described their experience as trying to work harder or "grinding" to find a path to success. They felt the need to spend more time making the experience work, or at least feeling like they were spending more time. In truth, something else might have been happening. In a 2013 study of procrastination, researchers Pychyl and Sirois found that when under stress (maybe because of a deadline or being in a less-than-optimal working situation), we will tend toward procrastination.[42] However, procrastination isn't what we assume. It isn't about idly wasting time, or being lazy. In fact, procrastination is about losing time on the tasks at hand due to our urgent need to "manage negative emotions." In other words, we will tend to feel like we have less time in the day because time is being lost to protracted moments of worrying about our place in the org, our worry about whether our next meeting will be better, and managing our increasingly negative mood or loss of confidence.

Adding further complexity to this obsession we all have of working harder in the face of *wrong fit* is the ancillary impacts of doing so. Working harder to fit in requires more energy, creates more stress, pulls even further on our time and can dominate our thoughts while at work and at home. As a result, my interviewees reported big dips in overall engagement, well-being, and health. When describing the impact of *wrong fit* experiences, interviewees consistently mentioned that over time, they experienced moments of burnout, issues in their home life, a loss of confidence, and in many cases despair, depression, and a loss of capability in their craft.

In the end, it's crystal clear that working harder to fit in does not produce *right fit*; rather, an even greater gap between the talent and the company gets created. So, if you find yourself struggling to find fit, focus your time carefully. Take a hard look at your calendar and your approach to your day. You might find there is more time if you adopt these strategies:

- **Examine the last month of your calendar and look at who you met with and the purpose of those meetings.** How many meetings are with BFFs, doppelgangers (a coworker who shares common ways of working/sensibilities with you), mentors, leaders you respect, or your manager? How many meetings are about work that you truly care about? How many meetings put you in proximity to the consumer or customer? How many meetings provide you a chance to learn? How many hours in total are you spending thinking about, or participating in meetings for your job?
- **Think about the rhythm of work and life you aspire to have.** How many hours do you want to spend at work? What hours work best for you? How do you want to feel at the beginning of your day? What do you need to do to leave your work at work when you close your laptop?
- **Treat your calendar as a prototype**. Try to create a next week that is closer to your ideal in terms of time, types of meetings, and people you work alongside. At the end of the week, examine the outcomes. Did anyone notice the changes you made? Were you missed at meetings you declined? Did you find your way into work or meetings that felt more meaningful? How do you feel about the week? What do you want to keep from this prototype? What do you want to do differently next week?

These inspirational buffers, like the relational buffers to follow, are mutually reinforcing—meaning that as you dig into one of them and see benefits, they increase the availability and power of the others. However, unlike relational buffers that feed your connection to others, inspirational buffers increase your capacity for better and more value-added work by building energy, excitement, and deeper insights in you. In other words, inspirational buffers are natural motivators. From Todd Thrash's great work on inspiration, we know that inspiration is not the "lightning strike" that we believe it is. It's actually a motivational process that moves from seeing a source of inspiration to being inspired and then to taking action to transfer that inspiration to something new, different, better, or more meaningful.[43]

REAL STORIES OF FIT
A Right Fit Story
40, male, travel

A strong sense of purpose and connection to a product can be the ultimate buffer for fit and a path to building strong attachment with talent. This interviewee cited a strong and consistent connection to purpose in his *right fit* experience, almost from the very first moment. When asked about how purpose impacted his experience, he said, "Being new to the [travel] industry, there were some true travel nerds, people who are tracking prices and types of planes . . . they were obsessed. And, I liked how passionate people were about travel. They would work really hard on flights for others and then hop on a plane cross-country for a day. It wasn't my thing, but seeing people be so passionate was inspiring."

This connection to travel was resident in both the people the interviewee was surrounded by and in the core elements of the early experience. His multi-day orientation wasn't a run-of-the-mill experience. Instead, it was connected to the industry and had employees play tourist for a day. The interviewee said, "When I first experienced it, it felt like a scavenger hunt around the city . . . nothing super exciting. But, I came to appreciate that it was meant to show what the company was about . . . creating fun adventures."

This sense of connection to the thing that a company does was a "red thread" or connection for this interviewee across his experiences, and in some ways made even the *hard fit* or *wrong fit* experiences right—for a moment, anyway.

CHAPTER 8

Relational Buffers and Enhancing Fit Over Time

REAL STORIES OF FIT
A *Wrong Fit Story*
45, female, food and beverage

Relationships have the power to make our day or break our backs at work. In this interview, the leader's *right fit* and *wrong fit* experiences happened at the same company. She held a firm belief that "*right fit* is rooted in a feeling of psychological safety," which she defined as an environment where "you can be yourself, you can fumble, you can laugh, and you are having a good time, but you are also challenging the heck out of each other."

In her worst fit experience, her leader's behavior eroded the psychological safety that this interviewee had enjoyed for many years. The company had promoted this individual very quickly because she got results but "left an aftermath of bodies behind her." Interestingly, the interviewee didn't blame the leader for the *wrong fit* experience—she blamed the company. "I watched the company condone this leader's behavior by promoting her while espousing people-focused values and all the rhetoric around leadership behavior. I lost massive respect for the company. Candidly, that is the reason I left."

The power of relationships is clear in this example, and it isn't just about toxic individual leaders or competitive teams. The system (i.e., the senior leaders) has a responsibility to condone behaviors by holding all individuals to the values and ways of working they promote.

A. A. Milne, the author of the *Winnie-the-Pooh* series, wrote, "After all, one can't complain. I have my friends."[1] Behind the colorful characters and witty adventures, A. A. Milne primarily wrote about friendship and how much we (and Pooh) need people in our lives to be happy, fulfilled, safe, and motivated to be or do more. This need for connection extends into our companies and our *right fit* experiences. Close your eyes and picture your most *right fit* work experience. My guess is you pictured the people as much as you pictured your office or the brand. This is because our experience, as humans, is a human one. One of my interviewees summed up the relational element of work when she was describing what made her *right fit* experience different: "These are people who care about people, and they're hiring me because I care about people. I was able to immediately see myself as part of the whole thing . . . like there's this magic connection . . . this is my place."

Whether you are currently in "your place" (i.e., in a *right fit* experience) or are striving to get there, relationships can help—they help us connect to purpose (through people who live and breathe the company), help us gain skills (though people who are masters of craft), and help us to see how we can be a success (through people who are your doppelgangers). Like inspirational buffers, the relational buffers will aid us on our journey to *right fit* and to build a deeper attachment to our role, our team, and our company. And, they will increase the chances of us having fun along the way.

As a reminder, this chapter will cover these relational buffers:

- A supportive leader/manager
- Meaningful mentors
- Workplace BFFs or doppelgangers
- Making sure "life outside of work is magic"

How to Make Your Manager Great and Mold Them for the Future

A quick search for "great managers" on Amazon showed the following titles: *Everyone Deserves a Great Manager, Great Managers Are Always Nice, The Leader Lab: Core Skills to Become a Great Manager, The Miracle Manager, 1 on 1 Management: What Every Great Manager Knows That You Don't, When They Win You Win: Being A Great Manager Is Simpler Than You Think, The First-Time Manager, It's the Manager, The Making of a Manager*, and on and on.

There are plenty of words out there on how to be a caring, great, nice, winning, first-time, in-the-know, miracle manager. I won't be adding to them here. Instead, I want to offer talent a look at how they can shape the manager they have into the manager they need.

You see, I'm a firm believer that the team makes the manager, not the other way around. Imagine if you gave me the absolute best manager in the world today, the one who has read all the books on Amazon (though I'm not sure that is humanly possible) and has managed to put all those practices into play in a way that is truly, mesmerizingly engaging. Then, I give you a team of degenerate, disengaged, dysfunctional, and disrespectful team members. Odds are the team will win (in this case, they would likely render the manager to average, if not low, performance). Now, this extreme example isn't reality, not even close, but it does make an important point . . . that is, the team makes the manager. The team has the power to shift a manager's behavior, change their ways of working, and create an environment that is collaborative, inclusive, and highly productive. It takes time, energy, and effort, to be sure, but it can be done.

The Power of Positive Reinforcement

First, let's start with what you can do. The easiest way to shape your manager's behavior is to reinforce the behaviors you want to see more of, every chance you get. One of my teams used to tell me that the easiest way to get me to do anything was simply to tell me, "this would mean a lot to us, and you would be really, really good at it." As I reflect on my interactions with them, I see that it almost always worked. It worked partially because I adored my team (and truly would have done almost anything for them), but mostly because of a little-known secret about managers—they are all looking for feedback.

> **COMPANY INSIGHT**
>
> Often, expectations for managers are shared with managers but not with their teams. What if you trained everyone on what makes a great manager and gave teams the tools and assets to reinforce the right behaviors when they see them (e.g., reimagined recognition or employee sentiment systems)? Remember, day-to-day life is the greatest classroom on earth—all we need is a group of people around us committed to helping us learn. Enlisting the team as the coach is a potential first step.

As leaders move up and through the organization, individual feedback will typically have an inverse relationship to seniority, meaning that a CEO will get a lot less feedback than an entry-level new recruit. Now, this might seem counterintuitive, because it is. One would think that as the stakes go up for a person's role, more feedback should be sought and offered. It isn't that there isn't feedback, but the majority of feedback is less about you as an individual and more about your leadership and its ability to produce results at the team or organizational level.

For most managers or leaders, they may understand that their teams are performing, but they may know very little about the why behind it or how they are contributing to that success or or detracting from it. Even the most self-aware leaders tend to misattribute their own strengths and development areas. In numerous research studies about the discrepancy between self ratings and other's ratings in 360 instruments, researchers almost universally find that a leader's self ratings are elevated, meaning they are higher than their raters'.[2] Given this elevated sense of effectiveness that many (or most) managers carry about themselves, it's important to help them calibrate by providing them a better sense of where they are great and where they might be better. In other words, conditioning the behavior you would like to see. Social science is a great guide here.

Operant conditioning is a well-studied area of social science that dates way back to research of B. F. Skinner in the 1940s and is defined as a principle that states, "behavior that is followed by pleasant consequences is likely to be repeated, and behavior followed by unpleasant consequences is likely to be diminished or disappear over time."[3] On the surface, this might seem like a blinding flash of the obvious, but through his ingenious measurement technique (dubbed "the Skinner Box") he was able to discern whether a stimulus would have a positive impact (reinforcer), a negative impact (punisher), or a neutral impact (neutral operant) on future behavior. Core to Skinner's contributions was the idea that positive reinforcement is the most rewarding stimulus. The concept that rewards increase the likelihood of a behavior being repeated was fundamental to modern motivational theory and spanned areas from education to the workplace.

In an examination of the research on reinforcement and motivation, Judy Cameron and W. David Pierce offer an interesting separation of reinforcement and reward in applied settings. They argue that a "reinforcer" is an event that increases the frequency of the behavior it follows, while a reward is a positive event that evokes emotion but doesn't have a clear link to any behaviors.[4] To put this in context, let's say your manager just finished a meeting that you really enjoyed. By saying "good job" or "I liked that meeting," you are providing a reward as the comment will increase positive emotion but does nothing to aid repeatability. However, if you were to reflect on what you liked about the meeting and the role your manager played, you might say something like, "I really like how you opened the meeting by asking each of us to share something that inspired us. It helped us generate more ideas than I expected." That comment is positive reinforcement, as it zeros in on a behavior that can be reintroduced or repeated.

As a team member, you have the opportunity to mold your leader by being choiceful about when you give them feedback (closer to the behavior is more powerful) and the kind of feedback you give (reward or reinforcement). If you focus your feedback on positive reinforcement of behaviors you would like to see repeated, two things will happen almost automatically. First, you will increase the likelihood that when your manager is presented with a similar situation, they'll do more of what garnered them the positive feedback. Secondly, you will be seen as helpful, which will increase their level of trust for you as a team member. Here are a few additional thoughts on how to mold your manager:

- Reflect on all the managers you have had over your career (or return to the Ideal Manager Excursion from Chapter 4). List the behaviors that engaged you and those that didn't. Use that list to catch your current manager doing great things. These are likely to be sound manager behaviors that would help them with anyone, and they are things that will improve your day-to-day as well. Win-win.
- Get in a rhythm of giving positive reinforcement when your manager does something that positively impacts your experience. Every manager wants to be great for their team, and very few are getting nudges in the right direction. They will lap up the feedback.
- When your manager is looking for places where they can be better or do better, be clear about the top three behaviors that you would like to see changed and share with them the better practice. Don't limit the conversation to just what they are doing wrong or aren't doing at all, as it doesn't give them direction for the future.

The Search for Belonging through Mentoring

In every organization I have ever spent time in, there is a group of people who are shining examples of the best of the organization. Maybe they spent their entire career there, have mastered a craft core to the company's mission, or represent the essence of the mission and values. Sometimes you find the unicorn that manages to do all three flawlessly. Regardless, when you are looking to buffer a *hard fit* experience or keep *right fit* through transitions, knowing and spending time with these sorts of individuals in a mentoring capacity can be a huge energy boost and keep you connected to the bigger promise when the context around your day-to-day shifts or moves.

Mentoring relationships are essential to career progression and engagement. You don't have to look much further than a recent article in the *Harvard Business Review* by Marianna Tu and Michael Li titled "What Great

Mentorship Looks Like in a Hybrid Workplace" to see its importance in our new world. Based on their work with first-generation college students, Tu and Li found mentoring is not just a powerful tool for career development, but, more importantly, it also increases the rapport (respect and trust) that is felt between the individuals.[5] This can, in turn, help increase engagement, reduce loneliness, and help individuals stay resilient in the face of major challenges like the COVID-19 pandemic, a downturn in the economy, or a large-scale transformation of the company.

Further, according to a recent survey by SurveyMonkey and *CNBC*, more than 70% of talent who have a mentor are satisfied with their jobs, feel they are well paid, believe their contributions are valued, and believe their companies provide them with excellent or good opportunities to advance their careers. These trends hold across demographic categories like age and tenure. The most interesting piece of data is that across individual contributors, managers, senior managers, and vice presidents, those who have a mentor are less likely to consider quitting their job. Again, mentors create connections, and connections are the seeds of commitment.[6]

Mentoring has another powerful impact: it increases the level of commitment and belonging we have to the company we joined. In that respect, mentoring from storytellers (those who have been at a company for many years and have collected the all the tall tales or lived through them), models (those who bleed the mission and values of the company), and masters of craft (those who have built a skill set within a context that is pure art) have the ability to deepen our connection to a place, a purpose, and a story in a way that few others could. Rarely are these individuals in the top leadership positions and even less frequently are they used in the capacity of mentoring. They are usually on the fringes, roaming the hallowed halls, or locked away in their lab creating the next big thing. Over my career, I have often sought them out, invited them into my programs and built relationships with them over time. Rarely did I find them to be anything but available to help the next generation carry the torch.

COMPANY INSIGHT

If your company doesn't have a company mentor program, consider building one. Mentoring programs don't have to be expensive and can simply be an expectation of leaders across the company to help all talent learn and grow. The secret is to separate managing, coaching, and mentoring from each other and make sure that mentoring is focused on specific talent pools such as new joiners, diverse talent, or next-gen talent. Oh, and make sure you train the mentors—it isn't for everyone.

With that said, mentoring requires effort and structure for it to really work. So, if you're going to pursue a mentor, think through the following factors:

- What are you looking most for out of the relationship (career advice, connection to the company, inspiration in your craft, a model for leadership, etc.)? Without knowing this, it is difficult to choose the right person.
- Does your company have a formal mentoring program or technology that can aid you in your search? If so, use it. If not, look for a mentor who is in your network even if they are a "weak connection," meaning they might be a friend of a friend or an acquaintance.
- Are you clear about how mentoring works and what makes a relationship a success? If not, there is plenty of information out there to peruse. My best piece of advice is to own the relationship and time bound the first set of engagements. It is easier for a mentor to commit if the responsibility is just three or four sessions to start. Also, keep the sessions short (forty-five minutes each) and come in with a clear agenda. The agenda should be question based and focused on real areas where you are struggling or looking for wisdom.

A Workplace BFF or Doppelganger

Did you know that the Bureau of Labor Statistics's Time Use Survey shows that the average American now spends less than four minutes a day "hosting and attending social events?"[7] That is twenty-four hours a year. Huh? That same study investigated a broader category of "socializing and communicating" between two adults, where communicating is the main purpose of the activity as opposed to being incidental to some other activity, like working—think the heart-to-heart with a spouse or happy hour with a friend or a coffee with a colleague out of the office. The study found that, on average, Americans spend about thirty minutes a day in this sort of activity.[8] That's less than watching television (three hours) and even grooming (one hour for women, forty-four minutes for men). The irony is that study after study shows us that good social relationships are one of the most consistent predictors of a happy life, with some going as far as stating it is a fundamental building block.

The point: Regardless of if you are in a *right fit* experience or currently struggling with fit, more relationships will increase your chances of being happy. Gallup recently reported that having a best friend at work (someone you enjoy spending time with and/or don't want to let down) has become more vital to engagement due to the support needed to face the traumatic experiences stemming from the COVID-19 pandemic. Further, our best friends at work have helped us feel connected and seen as companies shifted to remote or hybrid ways of working. Lastly, when we have a best friend at work, we tend to feel more accountable to our work and our company as we don't want to let them down.[9]

In a similar vein, the *New York Times* reported on the "Magic of Your First Work Friends" and how they helped to crystallize who we would become in the years that follow.[10] Fundamental to those relationships lasting a long time was proximity. When you're young, living in the same city and having the same experiences, it's pretty easy to find time in between everything else to see each other, value each other, and grow with each other. When the pandemic hit, Gallup reported a drop of four percentage points in employees who felt they had a best friend at work.[11] Now, three years into the pandemic, those who have a best friend at work are more than twenty percentage points more likely than those without a best friend at work to recommend their organization as a best place to work and are about twelve percentage points less likely to look for a different job.[12]

So, a best friend at work is an obvious buffer, and the more of them you have, the greater the impact on your happiness and overall commitment to the company.

Beyond your BFF, there is another type of person that can help you gain a stronger sense of fit, and that is what I call your *doppelganger*. In this context, a doppelganger is someone in the organization who works like you work: they have the same sensibilities, values, beliefs, and often the same sorts of skills. One key difference is that they seem to move through the organization with greater ease. I have encountered these individuals in each of the companies I have worked within and sought them out early, as they were key enablers of my confidence remaining high, even when my days felt long and hard. You see, a doppelganger represents future possibilities as they are successful, and you can be, too. Often these individuals also become best friends at work as you see, feel, and struggle with many of the same work issues.

Whether you're seeking a doppelganger or a BFF, here are a few tips and tricks to finding them and keeping them as buffers:

1. **Look for them early and often inside your team, your department, or your function.** When we share a craft, we are more likely to share values, beliefs, skills, and mindsets. Designers tend to understand other designers, and CFOs often find it easier to relate to CFOs.

2. **Invest your free time in them and the relationship.** Time is a finite resource, and it gets taken by others quickly if we are not careful. So, find a way to connect, a reason to spend time together, and make sure it is in your calendar. I used to do writing with my doppelganger. We would give each other an assignment and write an article or an essay. The time spent was fun, it allowed us to get to know each other, and we forged a nearly unbreakable bond.

3. **When you're feeling a dip, dip into their energy.** When we start to lose our feet or feel like our fit to a team or a place is waning, we can often go quiet, disconnect, or look for solace outside of our company. These are all fair strategies to keep our sanity and our sense of self, but they can sometimes exacerbate the issue. Your doppelganger can help reinvigorate you—or at least, help you refocus your energies on work.

Make Life Outside of Work Magic

This is not a book about work-life balance, not even close. And, you should know up front that I'm not a big believer in the concept. Life is just life. It is a series of choices about what gives us energy, fulfills our dreams, provides us goals to strive for, and connects us to the values and beliefs that matter most. Well, that is what it is supposed to be at least. The truth is life rarely is perfect on every front—home life, work life, social life, personal health, financial health, etc. Why is that, you ask?

Well, Peter Block, a famous consultant, once said, "If you don't say no, then your yes is meaningless."[13] That quote has stayed with me ever since I heard him utter it the first time. What he meant is that every choice for something is removing the choice for something else. If we maximize focus on our personal health by training for a marathon or working out with a trainer every morning to lose twenty pounds, that time is not available for other things—it is time away from family or friends or work or the ever-popular side hustle. However, in our "more is more is more" mentality, we have come to believe we can have it all. Well, we can't, not really. But, what we can do is be more conscious of our choices, our yes's and our no's, so we can respect where our time is going.

I remember working at a Cleveland steel company during my first consulting job. I was there to help select line shift leaders through an assessment center. Over the course of the three months I spent there, I saw a group of people who had a very different orientation to their jobs than I did. They clocked in at 7:00 a.m. and out at 4:00 p.m. They worked hard, took an hour for lunch, and then left their job to pursue their lives. Their job wasn't their identity; it was a means to an end. It had purpose, but it was not primary to their lives and livelihood. As an ambitious, career-focused twenty-six-year-old, I was stunned, but learned to appreciate the power of their choices. You see, many of the shift leaders I met could have been running the mill. They were charismatic, savvy, interpersonally gifted, and super smart. They just wanted different things, and one of them was to leave their work at work.

For those of us who have made a commitment to work being a larger part of our lives, an end in and of itself, Scott Schieman of the University of Toronto offers some interesting insights. He did a study on work trends and found about 50% of people bring their work home, and many reported disruptions in their home life as a result.[14] Of particular distraction is the mobile devices that connect us, on the move, to our organizations. The average person checks their phone forty-six times per day and spends nearly five hours per day on their mobile devices.[15] In additional research by the team at Harvard Business School, Erin Reid and Robin Ely concluded that we work an average of 1,835 hours a year, up 9% from 1979.[16] So, for all the technological advances in work, they have resulted in us spending more time working. Not surprisingly, in Gallup's latest poll on life ratings, the number of Americans who are thriving has plummeted to a twelve-year low and is the lowest since the 2008 Great Recession.[17] The rapid downward movement is marked by a particularly sharp decrease in satisfaction with their current lives, as well as decreased feelings of resilience and optimism.

So, when we are in a less than ideal fit experience, it's vital to have some happiness and stability in the hours outside of work, especially in today's climate. A 2009 study by Kansas State University showed that employees who are engaged in their work have a happier home life. Most of us intuitively understand that when we are highly engaged and valued during our working hours, there are spillover effects in our homes. More interesting was the interaction effects the team saw between work and home. They concluded that stress at home and stress at work compound to make us more stressed in both domains. They also found that work engagement is heavily related to daily mood, and daily mood is positively correlated to one's ability to facilitate work and home.[18]

So, in order to have the energy needed to push through a *hard fit* experience or manage *wrong fit*, we need to maximize the happiness that can come from the hours outside of work as much as those within work. Instead of focusing additional hours on grinding to get ahead, we should think about using those hours to "build a happy home life." Now, I am the first to admit this is super hard to do, but there are some strategies that can help:

- **Set boundaries on your work.** Be fully focused and fully engaged in fewer hours, not more. Set these boundaries with your partner, spouse, or good friend and have them help you remain committed to them.
- **Don't let your outside work hours be filled with sensory pursuits.** When we are under stress, many of us will tend to focus on sensory pursuits that require little effort for just a bit of entertainment. When we are tired and down, the easiest thing is to mindlessly surf the internet, scroll TikTok, or binge Netflix. Don't. Have a list of activities that you will do during your nonwork hours. Make them active and make them collaborative if you can. I like to cook, walk the dogs, play pickleball (I know, I know), write, listen to vinyl, and have a good meal out with my wife or kids. Make sure you are doing at least one of these things every single day.
- **Create consistent space for yourself.** Imagine if I gave you thirty days off, took away your phone, removed you from your family, and said "spend your time doing all the things that bring you (and only you) joy." How would you spend your days? Seriously, map them out. What would you do? Take this list and carve out one or two hours a week to do these things for yourself without fail, even if you feel too tired. These are your bucket fillers, your energizers. This is your time.
- **Lastly, stash your work phone when you walk in the door or set up "focus modes" to minimize distractions.** Put it somewhere

hard to get (like in a cabinet or upstairs in your bedroom). It is a symbol of stress, and you will find yourself wanting to pick it up, look at what's happening, and respond. Or, if you can't part with your beloved phone, set up "routines" or "focus modes" in your phone—a work routine might have social media apps disabled and "do not disturb" turned on so you can better focus on your work. Truthfully, unless you're a surgeon, fireman, special assistant to the president, or on the verge of curing cancer, it can wait. I promise.

Whether you focus on the inspirational buffers from the previous chapter or the relational ones you reviewed here, they are here to help you retain *right fit* if you have it and move toward *right fit* if you don't. It is super easy to put these activities aside until you are in a stuck place (I would probably do the same). However, just like preventive medicine, the best time to start is yesterday, the second best time is right now. Choose one of the buffers and put effort behind it. Once it's a habit, try out another. If the interviewees are right, you will see a higher level of attachment or commitment and less stress, anxiety, and frustration. You will be a step closer to harmony in work and life.

REAL STORIES OF FIT
A Right Fit Story
35, male, education

Right fit experiences don't always start off that way. In the case of this interviewee, his *right fit* experience remained hard up until the day he left. However, due to the buffers he had in place, it was consistently one of the greatest learning experiences of his life. "For me personally, as a public school teacher, I was spending mental and emotional energy trying to maneuver through the context . . . where expectations weren't clear and there were constantly changing mandates. And, there was this emotional burden of real kids' lives being at stake. I was trying to be good at it [teaching], but you don't feel like there are a lot of wins in the day."

Instead of giving up or leaving teaching, this interviewee put in some buffers to help him remain engaged and have more impact. His first buffer had to do with focusing on things he could control by "scoping down my view of the world to only what was happening in my classroom, what is in my control." Peer relationships were vital as well, but only after he realized that he wasn't alone. He said, "We assume we are the only one having that challenge. I lived with four teachers and so we all came home and had a beer and talked about what happened. We talked about how terrible we were, realized we were all in the same boat, and then got the energy to get up and do it again." He shared that he was lucky to have that built-in support group. If he didn't have it, he said he would have felt "this is about me; everyone else can figure this out except for me."

At the end of the interview, in a moment of reflection, this interviewee shared a last buffer: his development and growth. Through all the *hard fit* moments and exhausting ordeals, he continued to learn and look for experiences that could help him grow. He became the guy that the school system said, "Hey, that's broken over there and we don't have a leader to put there yet. Can you go over there and not make it any worse?" He did more than that, and it helped him find *right fit*.

PART 5

COMPANY
+
RIGHT FIT

CHAPTER 9

Crafting and Communicating How the Company Works

REAL STORIES OF FIT
A Wrong Fit Story
45, female, consumer goods

"[Ways of working are important] because it's your day-to-day experience. You can live in a big house, but if the head doesn't work every
day, it's unbearable." This is how one interviewee, a C-suite leader at a
renowned brand, described the importance of ways of working in creating an employee experience that breeds commitment and gets your best
out of people. In her *wrong fit* experience, the ways of working were neither clear nor familiar to her. She offered, "Though the company I am at
stands for so many wonderful things, from maybe day three, I thought to
myself, 'Wow, that surprises me. I don't really know how to approach this
meeting.'" When we dug a little deeper into how and why it felt off, the
interviewee shared, "How you say something is extremely scrutinized.
So, I often felt like the thought police were sitting over my shoulder. It's
terrible. It erodes your self-confidence. I stopped trusting myself."

Throughout this interview and many others, the biggest insight was
that it wasn't that the ways of working were evil or misguided, they simply weren't clear or the practice of them were different than what was
espoused. This interviewee summed up the dilemma that this creates for
top talent when she offered, "I thought, this is a great company. It's got
a great brand. It is number one in everything. [If it isn't working,] I should
probably just try harder." Further, she justified the hard moments through
externalities, like changes in leadership, to give herself the permission to
keep pushing. She kept telling herself "it must have been them and not
me [or my fit at the company]." Over time, she saw the flaw in that logic
as the system was still the system, and doing her best work was still hard,
if not impossible.

One piece of advice she shared was to note how you personally react
when friends or ex-colleagues that you respect call or ask about a job
at your company. "I couldn't say bad things about my company, so I just
didn't call them back or skirt the question. . . . That is an important and
subtle signal that something is off."

Just behind quiet quitting and the Great Resignation is another HR buzzword that has been finding its way into our lives—"the employee experience." Now, the rise of this term makes sense given the shift companies have made to exploring digital transformations, digital platforms, ecosystems, and the user experience embedded in all of those new ways of reaching our consumers. We have seen value in becoming far more consumer- and user-focused and are feeling the rub between how we treat our consumers versus how we treat our employees.

However, we are still in a state of ambiguity about what the employee experience really is, how the term should be defined, and what success looks like when we get it right. In this chapter, we will explore how companies can create environments that become fertile grounds for *right fit* talent. The primary purpose of this chapter and Chapter 10 is to help HR, recruiters, managers, and leaders within companies learn what they can do to cultivate *right fit* for more talent over longer periods. This does not mean this chapter isn't for talent; it absolutely is—it gives a peek behind the curtain, so to speak, and can provide helpful insight about where progressive companies are heading and what you should come to expect from your place of employment in the future.

What Is the Employee Experience, Anyway?

During a quick search of the term in fairly well-respected publications and consulting firms, I found the following definitions:

> "The way in which employees internalize and interpret the interactions they have with their organization as well as the context that underlies those interactions."[1]

> "The journey an employee takes in your organization. It includes every interaction that happens along the employee life cycle, plus the experiences that involve an employee's role, workspace, manager, and well-being."[2]

> "A holistic understanding of what employees do—the physical environment, the culture in which they evolve and the work and activities (increasingly through a digital means) that they perform."[3]

"What people encounter and observe over the course of their tenure at an organization."[4]

"Everything that the worker learns, does, sees, and feels from the moment someone looks at your job opening to the moment they leave your company."[5]

For the purposes of our conversation here, we'll use a super simple definition of the *employee experience* that is time-bound. The employee experience is any and all touchpoints an employee has with the company in a single year, including technology, workplace, policies, programs, gatherings, and day-to-day interactions. This definition has some vital components. First, it limits the conversation to a finite period as opposed to focusing attention on the vast universe from recruiting to retirement. Secondly, it focuses on the physical, digital, human, and administrative elements that make up work. Lastly, it excludes any nod to culture, since we treat culture as an outcome of these interactions as opposed to an element within them.

To help us further align the employee experience conversation to *right fit*, I'll use this chapter to showcase a new and more compelling way to bring a new joiner into a company, onboard them more effectively, and create a way to honor their individuality and help them to work effectively in your organization. Employers and talent should strive to create a relationship that is built more on commitment through a connection to purpose and ways of working versus the arms race to offer the best perks that has accompanied many companies' approaches to date.

The hope? Well, it is simple. To help talent find the right company, help the company bet on people who work like they work, and reduce just a little of the $7.8 trillion of lost productivity in our workplaces. To do this, we will focus over the course of the next two chapters on sharing some progressive (and often counterintuitive) approaches to key areas of the employee experience. Those are:

- Chapter 9: Crafting and Communicating How the Company Works
  - *Work principles, practices, and platforms*
  - *Powerful first impressions*
  - *Realistic job previews*
- Chapter 10: Reimagining Fit—Recruiting and (Re)recruiting for *Right Fit*
  - *Preboarding, orientation, and onboarding*

- *Viewing "team" as a verb*
  - *Manager as team leader*
  - *The rise of the team member*
- *Redefine high performance*
- *Maximize moments that matter*
- *End meeting mania*
- *Mine the power of transitions*

Stop Losing Productivity, Start Making Work Practices Explicit

In one of my interviews, the regional president of a large consumer goods company shared a revelation with me regarding the importance of explicit work practices. When asked if more explicit work practices would help, they said, "We are a Montessori company. Do it yourself. Don't expect you are going to find manuals, they don't exist. . . . [but] if [they did and if] we interviewed with that level of transparency [about how we work], things would be very different. Easier."

This acknowledgment that work practices are often implicit and inconsistent across functions and leaders and tend to be left for new joiners to pick up and figure out as they bump into the company leaves us with a question. Why? Well, it is mostly because work practices often emerge organically via how the CEO or founder and the executive team choose to work with each other day in and day out. In the early days, when a company is first forming, those interactions are natural, fluid, easy. They grow organically from the founding team's individual experiences, hopes, aspirations, interactions with each other, and search for greater effectiveness. In other words, they start mostly unwritten and mostly remained so—passed on more through interactions and artifacts than through formal articulation.

There are numerous stories within many of the recently founded productivity-based platforms (think Basecamp[6] or Shopify[7]) whose core products were actually developed to help internal employees do better work together. Basecamp was originally created to help a creative agency do project work, and Shopify was originally created to help an independent snowboard shop run their operations. These are examples of work practices (ways of working and the technology that supports them) being developed organically and in the flow of growth. What fascinates me about these two stories (and countless others) is that the practices grew out of both necessity and personality, a phenomenon that is more prevalent than I would have imagined.

As companies continue to grow, the founder and the original band of employees become a smaller and smaller percent of the overall company. With each passing day and with each new recruit, it gets harder to consistently teach or develop consistent unwritten practices (practices are built in proximity or learned through modeling and mentoring) as the contact points with the people who built the company become less and less frequent.

Further exacerbating this is that every leader hired into the company already has a way to do most things. External hires have ways they like to create strategy, sell new ideas, run meetings, solve problems, gather, socialize, give feedback, develop people, etc. And, unless someone points them to a different or better way of doing those things, guess what. Those practices become part of the new company. Now, if companies all truly worked in independent widgets or separate products, multiple ways of working would be fine, but they don't. Most work travels across the horizontal of a company with multiple teams inputting into an overall initiative's success. If the leaders of two functions work in two different ways, imagine what that does to the teams below and around them. Work just got really hard, really fast.

Companies can do a better job making ways of working more consistent, but it will take some work because most have let it become far too implicit (where it has to be bumped into by new joiners as they come in and constantly managed by those who are already in the system). Or, ways of working are left to the discretion of the leader to create (which increases coordination costs and makes collaboration across boundaries more difficult).

Creating *Right Fit* Doesn't Mean Being the Right Place for Everyone

I would like to stop here and acknowledge that we live in an age where talent wants to bring their whole self to work. It is a laudable pursuit and one that I support in principle as it is rooted in belonging and psychological safety—two constructs that are enormous accelerators of engagement and commitment. However, I do not believe that every organization should morph to fit every talent (become a run-of-the-mill, one-size-fits-all shell of itself), nor that talent should expect to choose how they want to do their work day-to-day once they commit to a company. Before debating the point, we must first ask the question "why do organizations exist?"

We must never forget that companies exist to create value for shareholders and stakeholders. Talent is vital for their success, but not the reason for their existence. Almost unintentionally, we collectively have confused "creating a place where talent can thrive so companies can bring more value to the world" with "creating a place where everyone can come and explore their own purpose in their own way." Companies can be accelerators of individual purpose, but they can't be instruments of it.

This is readily apparent in a recent McKinsey study of two hundred of the best CEOs. It asked them a series of questions about trends that are driving their actions in 2023 and beyond. A few of the most interesting findings were that CEOs are refocusing their talent on performance with the belief that the best and brightest will welcome it, creating more consistent ways of working to create more meaning and connection, and see increases in technology spend (platforms) to drive the automation of work and reduce administrative burden while increasing speed.[8]

Further, we are also in a time when work is done horizontally, not vertically. Gone are the days when work is done on an assembly line or completed start to finish by a single team. Most companies' end products or services are shared, with thousands of people touching them from design through to the point of purchase. Thus, the more we work differently in each team or department, the higher the coordination cost and the greater friction to creating value.

TALENT INSIGHT

Think about how you view your current company. Do you see it for its purpose or as an instrument of your happiness? The latter can only be true in the context of the former. That is why we must search for a place that we believe in and that connects to who we are and how we work, versus choosing the place that everyone else reveres. There is no best place to work, not really. So, continue to search for the best place for you. Go back to Chapter 4 for inspiration.

With those two points in mind, companies must define the way of working that is most natural and most effective for them. Then, they must search out talent that work like the company works, both for the growth of the company and for the energy and engagement of talent over time. If companies create more natural and consistent ways of working, talent can more fluidly practice their respective craft (as opposed to using their creative energy to manage the context), and both parties will gain higher energy, commitment, and meaning over the long term.

Let's take a look at a few ways companies can both define their ways of working and make it easier for the *right fit* talent to find them.

Work Principles, Practices, and Platforms

As noted, how we work day-to-day tends to be the least consistently designed element of the employee experience. Yet in a changing, constrained, or disrupted environment, consistent and effective ways of working have become paramount. Over the last decade of rapid growth, companies have invested in bringing more talent and surrounding them with better resources and more abundant perks while letting ways of working evolve more organically—from work practices to platforms/technology. They exist to add value, but they're not always thoughtfully designed and connected.

So, what happens when perks are removed or work changes significantly, as was the case when the world flipped due to the COVID-19 pandemic in 2020, or the global economy turned toward a recession in 2022? In these moments, companies and talent have to shift into higher gears and find more focused ways of interacting. The experience a company sets up falters as consistent ways of working are elusive and the employee's struggle to keep their feet.

We can't recreate the office environment virtually or move quickly with massive shifts in the macroenvironment when we all view work differently, have different' practices, or rely on extrinsic motivators to buttress engagement. As we look ahead, we'll undoubtedly see more disruption and a more frequent need to shift and move together. To keep agility high and ensure talent can continue to be creative, the employee experience must be consistent—we must see *how we work* as the fuel for both productivity and commitment. Freedom is good, but if

TALENT INSIGHT

Instead of being a victim of the system (tools, processes, platforms), seek to deeply understand the operating system of the company. The most productive talent and best leaders optimize the tools they have as opposed to complaining about them or bringing in alternatives "under the radar."

COMPANY INSIGHT

Whenever you face an unexpected challenge (COVID, recession, etc.) or institute a large-scale transformation, create a space (physical lab) or the time and intention for your talent to experiment with new ways of working. Often, they want to go on the journey with you but don't have the confidence they can to succeed in the new world. Provide that to them in information, space to experiment, and grace.

everyone in a company can choose their own way of working, then freedom quickly becomes chaos. We can start this paradigm shift by looking at how a company works with a clean slate and redefining the following elements:

- **Work principles:** Think about these as norms or teaming ground rules at the company level. These are the organizational guidelines to frame how it should feel to work in a group or a team at the company. Principles help create a productive environment where everyone stays aligned to a single philosophy of how work gets done. It is the corporate equivalent of rules to a sport, etiquette at a dinner party, or laws that govern how we drive. These principles are over-arching statements of intent like "the consumer decides," or "asynchronous first, meetings second," or "we work in full sentences, not beautiful decks." These principles are often set (but not often codified) at a company's founding and are core to what differentiates a firm. Without work principles, chaos eventually reigns.

- **Work practices:** We covered these in depth in Chapter 4, but if work principles are "the way work should feel," then work practices are the "how work gets done." Work practices are the methods, models, and mindsets that we use day-to-day. Designed well, these practices should tell talent how a company:
  - *Makes decisions (top-down, consensus, individually, etc.)*
  - *Solves problems (data analysis, human-centered design, scrums, etc.)*
  - *Communicates ideas (two-page memo, white paper, walking deck, informal storytelling, etc.)*
  - *Resolves conflict (person accountable decides, superiors break ties, disagree and commit, etc.)*
  - *Manages projects (scrum, waterfall, Six Sigma, etc.)*
  - *Gives feedback (third-person/hearsay, first-person/in the flow of work, via technology, it isn't [smirk], etc.)*
  - *Builds relationships (beginning of meeting, at the bar after work, in the cafeteria, through working together, etc.)*

- *Recognizes employees (through performance systems, via internal comms, during town halls/large meetings, through recognition systems, etc.)*
- *Spreads information (top-down, to everyone all at once, to a select few, through formal channels, through informal channels, etc.)*
- *Develops people (through experience, through coaching, through formal programs, etc.)*
- *Etc.*

- **Work platforms:** The technology that is used to do work. For example, the tech stacks that enabled pre-COVID work were optimized for physical, face-to-face contact, which meant they needed to be just good enough to enable good conversations. We know that work in a hybrid or remote world is vastly different. In a physical environment, the platform is the ground (it disappears into the experience), whereas in a hybrid or a remote environment, the platform is the figure (the center of our attention and our main connection point to our company)—it is our experience of our company. Lucky for us, there have been profound innovations in this space that have created a plethora of application programming interfaces (APIs) that can be combined to create a simple, powerful, and inviting experience for talent to do their jobs with joy. Unfortunately, most of us are still trying to fit our pre-COVID platform experience into the square hybrid/remote working hole. And, it just feels clunky.

The best managers and leaders in a company are often scrambling to keep engagement high while meeting the demands placed on them by the company's growth aspirations. They pull on, prototype, buy, borrow, and create principles, practices, and (yes) even platforms. During the COVID-19 pandemic, one of the companies I worked at did an inventory of twenty-plus learning management systems and about ninety-five different APIs linked to learning alone, not including the APIs and third-party software related to project management, meetings, and asynchronous work). The best way for your company to work is out there, waiting for you. Some team has figured out a more effective, more efficient, and more powerful way to work by combining:

- The principles, practices, and platforms (PPPs) the company was created on
- The PPPs that were added during the inflection point or disruption (e.g., COVID-19 pandemic)
- The PPPs that were brought in under the radar or developed by the team itself

Figuring out how you will work in the future should begin by studying the company's most engaged, committed, and productive teams of today. As noted above, given how loose companies have been to date with how work actually gets done, teams have been out there on the fringes discovering a better way and creating better practices. We don't need to recreate; we need to uncover, make consistent what has already been innovated on, and scale a more consistent way of working so we can minimize the confusion, lower coordination cost, and decrease the administrative burden felt by our people as they try to drive growth. So, how do you find those *positive disobedient teams* (the teams most progressively pursuing new and better ways of working)?

- Look for teams or functions people seem to be migrating to more frequently. This will indicate that there is an emerging narrative out there that makes it a great place to work.
- Examine the engagement data for those teams that saw increases in engagement over the last year and held steady over a significant period of time.
- Then, inventory those team's work principles, practices, and platforms. Where have they innovated? What have they let go of? How are they using the platforms differently? What are their answers to the "how they work" practices?
- Then, create an 80% framework for the company where most, but not all, of the principles, practices, and platforms are the same.

TALENT INSIGHT

If you are a talent in an organization that is experiencing change or transformation, look for the outliers—the teams that are succeeding in the face of adversity, the leaders who are held up as the best to work for, or the individuals that seem "better off" when compared to the average. Then ask yourself how you could work like they work or do what they do, as their approach is likely the secret decoder ring of success.

Powerful First Impressions

First impressions matter. They happen insanely fast, and they are nearly impossible to break once formed. Research out of Princeton University found that people make judgments about qualities such as trustworthiness, competence, and likeability within a fraction of a second upon seeing a person's face.[9] Trustworthiness is often judged the quickest. And, when participants were given more time to make their judgments, they typically don't change. Interestingly, the quick assessment is thought to be rooted in our early evolutionary need to assess danger quickly so we could survive as a species. However, that theory doesn't explain why, in relatively safe environments, we continue to use facial features to determine one's character, even when we know that relationship is tenuous at best.

These quick judgments extend beyond first impressions of people we meet through to our choice of products we buy, homes we purchase, and cities we live in or visit. In one study by BMO in 2013, they found that 80% of potential buyers know if a home is right for them as soon as they step inside it.[10]

> **TALENT INSIGHT**
>
> Our minds are wonderful and beautiful instruments that can find patterns and make sense of a situation in the blink of an eye. However, they can also lead us to first impressions that might be wrong. Take your time in your assessment of a company or an opportunity. Make sure you are triangulating all of your gut reactions. What tells you the person is trustworthy? What tells you talent at the company is engaged and happy? It pays to be a bit more critical in the first moments. If you need a little inspiration, head back to Chapter 5.

Though we might be led to believe that these decisions, given their weight, deserve more time and careful attention, a paper published by Ap Dijksterhuis and Loran Nordgren in 2006 might say otherwise. Through their research, they present a new theory of human thought, termed unconscious thought theory, that asserts conscious thought is more helpful in simple buying situations (buying cereal or towels) and unconscious thought is more effective in more complex situations (buying a home or choosing a life partner). This is because the conscious human brain doesn't actually do that well with holding many factors at once and in balance, and it tends to place more emphasis on the attributes of a product or a person that are most easy to verbalize.[11]

So, how do first impressions relate to fit? Impressions play a vital role in determining how much we trust the people we meet, the products we might buy, and (here is the punchline) and organization we might join. The first impression of a company will be made almost immediately and usually before a recruiter or manager ever gets a chance to speak with a talent. So, those first impression assets (career websites, employee brands, LinkedIn company pages, etc.) matter more than we might appreciate. And, if they don't authentically represent the second or third experience we have with the company (job descriptions, initial interviews, etc.), the opportunity to lose talent is enormous.

Do the company's "early impression" assets truly represent who the company is and how the company works? Do they tell an honest story about the experience talent can expect upon joining the ranks? Do they showcase real examples of what working there will feel like?

Or, do they overemphasize optimism, aspiration, possibility, and marketing?

Here is the deal: making a balanced first impression is key. Companies should engage prospective talent with who they are today (so talent can have a realistic preview of their day-to-day) and where the company wants to be tomorrow (so they know what lies ahead). What companies should not do is present an aspirational version of today as if it is the truth.

There are two reasons for a company to reconsider its approach if it is tilted toward aspiration. The first is that there are numerous independent sources of information about a company available to prospective talent today (think LinkedIn, Glassdoor, Indeed, Comparably, TikTok, etc.). If the company's website veers significantly from reality, the company can look misleading, out of touch, or simply unaware about its own culture. The second is that without an honest presentation of who a company is today, the company will likely hire talent that will immediately feel dissonance between what they thought they were "buying" and what they actually "got."

One of my favorite analogies to how this might feel happened a couple of years back on Amazon. Furniture buyers around the world suddenly were seeing amazing deals on couches, benches, tables, and chairs.[12] People were abuzz with the seemingly impossible prices and jumped on them, thinking it was a glitch in the pricing algorithms. Turns out, Amazon and their resellers had gotten into the tiny furniture business. People shared hilarious pictures of themselves sitting on couches that are made for dollhouses. The buyers felt duped—frustrated that the descriptions were inaccurate or left out key information. And, the sellers had to go back to their product descriptions and reorient them to ensure the most salient points (like size) were clearly displayed.

Creating a more realistic (yet inspiring) first impression of the company starts with the career website. This is the funnel for the candidate experience, and anyone looking for or looking at a job will go there. Here are a few tips and examples of progressive approaches to these sites:

1. **Make values the ground and work PPPs the figure.** Values guide us as individual talent and they should do the same for a company. Values should be less words on a wall and more filters for decisions

day-to-day. When they are real, they are embedded in every decision and every action universally and without doubt, and they will show up through a company's choices about work principles, practices, and platforms. The best companies know how they work best. They see their ways of working as a differentiator—a way to find and retain the talent they need. And, they are explicit about them. For instance, Hotjar, a player in the growing field of automated site user experience, uses their blog to share how they work from how they run meetings to the tools that they use to collaborate.[13] So, anyone who works there knows how to work to be more effective and anyone thinking of joining knows what to expect.

2. **Make the company's purpose and how it makes money (have impact) overt.** Employees, prospective or otherwise, often do not know enough about a company before raising their hand. We might be consumers, but we don't understand the reason a product exists or how the company actually makes money. Making this overt early and often in recruiting can create a buffer that (as stated in Chapter 7) can pay dividends for years. For instance, Google is best known for its website, email applications, YouTube, and phones, but most people don't know that much of the revenue comes from Google selling ads. It is a sales organization as much as a technology organization. And, through Google Bets (funded through the strength of Google's revenue), they're able to invest in amazing technology applications from live translation to fully autonomous cars. Companies should let prospective talent know early and often how the company creates value and why the world is better with the company in it. Those stories should be powerfully written and shared unabashedly.

   In September of 2022, Yvon Chouinard placed Patagonia in a trust and ensured that all profits from the company flow into a nonprofit aimed at funding environmental causes.[14] In doing so, he shifted the perception of what the company is and why it exists. Even more impressive is how fast Patagonia moved to help everyone understand the decision—consumers, stakeholders, partners, and talent (both internal and prospective). Their website showed a letter, an accompanying Q&A, and links to the "new owners." It speaks to the purpose of the business s and how profits will be used, not about the products directly. This sort of explicit description of purpose and path to growth/profit is exceptional.

3. **Listen to and learn from prospective talent; they are the company's future.** Career websites are typically one-way streets to

nowhere. What a missed opportunity. Prospective talent is knocking at the door, and there is seemingly little or no interest in having a conversation with them. Imagine if a company picked prospective talent's brains (What is their ideal workplace?), learned from them (What is the coolest thing they saw in the last three days or what are they missing at their current job?), or learned about them (Who are they and what do they want to do?). I would guess there are significant and vital insights that could come from more of a two-way dialogue. Though I have yet to see a career site master this, there are a few intriguing things happening. For instance, a small Hungarian creative firm named Mito provided a space for "random clever people"[15] to introduce themselves, even if no jobs were currently available.

4. **Introduce prospective employees to the real company in real ways.** In many ways, it's the people that make or break an experience. Getting to know real employees and seeing how they work early in the recruitment process will help. Getting a bird's-eye view into how the company gathers, socializes, and does work is super compelling to a candidate who is considering joining. Though many companies have "company-mentaries" on their websites (think short-form, often narrated, and way overly produced versions of their offices and life), there are those that go a little bit further. Some, like Apple,[16] use their creative muscle to take us inside a beautiful version of their company from multiple angles and perspectives. Others, like Quantum Metric,[17] take you into muse-based vignette stories that allow you to relate to a parent, an engineer, an extravert, or a technologist. And, some places, like 37 Signals,[18] like to share a "manifesto" for work that goes deep on values and behaviors while interspersing them with real photos of talent in the company. It is an experience, to be sure.

5. **Create a network, a way to bind talent to the company beyond the moment.** Companies never really know what kind of talent they'll need in the future. Workforce planning helps, but it's a barometer for how the winds are shifting, nothing more. Disruptions in the industry, increases in demand for a certain skill worldwide, or attrition can all put companies in debt when it comes to acquiring talent. So, even if there's nowhere for gifted talent right now, how does a company keep a conversation going with them easily and at scale? The simple answer is building a community and offering it as a service and engaging them personally from time to time.

One cool prototype in this space belongs to Red Bull,[19] who has created talent communities for each of their functions so prospective talent can stay connected, be the first to hear about jobs, and learn more about how each of these functions are contributing to the Red Bull mission. Another brilliant career site innovation belongs to the fashion brand LVMH. Among many cool aspects of the deep and rich experience is the INSIDE LVMH[20] platform, which allows students and early career professionals to interact with the company and learn about its maisons, mission, values, and business by creating a constant flow with prospective talent.

Realistic Job Previews

Job descriptions are a seemingly necessary evil of the recruitment process and are the bane of many leaders' existences. They feel cumbersome, are time-consuming to create if done correctly (which they rarely are), and often produce a picture of a role that answers the question of "What would anyone with this title possibly do in the next ten years?" instead of answering the most important question of "What will the person in this role need to know or have done to meet these three primary objectives in the next eighteen to twenty-four months?"

So, how did we get here? Well, we mostly have Frederick Windlow Taylor and Lillian Moller Gilbreth[21] to thank for their work in the early twentieth century. The job description was originally created to help manufacturing business owners to better understand the knowledge, skills, and abilities needed to perform. They collected most of their data through ingenious time and motion studies. Time and motion became the prevailing buzzwords of the time and resulted in the creation of a time motion officer (the early ancestor to our chief people officers of today). This work was used by Morris Viteles in his book *Industrial Psychology* to introduce the idea of a job analysis and with it the job description.[22] Interestingly, over the last hundred years, we have innovated very little in this space even though the majority of roles have shifted to knowledge versus physical labor and are greatly altered from the moment a person sits in their seat on the first day. So, why do we keep using them? Mostly because they're an accepted practice, even though I have yet to talk to a CHRO (chief human resources officer) that believes they are truly helpful. In one of my interviews with a CHRO, they even went as far as to say, "Why are they still used? Because they are a stage gate to getting a job filled, and we need to move fast. We are lazy. We tell our HR person to go out and find one that is 'good enough.'"

The only place where we have seen some movement both in research and in practice is the *realistic job preview*. The realistic job preview is defined as "the presentation of both positive and negative information about the job and the organization to prospective applicants."[23] It's supposed to be used before the offer to set a clear expectation about the day-to-day environment to prevent the new hire's jarring realization that the job described bears little resemblance to reality.

A recent study by Lighthouse Research found that if candidates could view a video of some aspect of the company they are joining, they would choose to watch a video of the hiring manager for the job, followed closely by a job preview.[24] Additional research by Jobvite, a recruiting software provider, found that the reason new joiners leave is that the day-to-day role isn't what they expected (43%), followed closely by an incident or bad experience that drove them away (34%), or a dislike for the culture (32%).[25] Interestingly, a more realistic (yes, true) preview of the job, the company, the manager, and the work would go a long way to alleviating these first trust-eroding moments that have been created by hiring processes and job descriptions. So, why hasn't the realistic job preview caught on?

The answer is unknown. What is known is that unrealistic or idealistic job descriptions or previews set the hiring team up to key in on the wrong attributes, skills, and experiences. Old-school job descriptions create dissonance between the recruiting process and the first ninety days on the job, which can set the new recruit up to lose all of those "good vibe" engagement and commitment feelings early, thus almost ensuring a swift departure. And, employees can often perform badly because they are basing their work on their recruitment versus the real environment or priorities. I guess, the easiest answer is that tools like realistic job preview are not used because they require too much learning, system rework, and effort.

As I reflect on a few of my roles, if I was given a realistic job preview, I likely wouldn't have made the leap. In one case, the role changed during the recruitment process, but the conversation continued as it started. As I came into the role and saw the difference between the job I originally pursued and the job I received, it was obvious I had made a mistake. Not surprisingly, I stayed there a much shorter period of time than I might have otherwise. And, I was lucky to have other options. If I didn't, I might have stayed put, swallowed my frustration, and become one of the actively disengaged that make up the $7.8 trillion in lost productivity.

So, what's to be done about this? Well, for starters, we should revisit the realistic job preview and enhance it to make it a replacement for the job description as opposed to something used toward the end of the process when confirmation bias keeps a powerful hold on psyches and choices. If I were to recreate the job description for fit, there would be five main categories of information (and order of them is important):

1. **The nonnegotiables.** This bit of information allows the organization to set the bar at a certain level for the role. I put this piece of information first, as it will tell people the minimum criteria that must be in place to be considered. Being unambiguous here is important, as is ensuring you follow good employment law. This information will help talent to determine, "Am I in the talent pool that will be considered for this role? If not, how can I gain those skills before I apply in the future?

2. **What we do.** First, and foremost, explain what the company does and how our product or service flows through the system—focusing particular attention on the role and how it adds value inside of the larger picture. This description will help the candidate understand how and why the work they'd be responsible for is meaningful to the company.

3. **How we work.** Take a chapter out of Hotjar's playbook and be super clear about how work gets done. Answer the fundamental questions through the type of person that succeeds here and how they get stuff done. Of particular interest is prose-based work principles, practices, and platforms. You would be surprised at the number of talent who care deeply about what technology is at play in their day-to-day life. This section of the fit description will help talent to answer the question of "Will I be able to work how I know how or like to work?"

4. **What capability we need.** Focus on the capabilities that are actually needed, what the company is looking for in the right candidate. I have always argued that with any external talent, a company is hiring the "narrative" of the person as much as the person themselves. So, write the narrative the company wants. Get clear about the vital experiences and more important knowledge vis-à-vis the team already in place. This information will help talent answer the question, "Do I have something unique to offer the team?"

5. **The three top deliverables for this position or this team.** Instead of typing endless bullets of everything a job could do or all the responsibilities a single person might have, focus on what must be delivered in a new, better, different, or more meaningful way in the next eighteen to twenty-four months. Why that timeframe?

Well, because that's truly how long roles often last without a reorg, scope increase, or a talent move. Providing this information will help talent answer the question of "What will be expected of me out of the gate? Where do I need to be great?"

An emerging changing consulting firm called NOBL Collective[26] has showcased some chops around realistic job previews. Instead of focusing job advertisements on core job responsibilities, education/experience, and requirements, theirs focus on three core elements—what the company strives to do (purpose and way of operating), who you are and what you like to spend time on (how you work), and their promise (what you can expect in return).

One line from a recent role profiled that exemplifies their approach was:

> We want NOBL to be the place where you do the best work of your career. We're successful because the people on our team are kind, smart, and quick studies. They're comfortable working in an ambiguous and highly dynamic environment and inherently optimistic about what our uncertain future holds. We hope this way of working appeals to you too.[27]

The beauty of NOBL's job advertisements is that they read like descriptive and engaging consumer profiles, not bland HR job descriptions. They are inviting and personal. They give the candidate enough information to decide if they are the kind of person that would thrive at NOBL.

Between the way the company crafts and communicates how it works, how it engages with prospective talent, and how it describes roles realistically (or not), there is a good chance that the company and talent will share expectations. Now, many of the CHROs and C-suite leaders I spoke with are worried that presenting a stripped-down and honest version of the company would make recruitment more difficult. One of them even said, "We are scared that talent won't come or won't revere us in the same way." Oddly, almost universally, my interviewees wished for that sort of preview. You see, talent wants to come to companies to help—to help create better products or services, to enact disruptive strategies, and to create better places to work. They are imperfect and they should expect the companies they join to be as well.

REAL STORIES OF FIT

A Right Fit Story

45, female, industrials

When asked about whether there are good or evil cultures, this C-suite leader said, "I can't really think of any companies that were designed to go out and just be nefarious [in terms of culture]. Companies aren't good or evil, nor are their ways of working right or wrong. [As talent] we prescribe the value to both. It's the value you put against it. You have to know yourself really well."

This point resonated with me personally and as a summary to the experiences of the interviewees I interacted with for the book. When talent was in a *wrong fit* experience, they judged the interactions as good or bad practices by the company, when in fact they were simply right or wrong for them. The question posed by this interviewee was that it all comes down to "How much do you [as a talent] want to open yourself up to it [the ways of working of the company]? It is a very personal thing . . . it has got to work for you."

This leader's *right fit* experience sums up how personal fit really is. She explained, "I had every reason to believe my move within this company wasn't going to work. I had to move locations, change leaders, shift from supporting a business unit to running a region, move my family, and do all of this in a new country where I knew nobody. Yet, in my first interactions with my new leader, he was humble about what he had learned, who he was [and wasn't], and how work got done. It felt like a safe place." Over time, the feeling of safety gave way to "effortless [work]. It didn't mean it wasn't a lot of work . . . you're just not fighting complexity you have to manage."

CHAPTER 10

Reimagining Fit— Recruiting and (Re)recruiting for *Right Fit*

REAL STORIES OF FIT
A Wrong Fit Story
Female, 44, Consumer Marketing

Joining a new company is terrifying on our best days in our most *right fit* environments. It is hard to be new. For those of us who successfully make it over that hump and get some semblance of belonging, we forget how hard those first moments were, how uncertain each interaction is, and how much you desperately want someone to see you, value you. Well, imagine what those moments feel like in *wrong fit*.

This interviewee described how bad her experience was: "I had gotten laid off and had a friend recommend me to this gig at a rising tech company. The interview process was unremarkable. The job didn't fit my core skills, and I hadn't ever worked in tech, which I shared repeatedly. Their answer was 'That's fine.' I had like an hour of onboarding. Everyone was really busy. No one had time for me. No one was assigned to take me to lunch." In attempts to make inroads, she said, "I turned to people near me and asked, 'Can I help you today? Is there a book I can be reading? A website I should look at?' I didn't really have a job."

Though this was frustrating to this talent, it was the inconsistency of espoused values and ways of working that made it unbearable. She saw behavior that didn't align to the company's values but it wasn't called out, and she got reprimanded by her boss for sitting in her chair in a meeting room. Even though people saw her sit there, no one said anything to her. "No one helped me. It went from bad to worse."

Unfortunately, often *wrong fit* does.

The crafting and communicating of who the company is and how we work is a vital first step, but is insufficient to create *right fit*. To do that, companies must make the aspiration a reality every day, for every team, by ensuring the version of the company we sell to talent during recruiting matches the one they see on day one and the one they live every day after. This isn't a one-and-done set of activities; due to the level of distraction, the rate of growth, and the amount of transformation companies will experience in the future, leaders must (re)recruit their talent at every opportunity. This chapter is intended to help you do just that by reframing some key elements of the employee experience with (re)recruiting in mind. Though the list of opportunities is vast, the chapter will go deep into the following areas:

- Preboarding, orientation, and onboarding
- Seeing "team" as a verb
  - *Manager as team leader*
  - *The rise of the team member*
- Redefine high performance
- Maximize moments that matter
- The end of meeting mania
- Mine the power of transitions

Preboarding, Orientation, and Onboarding

I remember arriving at my first day onboarding at one of the top brands in the world, and I was stunned. It was a few tired videos that were obviously from past marketing campaigns, a few random speakers, and a lot of information about my benefits. Oh, and there was a really pitiful exercise on how a matrixed organization works and why work is so complicated. I remember walking out of the day wondering if I'd made a colossal mistake. This kind of onboarding experience is not unusual in organizations, since the mindset is often that onboarding is about getting the basics out of the way so a person can get to work. However, if companies step back and think about onboarding in the context of growth, it is the lynchpin of so much more. First, they have to accept a few truths:

- **A company will never have a more excited and engaged employee than the moment they walk into their first day.** They have likely spent the prior month sharing their news with family, friends, ex-colleagues, etc. They are ready to start fresh, have an impact, and help their new company be great. The Society for Human Resource Management tells us that employees who felt their onboarding was effective were eighteen times more likely to feel committed to their organization. They were also much more likely to feel a strong connectedness, like they were integrated into the company's culture.[1]

- **If a company just focuses on the new joiners, their culture will transform automatically over the next few years.** Recent layoffs aside, research into some of the fastest-growing software companies shows they have doubled in size from a headcount standpoint, on average, four times within six years.[2] If you account for voluntary and involuntary turnover alongside growth, companies could replace their entire organization with new people in a short period of time. The latest stats from Gartner tell us that the turnover rate could increase by 20% in 2022 and stay high, meaning that the average turnover of 18% pre-pandemic could move to 22% to 24%.[3] If a company is growing by 20% on a base that is turning 22% to 24% of your current employees, you could conceivably replace nearly 50% of your workforce in a single year. The point is, invest in the mindsets and skills of new joiners during growth, and you can change the entire way the company works in a short period of time.

- **Anything the company spends on onboarding will be far less expensive than the hidden cost of losing new employees within their first six months.** According to SHRM, the average cost per employee of onboarding is $4,125—this includes laptops, tools, phones, physical equipment, time investment of HR/IT, first day orientation, and training resources. However, the real cost is likely upward of $10,000 per employee. Even then, SHRM estimates that if an employee leaves, it will cost the company, on average, six to nine months of that employee's salary, accounting for the time invested in getting the person productive and the gap of not having the role filled when they leave.[4] If the person leaving is an entry-level employee making $36,000, the cost is $12,000. If the person leaving is an executive making $300,000, the cost is $100,000 or more. And, these figures do not account for the collateral damage of other talent having to take on their day-to-day duties, how an exit shifts the engagement and dynamics of a team, the cost of recruiting yet another talent, or the dip in productivity that comes from bringing on another new team member in the future.

It is important here to separate employee onboarding from orientation from a new term—cultural immersion. *Employee preboarding* is all the things that must occur for an employee to get up to speed enough to do their job. *Employee orientation/welcome* is the initial introduction to the company that typically happens in the first one or two days on the job. Both of these elements are table stakes, where the real differentiators in this space are pulling in a third area, what we call *cultural immersion*.

Cultural immersion is the set of experiences, events, and tools that allow a new joiner to understand the ins and outs of what is expected, what is valued, and how work gets done. Now, many companies will claim that they do this, but before you do, let's look at a checklist of what might be included in each of these areas:

Companies have come to believe that if they simply introduce the cultural elements of the company on the first day (values, leader expectations, etc.), they can expect those cultural elements to be honored in the day-to-day interactions from day 2 onward. Now, it's easy to claim that companies are introducing talent to the values, systems, and ways of working in the orientation with the expectation that managers and teams will provide the immersion needed. But, this rarely happens effectively because each of those individuals has varying levels of appreciation for how the company works, and a vast majority have interpreted the values to their own liking or preferences. So, at best, every new joiner is getting a slightly different view of the values and work principles, practices, and platforms. At worst, they are getting completely different ones.

Imagine what would happen if the company itself thoughtfully immersed talent into its ways of working and culture as opposed to simply welcoming, orienting, assimilating, or onboarding them? What if talent were prepared and confident in the rules of the road so they could hit the ground running, knowing beyond a shadow of a doubt that they had everything they needed to succeed? How can a company move beyond a two-day orientation to really helping new joiners land effectively? How might a company make its culture immersion deep and rich and all about why the world is better with the company in it, how it makes money, and how it works? And, what if companies gave just a little space to career aspirations, helping new joiners to find a BFF at work, setting the appropriate line on productivity and wellness, and providing them a clear set of expectations for the first ninety days? Well, my guess is that we would see a level of early commitment that is unmatched in today's climate.

> **COMPANY INSIGHT**
> Deep relationships are at the heart of long-term commitment. Spend time thinking about both the who and the how of relationship building for your incoming talent, especially for your diverse or traditionally marginalized talent tools. Without a strong network where new joiners feel seen, valued, and connected, their engagement and loyalty will be left to chance.

Now, there is no one way to create an onboarding experience, and no company has mastered the "first moments" to fully ensure that their new talent can enter their first projects with the highest possible level of commitment, clarity of the way the company works, and confidence that they have something unique to add and gain from their new role.

Fundamentally, onboarding requires supreme focus on the aligned outcomes the CEO, CHRO, or executives are looking to achieve. Once those are in place, a company can build an employee journey or experience that brings those outcomes to life in the most meaningful way given the company's culture and working principles, practices, and platforms. Now, there are a few companies doing exciting and innovative things in this space. Check out my favorites:

- Buffer[5] implements a "three-buddy" system where every new joiner gets a role buddy, a leader buddy, and a culture buddy as part of their six-week onboarding bootcamp. They even share their buddy program online.
- Quora[6] believes in giving new joiners a chance to make meaningful contributions early by giving them a feasible project to tackle in week 1. Additionally, they give ten onboarding talks over the first few weeks to provide new joiners the fundamentals of success.

ONBOARDING

-30 to Day 0 Preboarding (What allows talent to be ready to work?)	Day 1–3 Orientation/Welcome (What allows talent to know the company?)	Day 4-90 Cultural Immersion (What ensures talent will be successful?)
☐ Equipment assigned	☐ Company purpose overivew	☐ Work principles, practices, platforms deep dive
☐ Credentials issued	☐ Company origin story/ history	☐ Self awareness/work style assessment
☐ Set-up on company tools/platforms	☐ Operating model overview (how we make money/impact)	☐ Time (outside of tasks) to build trust with the team
☐ Tax/I-9 docs signed	☐ Product/service overview	☐ Trusted sponsor network built (BFF, mentors, key colleagues, etc.)
☐ Benefits overview/ choice	☐ Values (linked to behaviors) overview	☐ 30/60/90 day check-ins completed
☐ Desk/office assigned	☐ Leader "rules to the road" stories	☐ 12-month realistic job preview created
☐ Company swag received	☐ Manager/team meet and greet	☐ Coached through first big win/ key deliverable

Figure 10.1: A Sketch of the Ideal Onboarding

- Patagonia[7] encourages new employees to test out the products in the field immediately by giving them a chance to shop for discounted products and then giving them time to test them outside via surfing, fly fishing, or any other activity they might enjoy.
- Square[8] focuses their onboarding on three phases—the company, the team, and the individual. Square does a fantastic job of orienting new employees to the company via the vision, procedures (ways of working), and the deliverables or responsibilities of their role.

Viewing "Team" as a Verb

The prevailing winds of change around how we work have been well documented, written about, discussed at conferences and in boardrooms, and struggled with by well-meaning managers and leaders who just feel unprepared for the moment they find themselves in. On one hand, they have a new generation of employees who have a different definition of work and higher, sometimes unrealistic, expectations for their leaders and their companies. On the other hand, the company has higher expectations about creating a workplace that is more and more about the larger purpose, the customer, and optimizing performance (just look at the tech layoffs of early 2023 and the press around the search for operational efficiency).

Caught in between all of that chaos are team leaders and their teams, who are trying to stay engaged, committed, energized, and productive. One of the major assets in *right fit* from an organizational standpoint is the relationship of the team leader (or manager) to their team (talent). You will notice the shift in language here—it is purposeful. The idea of a manager is someone who is overseeing and distributing work, delegating tasks, and ensuring optimal levels of productivity. Given our lack of proximity to each other (even when we are working in the office) and the shifting needs of employees, the moniker of "the manager" is both unfulfilling and not fit for purpose. So to ensure *right fit* over time, the company must invest in building both strong team leaders and strong team members—each of whom knows their roles and responsibilities in building a strong and vibrant team climate.

Manager As Team Leader

The team leader is a role that is not for the faint of heart—cheerleader, counselor, confidant, mentor, leader, coach, friend, culture carrier, etc. As teams become more distributed, work becomes more asynchronous and virtual, expectations to balance productivity with energy heighten, and commitment to our organizations wanes, team leaders are the lynchpin of engagement, retention, and growth. It used to be that there were multiple connection points to the company on a daily basis—campuses, cafés, full team meetings, face-to-face training—but now (even in the back-to-the-office sect), we are both less enamored with the "perks" and more willing to be less proximate. So, the team leader becomes the sharp point of the spear or the tip of the funnel, whereby many of the judgments about the company and fit will be filtered through. And so we arrive at some big questions. Have companies prepared their team leaders for this role? Have they been provided with the tools, resources, platforms, and training they need to model "the company"? Are the nuances of this role clear, given the changing dynamics of work? Have these roles been scoped appropriately?

For most leaders in most organizations, the answer would be no to most of these questions. It is not that there hasn't been focus on training managers; it is that the role, the expectations, and the pressure have shifted dramatically. So, companies and leadership should look toward shifting as well. Here are some thoughts on how:

- **Find the best and brightest and make them designers.** There are team leaders in every company right now who are exceptional, whose team reveres them, and whose performance outpaces the norm. They have shifted and adapted and found a "better practice" to help them and their teams succeed. These are the muses. How they work should be examined closely, and they should be invited to design for the rest.
- **Reframe the role from manager to team leader.** We must look at the "team leader" level within the company (synonymous, for the purposes of the book, with frontline manager) and reset the expectations, responsibilities, ways of working, and spans/layers (or how many team members they lead and how deep their organizations are). Leading people is infinitely harder than it used to be, so these roles should be full-time roles, and the teams being led should be be a bit bigger.
- **Make team leaders the first group re-recruited.** We are at the point where all employees must be re-recruited back to the company during any major transformation, whether that transformation was planned or in reaction to a disruptive event. Once the purpose, strategy, values, work PPPs, and mode of working have been set, build capability in team leaders to bring those things to life—stewarding culture is a capability, not a communication effort. These team leaders are the culture (as it is created in how they interact with their teams), and they are the strategy (as strategy is either participated in or not).
- **Find new and more frequent ways to measure engagement, commitment, energy, productivity, and inspiration.** Team managers will struggle, and they often won't be aware that they are pushing too hard, not pushing hard enough, or not keeping a pulse on their team due to the lack of proximity (either from hybrid ways of working or simply because managers can't be all places at all moments). So, we must help them have a way to see where they are and how their teams are doing more regularly. It doesn't have to be complex or a fifty-item survey, but we do need a way to measure our team's health quickly,

easily, and more often. As we know all too well, we can't impact what we can't see. I always think about the smiley faces that greet me in the international airports around the world asking quickly and easily for my opinion about my experience going through customs or security. I wonder if our measures of these areas couldn't be that easy. To make it work, it takes both honesty and trust by our talent and action by our team leaders. But why not find a way since the price of not having energy, engagement, commitment, productivity or inspiration is so great.

The Rise of the Team Member

Great managers are rare. According to Gallup, companies fail to choose the candidate with the right managerial talent for the job 82% of the time. This is a daunting statistic that gets even more dire when you add on the fact that 70% of the variance in employee engagement can be attributed to the manager (remember, most of the time, we join companies and leave our managers).[9] Given the impact the manager has on our company's engagement and performance, companies need to get creative, get inspired, and design a way to increase their chances of hiring and developing great managers. One of those opportunities might lie with the team members themselves.

Inc. Magazine reports that the optimal number of direct reports a manager should have is seven.[10] Interestingly, Gallup recently reported that teams with fewer than ten members have both the highest and the lowest engagement across their database.[11] They find that the level of engagement depends as much on the skills of the managers as it does on the size of the team. So, better managers will mean the possibility of increases in span of control, which has enormous implications on overall cost. How do companies make managers great? Maybe the missing link is through increasing the capability of team members.

Having been in multiple companies, all trying to find a path toward great managers, I noticed that they have often ignored the masses, the teams themselves. Why don't we work to build great team members? Why don't we invest in helping our talent to make their managers great? Why don't we respect that team membership is as much of an art as team leadership? Interestingly, in every organization I have worked in, no matter my level, I have been a team leader and a team member in almost equal measure. The context shifting between those roles is profound, and the skills needed to be a great team member are not totally overlapping to those of being a great manager. Team membership might be the panacea to our manager issue. What could the development of team members look like? Here are a few ideas:

- **Find the team members that everyone wants and create more of them.** There are individuals in your company whose names come up in every discussion about building a new team. If you asked just about anyone who is building a team, they would say, "I want them." Find out who they are, what they do, and how they show up. Then, use that profile to build ideal team member skills in everyone else.
- **Focus on developing the team together, through teaming.** We have become accustomed to building great managers by training them together. What if we flipped the script and focused our training dollars on teaching our teams "teaming"? What if we developed the manager and the team, together, in the context of the way the company works? This is not a return to the 1980s trust falls and forming, storming, and norming. No, it is about helping to create a working system so all the interactions between a team and the manager are shared and both team leaders and team members are skilled up for them. In other words, prioritize the day-to-day interactions—one-on-one talks, coaching conversations, project launches, problem-solving sessions, etc.
- **Assess for team membership in recruitment, regardless of level.** When we look for leaders or managers, we rarely stop to honor the idea that no matter their level, everyone is a member of a team (even the CEO is often a team member on the board). Many leaders I have met have lost the skills of team membership—a bias for action, being a servant leader, building on others ideas, committing to a larger purpose, executing strategy, catching others doing great things, creating the space for others, and following through on deliverables. They are unable or unwilling to release control or give up the mic. Assessing that capability will ensure they are both great team leaders and model team members. It's vital to keeping ways of working intact.

> **TALENT INSIGHT**
>
> If you're relatively new in a company or are looking to make a bigger splash, pay attention to the team members who are always in the middle of the action. Who are they? How do they show up every day? What do they do that other team members don't? The path to success is often right in front of you—you just need to determine if you want to work the way they work (and if it is a *right fit* or if you're pushing hard to fit in.)

Redefine High Performance

Back in 2007, Josh Bersin penned an article titled "The Death of Performance Appraisal" and put out a call to action for us to redefine the performance management approach in corporations.[12] He called for a move from "competitive evaluation systems" built on annual ranking, ratings and corresponding compensation and promotion moves for individuals built mostly on a bell curve (meaning everyone cannot be great) to "a coaching for development" model where goal setting, touchbases, feedback, and assessment are all aligned to allow talent to grow faster than the company. The only annual part of the process has to do with revising goals in alignment with shifts in strategy.

If we fast forward to March of 2023, we are largely still making the same call without huge shifts in the philosophy or practice. Gallup,[13] Gartner,[14] and others point to many of the same themes as Josh did in 2007 with largely the same conclusions. The system needs to change, and even more rapidly given the rise of hybrid, post-COVID ways of working. Now, technology has continued to advance with some real possibility of delivering fully on the promise of automation, flexibility, strong UX, machine learning, and instantaneous feedback/insights. However, this issue around performance is more about the mindsets of the leaders who run these processes and their seeming unwillingness to let go of antiquated, blunt instruments of productivity.

The move to hybrid and flexible working has exacerbated the issue and accelerated the need for more progressive approaches. In one of their latest studies, Gartner found that 64% of managers said they believed that office workers outperform remote workers—and that office workers should be first in line for the next raise.[15] This modern version of *proximity bias* (a term coined in the 1970s that describes how people treat those who are physically closer to them better) creates even more need for equity in our performance systems. Managers are wired to believe office workers are more productive even though piles of research (check out the work of Raj Choudhury[16] at Harvard) show that remote workers are as productive, if not more productive, than office workers.

So, what does all of this performance management mumbo jumbo have to do with creating a *right fit* experience for talent? Well, used correctly, a performance management process can become the greatest "better practice" sharing tool you have ever seen. It can remind talent of how the company makes money and what it values, capture the better practices around the principles and practices of how the company works, and help talent to develop each other by encouraging "stealing with pride" (or, focusing on scaling the better practices of others instead of creating everything from scratch again and again.)

Figure 10.2 is a visual of a typical annual performance process. Central to this process is the idea that performance management is about the individual in the company and comparing what they accomplished by the end of the year to what was set out for them. Now, there are many good reasons to use the standard company performance systems. It allows for every individual to be seen, to have clear goals or objectives to work on, and to have a universal cadence to the manager/employee relationship. It also allows for evaluation of talent at a single point of time. But, if you step back from the process that has been created, you wonder whether the premise performance management was built on is somehow flawed or archaic.

Back in the day, organizations mostly produced widgets so tasks could be easily broken down, distributed, and measured. However, this is a different world now. Talent wants meaning as opposed to mindless tasks. They want connection over consistency and flexibility over fixed schedules. Similarly, organizations are looking for collective success versus individual heroics and are interested in impact over individual accolades.

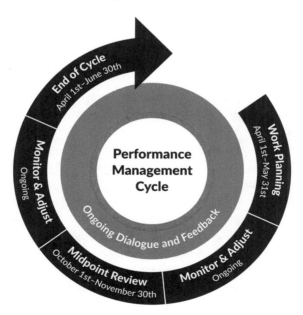

Figure 10.2: Visual of a Typical Performance Review Process
Soure: Tom Haak, "A Collection of Performance Management Cycles," HR Trend Institute (August 19, 2020), https://hrtrendinstitute.com/2020/08/19/a-collection-of-performance-management-cycles/.

My interviewees left me with a question for all the organization designers: "Is an organization an aggregation of individual effort or is it a collective act by individuals dedicated to a single mission?" If it is the latter, companies have some work to do before their structure reflects that idea. Here are some places to think about as performance is reimagined as a collective act:

- **Have one strategy and a collective of annual operating plans.** Due to individual orientation, every function, team, and project group in a company has their own mission, vision, values, and way of working. Why? Once the strategy is set for the company, everything else should be action to create value. No need for additional vision statements or missions below the one already shared. Teams simply need to know their place in the strategy and what the team (and individuals) will promise to do on behalf of it.

- **Think in outcomes, not in activity.** Performance goals are often created at the individual level and then sent up the ladder. When this happens, the focus is on the activities of the individual and the team as opposed to the outcomes. Imagine if every team had quarterly, annual, or twice-a-year outcomes and the project work to get there was only defined over time. There would be less preciousness about projects and fewer work initiatives continued beyond their usefulness. Talent would focus on the outcomes they are responsible for as opposed to the projects being checked off.

- **Focus one-on-ones on ensuring everyone is growing faster than the company.** No matter the size of your company (small start-up or mature business), the roles are likely getting bigger and more complex every day. You should establish a baseline for one-on-ones between team leaders and their talent and make sure those discussions are all about developing talent on the job. Most learning happens by moving key events to lessons of experience that change the way talent sees the world and how they will show up in the future. Imagine if team leaders were skilled at doing this and did it with regularity—everyone rises, work gets better, and more value is created.

- **Pay well and distribute bonuses to the team.** Companies have grand purposes and inspiring missions, but rarely do they measure themselves against them. If the company is a team, serving a single consumer, the company should all succeed together and fail together. If the company doesn't achieve its goals, then why should any one person get a bonus? Collective effort creates collective success and failure. It is not a question of "who did more?"—it is a question of "did we all do enough?"

- **Find and celebrate the "better practice."** I have often wondered why companies don't set aside a portion of the operating budget to give bonuses to individuals who show the rest of the company what great looks like. Somewhere out in your company, there is a better practice for everything—the positive disobedient who has found the better way to work, to coach, to do an operational task, to please a consumer, to make the company more efficient, or to live our values. What if you could find them, reward them, and then tell their story to everyone else as a development program (not an awards show)?

Maximize Moments that Matter

The cycles of commitment have changed radically since the onset of the pandemic. While companies used to simply onboard talent, set annual goals, engage with them a couple of times a year, and expect them to stay committed for a decade or more, that formula just isn't holding true any longer.

As Pete Davis tells us ever so eloquently in his book *Dedicated*, "This is the defining characteristic of my generation: keeping our options open."[17] He continues: "We can't rely on any job or role, idea or cause, group or institution to stick around in the same form for long—and they can't rely on us to do so either . . . It's 'infinite browsing mode,' but for everything in our lives."[18] He shares that there is an inherent tension in what we all want, which is a deeper sense of connection versus the fear of regret, association, and missing out driven by the sheer number of options available to us.

So, what can companies do? My best advice is to not see the infinite browsing versus counterculture of commitment as an either-or, but as a sliding continuum that works like the tide—ebbing and flowing, moving one direction and then the other. If we can assume that most people, at their core, want to belong, be committed, and feel a sense of community, then this willingness to browse must be created through tiny cracks in commitment or small disappointments over time. If the fear of missing out or regret is more prevalent in talent's consciousness than the reminders of why their current company, coworkers, and career matter, then they will lift their heads and look for something else. It is as true in our relationships as it is in our workplaces.

In a recent study, LinkedIn found that employees stick around 41% longer at companies that regularly hire from within.[19] Turnover, as cited earlier, has a tremendous impact on company performance, and turnover related to a lack of career opportunities (meaning this is talent that is high performing but stuck) costs an average-sized company $49 million a year[20] . . . and that number doesn't include the ripple effects of attrition—rebuilding a team, extra stress on coworkers, lost institutional knowledge, etc.

So, what can companies do? Shorten the cycles of interaction and take advantage of more touchpoints, transitions, and transformations. When we keep our cadence of commitment high, the fear of regret, association, or missing out can never fully take hold. Here are a few ideas:

- **Collect and curate the forums and gatherings.** Offsites, town halls, retreats, national meetings, team building days, and development programs are just a few of the ways that we gather to do work. These forums and moments have become even more important with our move to hybrid and remote work. However, we haven't yet maximized the value of them, as each is left to the individual leader convening to design it. What if every moment answered four questions before doing anything else:
  - *Why is the world better with us in it?*
  - *Who is our customer? How do we make their life better?*
  - *How do we make money/have impact?*
  - *How do we get work done?*
  - *What is our promise to our talent in return for their commitment?*
- **Ensure strategy is participated in, not just developed.** If you stop to think about it, the life or death of strategy isn't in the setting of it; it is determined in the number of day-to-day decisions that are made in service of it (or not). Many of us set strategy at the beginning of the year and check in on it once or twice, yet we marvel at why we didn't hit our marks and how so much additional work found its way into our team. Strengthening the link of strategy to functional operating plans to goal setting to recognition systems is a great place to start. Then, remind people in every moment possible what matters most. The year should start with a deep dive into who the company is, why the world is better with them in it, how they make money, and how they work. From there, annual operating plans should be set (as opposed to energy going toward every team working on their own mission, vision, values, and ways of working). Then, at the end of the year, collectively reflect on the ground you have covered, what you have learned individually and as a collective, and where you want to go, together, in the year ahead.

End Meeting Mania

Another compelling piece of data that causes cracks in company commitment are the sheer number of unnecessary meetings (or meetings that don't directly connect to purpose, profit, how we work, our sense of community). Based on research by UNC Charlotte Professor Stephen Rogelberg, it is estimated that there is a productivity waste of over $25 million per thousand employees every year due to useless meetings.[21] Think about that for a second: $25 million per thousand employees. In a company of five hundred, the real impact on the bottom line is $13 million dollars. If companies saved that and put it toward bonuses for their employees, the take home money per employee would increase by $26 thousand. That is a year of college tuition or a sizable part of an annual mortgage payment. In an organization of one million, that is $2.5 billion. Whether your company is large or small, what is clear is that meaningless meetings are rampant in our organizations, and the downstream impact is both direct and indirect—there are clear bottom line inefficiencies and a more insidious outcome of apathy or active disengagement over time. None of us sets out to be a professional meeting attendee as a career goal, but many of us have become just that.

So, what can a company do to change course and remove the meaningless meeting mania? Here are a few thoughts:

- **Change your company's relationship to time.** One of the biggest contributors to ineffective over-meeting-ing is that we see time as infinite and fail to assess the opportunity cost of any moment. If every team assessed the monetary cost of every meeting (based on a crude calculation of salaries alone) and asked if the time is best spent on the proposed agenda, we would often quickly answer no.
- **Get clear about why your company meets and what the outcomes are of each meeting.** In the age of asynchronous work technology (think Microsoft Teams, Slack, Basecamp, or Google Workspace), the ability to move work forward together without meeting is profound. We no longer need to be together in a room—we can be together in documents and online. So, companies then have to ask the question of "why do we meet?" What are the activities that require us to be in a room together? What cannot be done in another way?
- **Set a limit for the size of meetings and ask each person if they need to be in the room.** Our meeting attendee lists have tended to expand rapidly from the core members that need to be there, especially

with the rise of remote and hybrid ways of working. This is due in part to our generally low trust and psychological safety combined with our FOMO and need to be visible and have connection. We end up using vital and scarce meeting time for things other than value creation. By limiting the number of people at meetings, we could carve out more time in the day for other activities—some that would directly increase trust, psychological safety, and connection.

- **Measure and report on time in meetings as part of your P&L.** There are a number of measures that I always thought should be on a P&L statement and reported in quarterly earnings or monthly operating meetings. One of those measures is the amount of time spent in meetings. We get what we measure, and if we took a hard look at how often we met, it might spur us on to find a more efficient and effective way to get work done.

Mine the Value of Transitions

In almost every organization, a significant percentage of talent get promoted (~10%) or switch roles or jobs (~15%) inside of their company, so about one quarter of people move internally every year. Further, HR industry analyst Josh Bersin claimed that over 40% of the US workers changed jobs, roles, or managers since the start of the pandemic.[22]

Though external moves are typically orchestrated and designed with care, these internal shifts are typically conducted with speed and efficiency as the prevailing forces. In doing so, companies miss any opportunity to re-recruit our employees back to the company, the purpose, the way they make money, and each other. I have never served in the military but understand that part of the design of deployments is to allow soldiers to come back to a base, recharge, restock, reconnect, and prepare for their next mission.

I have always wondered why organizations didn't bring the same mentality to their transitions. During a transition, talent is most open to reflection, rejuvenation, learning, and recommitment, as they are unencumbered and unburdened—they are excited about what might be next and how the new experience might offer them a chance to recreate themselves a bit. Imagine if, in big and small ways, companies maximized these transitions to rebuild commitment, remind our talent of who the company is and why the world is better with them in it, and provide them a space for them to prepare for the next adventure.

The signal companies would be sending would be the most authentic display of well-being, career progression, engagement, and development. Instead, companies usher people through to the next role for continuity, often asking them to cover two roles at once so the dominoes can begin falling behind them more quickly. Companies end up exporting additional stress to the very talent that is already managing a difficult moment of transition. In these moments, talent should feel less stress, not more. They should see their leaders' commitment to them and feel their hope for the company. They should feel seen and valued, not overexposed and overburdened.

To remedy this, companies should see the time in between roles not as a nice to have but as an essential element to long-term performance and dedication. You can use these moments to help your talent be successful in the role and ensure they are dedicated to your cause. Here are a few ideas on how to handle transitions:

- **Respect the end of the effort and it will pay you back exponentially.** Any transition should come with a minimum of seven days off work to rest and another seven days of reflection, reconnection, and reset so talent can come into the new role with clarity and a plan for the first ninety days. Not only will this help talent accelerate into the new role, but they will be even more committed to playing big and working hard . . . as they will no doubt be appreciative for it.
- **Use the time in between to (re)recruit them back to the company as it is now and will be in the future.** During the time of reflection, remind talent of your strategy, how you make money, how you work, and the values you hold dear. This should not be lip service, but a true deep dive into all that has changed and all that has remained the same. And, if there are new capabilities that are emerging within the industry or in the company (i.e., digital, service, ESGE, etc.), use this time to build them as well.
- **Each talent should receive a healthy dose of self-reflection either through feedback from their past team, self-awareness instruments, or a combination of these assets.** Self-awareness is the key to building a culture of inclusion, equity, camaraderie, and engagement. Remember, talent will be most willing to hear it when they are standing in the space between roles.
- **Lastly, each talent should have real time with their new manager to set up their ninety-day plan.** It should have clear deliverables and

expectations and should focus on building a strong network and having a few small early wins with the team.

The Continuous (Re)recruitment of Talent

Change is the only constant. We live in a VUCA (volatile, uncertain, complex, ambiguous) environment. Agile is the new black. The future of work is upon us. I love all of the work prophecies; they make me feel like we are living in a corporate version of Hogwarts—like there is real magic in the world and true Joseph Campbell-esque hero's journeys awaiting us all. The truth is, work has always been changing, often radically and in punctuated moments in time, but almost daily. With every advance in technology (less than twenty years ago, most of us did not have email addresses), innovations in how we work (design thinking rose to mainstream fame in 2010), and new models for how companies can be designed (Slack went public as a company in 2014), companies rediscover a better and more efficient way to grow and serve customers.

However, these transitions don't alway coincide with the shifts in strategy or operating models within our companies. They are usually lagging those pivots or, even worse, happening in parallel but in a disconnected way.

How many of you have been a part of a major strategic pivot or shift in your function or your company? Here's how they typically go: A small group of senior leaders sense a shift in the market and design a new way to either gain market share or protect themselves against insurgents. They design a new product, service, or bundling approach, and that ignites a large-scale "shift to invest" organizational redesign. Often (but not always, thanks to some stellar Organization Development peers) top leaders move from a envisioning a new operating model straight to reshuffling the boxes and lines in the organization, which results in reorgs, layoffs, or some combination of those activities. And then we build beautiful decks and poetic speeches to land everyone in the new opportunities and reduce the fear, uncertainty, and pain as much as possible. And, then we go.

The missing piece is always "How we must work differently?" You see, companies leave the ways of working to be "figured out." Instead of building a new tech stack, incentivizing new behaviors and outcomes, and resetting how we collaborate, make decisions, solve problems, etc., we choose to simply move, trusting our talent will fill in the gaps and hop over the holes in our strategy to continue to serve our consumers. However, what tends to happen is talent try to force their old mindsets, ways of working, and networks into a new world. They end up being more confused, slower, and less willing to take risks. Now, eventually they find their feet and regain their focus, but it is never crystal clear if that was because the strategy was sound or the talent simply kept working the way they were working with some new lingo, titles, and products. I fear it is the latter.

Why this long diatribe? Well, it is because there is real productivity to be gained by "starting slow to finish fast" and ensuring the transformation of the ways we work are as clear as the strategic bets we highlight in earnings calls or with boards. According to a 2016 McKinsey survey, 80% of reorgs fail to deliver the hoped-for value in the time planned, and 10% cause real damage to the company. Further, those same reorgs tend to cause greater stress and uncertainty than layoffs, leading to reduced productivity in about 60% of the cases. One of the five essential steps to success in this article was to "get the plumbing and wiring right," though it was noted through the survey that this was the hardest part, as it means resetting everything from job descriptions to goals to incentive structures to technology to decision rights.[23]

So, in times of transformation, think about how you work before you launch. Ensure that we maximize the moment to do the difficult and detailed work to both assess how the company works today (how it really works) and design how it will work tomorrow. Then, ensure the incentive structures are set so your top talent are rewarded for leading the shifts and punished (yes, punished) for waiting it out or standing still. Lastly, celebrate those who are out in front and do it publicly. Showcase the better practice, the benefits of taking the leap, and the profile of the ways of working that will be heralded in the future.

REAL STORIES OF FIT
A Right Fit Story
55, male, design agency

"It was like an ease," this interviewee said. "I would always judge things by how it felt when I walked in the building. [With *right fit*,] there was absolutely no nervousness about who you were going to encounter because you were just gonna be psyched by whoever was there." He talked more about the day-to-day by sharing that "people showed up knowing what they were doing or where to go if they had questions. There was this synergistic quality among the people . . . you could delight in the brilliance of others."

When the interviewee described how this feeling of *right fit* was created, he first pointed to purpose, or "a sense of feeling that you are part of a collective that's aligned and inspired toward the same thing." The interviewee pointed to alignment on values that are lived by everyone. To describe this idea, we played with an analogy of the values of my family and how we would suss them out. He said, "I would want to talk to your dog walker, house cleaner, pool person and have them reflect on the experience there. Did they all have an unprovoked version of the same story? Is there durability of behavior over time?"

This idea of durability of behavior is so poetic. It describes the visceral feeling that we have when we are in companies that are consistent in how they work day-to-day. No matter where we go or who we talk with, it feels familiar and consistent. We can trust it and so it is easier to trust ourselves as part of it.

Fit, Fitting In, and the Fine Art of Reinvention

Something that bears repeating is the fact that we will spend thirteen years in the prime of our lives working. Likewise, another piece of information worth circling back to is the $7.8 trillion of lost productivity that we are losing annually due to disengagement. Adding to this already giant hairball of corporate chaos are the struggles to find an optimal post-COVID approach to work and a world where we will all, talent and companies, continue to be disrupted, interrupted, and under pressure to meet more demanding customer, shareholder, and stakeholder wants and needs. It is a world where companies have wandered from, or even abandoned, core employer practices in favor of brand-flashing perks and where talent is languishing, quiet quitting, infinitely browsing for something better, and ending more days stressed or burned out than fully engaged in their company, their craft, or their cause. This is no way to be.

Now is the time to reinvent ourselves, our companies, and the relationship we have. But, what do we do? This is where I love the universe, because right around the time I was working on the conclusion to this book, I caught up with a good friend of mine from the world of design, and we started to riff on the idea of fit, fitting in, and reinvention.

She regaled me with a story of her days in art school and a moment where she learned what reinvention takes. She signed up for a mid-level drawing class and the first day was asked to choose a single object that she would draw ten times a day, every day, for the remainder of the course. She chose, drew the object ten different ways on the first day, and she, like most students, came in the second day of class desperately wanting to change her object. But, the professor would not allow it. "You chose the item, now live with the item," is what he would repeat to each student throughout the first week.

So, day after day, for an entire semester, my friend drew the same object ten times. The lesson? Looking back, she said, "If we don't go through the pain of reinventing ourselves, we will never find the edges. We will never know how much is possible inside of a constrained, consistent space."

And, it was an apt analogy to end this book about fit.

My hope in this book is that all talent can find a place they, you, really fit—where it feels like you are writing with your dominant hand every day, where it is easy to practice your craft because the surroundings simply make sense to you. Once you have *right fit*, my other hope is that you don't take it for granted. You don't get seduced by the cooler brand or the bigger paycheck—that you don't move until the company heads in a direction where it no longer works the way you work, where you are spending more time fitting in than feeling the ease of *right fit*.

Nothing in this world is perfect, and all things that are cool and different today become boring and vanilla tomorrow. That doesn't mean they can't be fulfilling or meaningful or even exciting again. Any long-term relationship requires work and growth and grace and a willingness to compromise and wake up and try again.

Right fit means it is "right, right now." If you continue to keep an eye on it, you can see the subtle ebbing and flowing more clearly. You can understand why your engagement might be fading or why you might be attracted by that shiny new thing on the horizon. You can rediscover it or find buffers that protect against losing it. You can, against popular opinion, find what you need right where you are.

But, it isn't just up to talent; organizations need to shift as well. They must create places where talent doesn't need to leave to be seen and valued. Or, places where new talent can clearly understand how companies work and can find *right fit* instead of spending days or months or years trying to "fit in" to a place that works differently than they do. Maybe organizations can be created that remind talent more often of all the reasons they should remain dedicated to the place they are instead of dreaming of a place they could be. Maybe the $7.8 trillion of lost productivity could be found and could go to making the world just a little bit better and our lives, as talent, just a bit more meaningful.

Dedication is a daily choice. And, *right fit* is awaiting us all if we look really hard for it and work every day to keep it.

RESOURCES

BIBLIOGRAPHY

37 Signals. "37 Signals Manifesto." 37signals.com. Accessed March 15, 2023. https://1999.37signals.com/.

37 Signals. "Long Thoughts." 37Signals.com. Accessed February 7, 2023. https://37signals.com/thoughts/.

Abdou, Anouare. "This Study Says That a 5-Hour Workday Is Optimal— Here's How to Do It Right." *Ladders* (July 4, 2021). https://www .theladders.com/career-advice/this-study-says-that-a-5-hour-workday -is-optimal-heres-how-to-do-it-right.

Abramson, Ashley. "Burnout and Stress Are Everywhere." *American Psycho- logical Association Monitor* (January 1, 2022). https://www.apa .org/monitor/2022/01/special-burnout-stress.

Allas, Tera, and Bill Schaninger. "The Boss Factor: Making the World a Better Place through Workplace Relationships," McKinsey (September 22, 2020). https://www.mckinsey.com/capabilities/people-and -organizational-performance/our-insights/the-boss-factor-making-the -world-a-better-place-through-workplace-relationships.

American Express. "Business Class: The Series Solution—Latest Trends." *American Express Business Trends and Insights.* Accessed February 7, 2023. https://www.americanexpress.com/en-us/business/trends-and -insights/solutions/series-2.

Anderson, Brian. *From Recruitment to Onboarding, What Is the True Cost of Hiring Employees?* Bamboo HR (February 24, 2023). https://www .bamboohr.com/blog/cost-of-onboarding-calculator.

Anderson, Karen. "The Pros and Cons of Following a Boss to a New Com- pany," *The Seattle Times* (June 3, 2016). https://www.seattletimes .com/explore/careers/the-pros-and-cons-of-following-a-boss-to-a -new-company/#:~:text=a%20better%20boss.-,One%20of%20the%20 best%20ways%20to%20guarantee%20that%20you%20get,of%20 Career%20Horizons%20in%20Bellevue.

Andre, Louie. "112 Employee Turnover Statistics: 2023 Causes, Cost & Prevention Data." FinancesOnline.com (May 17, 2021). https:// financesonline.com/employee-turnover-statistics/.

Apple. "Careers at Apple." Apple.com. Accessed on March 15, 2023. https://www.apple.com/careers/us/.

Ariella, Sky. "27 US Employee Turnover Statistics [2023]: Average Employee Turnover Rate, Industry Comparisons, and Trends."

Zippia.com (February 7, 2023). https://www.zippia.com/advice/employee-turnover-statistics/.

Artz, Benjamin, Amanda Goodall, and Andrew J. Oswald. "If Your Boss Could Do Your Job, You're More Likely to Be Happy at Work." *Harvard Business Review* (December 29, 2016). https://hbr.org/2016/12/if-your-boss-could-do-your-job-youre-more-likely-to-be-happy-at-work.

Associated Press. "Americans Are the Unhappiest They've Been in 50 Years, Poll Finds." NBC News (June 16, 2020). https://www.nbcnews.com/politics/politics-news/americans-are-unhappiest-they-ve-been-50-years-poll-finds-n1231153.

Awesome Box. "AwesomeBox." AwesomeBox. Accessed February 7, 2023. https://www.awesomebox.com/.

Axios. "The 2022 Axios Harris Poll 100 Reputation Rankings." Axios (May 24, 2022). https://www.axios.com/2022/05/24/2022-axios-harris-poll-100-rankings.

Baker, Mary. "6 Predictions for the Future of Performance Management." Gartner (October 14, 2021). https://www.gartner.com/en/articles/6-predictions-for-the-future-of-performance-management.

Bamboo HR. "The Incredible Impact of Effective Onboarding [Infographic]." Bamboo HR (May 3, 2018). https://www.bamboohr.com/blog/effective-onboarding-infographic.

"Basking in Reflected Glory - IResearchNet." Psychology iResearchnet. Accessed February 7, 2023. http://psychology.iresearchnet.com/social-psychology/social-cognition/basking-in-reflected-glory/.

Beck, Julie. "The Psychology of Home: Why Where You Live Means So Much." *The Atlantic* (December 30, 2011). https://www.theatlantic.com/health/archive/2011/12/the-psychology-of-home-why-where-you-live-means-so-much/249800/.

Belli, Gina. "Here's How Many Years You'll Spend at Work in Your Lifetime," PayScale.com (October 1, 2018). https://www.payscale.com/career-advice/heres-how-many-years-youll-spend-work-in-your-lifetime/.

Bennett, Steve. "Talent Marketplace Platforms Statistics 2022—Everything You Need to Know." WebinarCare (February 20, 2023). https://webinarcare.com/best-talent-marketplace-platforms/talent-marketplace-platforms-statistics/.

Beres, Derek. "Mentally Challenging Yourself Curbs Anxiety and Depression, New Research Shows." *Big Think* (November 20, 2017). https:

//bigthink.com/personal-growth/mentally-challenging-yourself
-curbs-anxiety-and-depression-new-research-shows/.

Bersin, Josh. "The Death of the Performance Appraisal—Redefining Performance Management." JoshBersin.com (July 8, 2021). https://joshbersin.com/2007/09/redefining-performance-management/.

BetterHelp Editorial Team. "What Is Conformity and What Does It Do to a Person?" BetterHelp.com (March 8, 2023). https://www.betterhelp.com/advice/psychologists/what-is-conformity-psychology-and-what-does-it-do-to-a-person/.

Birkinshaw, Julian, and Jordan Cohen. "Make Time for the Work That Matters." *Harvard Business Review* (September 2013). https://hbr.org/2013/09/make-time-for-the-work-that-matters.

Block, Peter. *The Answer to How Is Yes: Acting on What Matters*. San Francisco, CA: Berrett-Koehler Publishers, 2003.

Brower, Tracy. "Finding a Job Is Tougher Now: 5 Practical Tips to Persevere." *Forbes* (November 13, 2022). https://www.forbes.com/sites/tracybrower/2022/11/13/finding-a-job-is-tougher-now-5-practical-tips-to-persevere/?sh=462412f331d5.

Brower, Tracy. "The Power of Purpose and Why It Matters Now," *Forbes* (August 22, 2021). https://www.forbes.com/sites/tracybrower/2021/08/22/the-power-of-purpose-and-why-it-matters-now/?sh=758b541f163a.

Brown, Brene. *Braving the Wilderness: The Quest for True Belonging and the Courage to Stand Alone*. New York: Random House, 2017.

Buckingham, Marcus, and Ashley Goodall. "Why Feedback Rarely Does What It's Meant To." *Harvard Business Review* (March 1, 2019). https://hbr.org/2019/03/the-feedback-fallacy.

Buckley, Thea. "What Happens to the Brain During Cognitive Dissonance?" *Scientific American* (November 1, 2015). https://www.scientificamerican.com/article/what-happens-to-the-brain-during-cognitive-dissonance1/

Business Insights. "Fundamental Attribution Error: What It Is & How to Avoid It." *Business Insights Blog* (June 8, 2017). https://online.hbs.edu/blog/post/the-fundamental-attribution-error.

Cameron, Judy, and W. David Pierce. "Reinforcement, Reward, and Intrinsic Motivation: A Meta-Analysis." *Review of Educational Research* 64, no. 3 (Fall 1994): 363–423. https://citeseerx.ist.psu.edu/viewdoc/download?doi=10.1.1.848.8473&rep=rep1&type=pdf.

Campbell, Emily. "Six Surprising Benefits of Curiosity." *Greater Good Magazine* (September 24, 2015). https://greatergood.berkeley.edu/article/item/six_surprising_benefits_of_curiosity#:~:text=Research %20has%20shown%20curiosity%20to,and%20greater%20psychological%20well%2Dbeing.

Campbell, Leigh. "We've Broken Down Your Entire Life into Years Spent Doing Tasks." *Huffington Post* (October 18, 2017). https://www.huffpost.com/entry/weve-broken-down-your-entire-life-into-years-spent-doing-tasks_n_61087617e4b0999d2084fec5.

Cappelli, Peter. "Your Approach to Hiring Is All Wrong." *Harvard Business Review* (May/June 2019). https://hbr.org/2019/05/your-approach-to-hiring-is-all-wrong.

Carhart, Dave. "People Are Quitting Jobs They Just Started. Here's What Managers Can Do." *Fast Company* (May 11, 2022). https://www.fastcompany.com/90750694/people-are-quitting-jobs-they-just-started-heres-what-managers-can-do.

Carr, Evan W., Andrew Reece, Gabriella Rosen Kellerman, and Alexi Robichaux. "The Value of Belonging at Work." *Harvard Business Review* (December 16, 2019). https://hbr.org/2019/12/the-value-of-belonging-at-work.

Center on Budget and Policy Priorities. "Chart Book: Tracking the Post-Great Recession Economy." Center on Budget and Policy Priorities (updated May 27, 2022). https://www.cbpp.org/research/economy/tracking-the-post-great-recession-economy.

Cerullo, Megan. "Unnecessary Meetings Can Cost Big Companies $100 Million a Year, Report Finds." *CBS News* (September 30, 2022). https://www.cbsnews.com/news/unnecessary-meetings-cost-big-companies-100-million-annually/.

Chamorro-Premuzic, Tomas. "10 Things We Know about Impression Management at Work." *Forbes* (April 7, 2022). https://www.forbes.com/sites/tomaspremuzic/2022/04/07/ten-things-we-know-about-impression-management-at-work/?sh=3d243f0a277e.

Chamorro-Premuzic, Tomas. "Does Money Really Affect Motivation? A Review of the Research." *Harvard Business Review* (April 10, 2013). https://hbr.org/2013/04/does-money-really-affect-motiv.

Chanty. "11 Brilliant Problem-Solving Techniques Nobody Taught You." *Chanty* (February 1, 2023). https://www.chanty.com/blog/problem-solving-techniques/.

Chatterjee, Rhitu, and Carmel Wroth. "WHO Redefines Burnout as a 'Syndrome' Linked to Chronic Stress at Work." *NPR Morning Edition*

(May 28, 2019). https://www.npr.org/sections/health-shots/2019
/05/28/727637944/who-redefines-burnout-as-a-syndrome-linked-to
-chronic-stress-at-work.

Chibana, Nayomi. "Recruitment Strategies: How IBM Uses Infographics
to Attract Top Talent [Case Study]." *Visme Blog* (March 15, 2018).
https://visme.co/blog/recruitment-strategies/.

Chouinard, Yvon. "Earth Is Now Our Only Shareholder." Patagonia.
com. Accessed on March 15, 2023. https://www.patagonia.com/
ownership/.

Cohen, Debbie, and Kate Roeske-Zummer. "With So Many People
Quitting, Don't Overlook Those Who Stay." *Harvard Business Review*
(October 1, 2021). https://hbr.org/2021/10/with-so-many
-people-quitting-dont-overlook-those-who-stay.

Coleman, Ashley. "The 8 Most Overlooked Reasons Why Marriages Fail."
Essence. Updated October 26, 2020. Originally published March 24,
2017. https://www.essence.com/love/relationships/most-overlooked
-reasons-marriages-fail/#53854.

Coleman, Jackie, and John Coleman. "Don't Take Work Stress Home with
You," *Harvard Business Review* (July 28, 2016). https://hbr
.org/2016/07/dont-take-work-stress-home-with-you.

Collective Hub. "Financial Solutions & Resources for Self-Employed Businesses." *Collective Hub* (May 17, 2021). https://www.collective.com/

Coletta, Jen. "Top Tips for Strenghtening EX in 2023 from Patagonia's
Former CHRO." *Human Resource Executive* (January 9, 2023).
https://hrexecutive.com/top-tips-for-strengthening-ex-in-2023
-from-patagonias-former-chro/.

Collins, Leah. "Job Unhappiness Is at a Staggering All-Time High, According to Gallup." *CNBC* (August 12, 2022). https://www.cnbc.com/2022
/08/12/job-unhappiness-is-at-a-staggering-all-time-high-according
-to-gallup.html.

Cooks-Campbell, Allaya. "What is Cognitive Dissonance and How Do You
Reduce It?" *BetterUp* (October 24, 2022). https://www.betterup.com
/blog/cognitive-dissonance.

Cooper, Joel. "Cognitive Dissonance: Where We've Been and Where
We're Going." *International Review of Social Psychology* (May 3, 2019).
https://rips-irsp.com/articles/10.5334/irsp.277.

Corritore, Matthew, Amir Goldberg, and Sameer B. Srivastava. "The New
Analytics of Culture." *Harvard Business Review* (January 1, 2020.)
https://hbr.org/2020/01/the-new-analytics-of-culture.

Cunha, John P. "What Causes Cognitive Dissonance." eMedicine Health.com (July 12, 2021). https://www.emedicinehealth.com/what _causes_cognitive_dissonance/article_em.htm.

Dagbo, Jeff, and Sam Acuna. "Company Culture: Private Equity's Intangible Value Creation Lever." Gallup (August 13, 2020). https://www .gallup.com/workplace/316883/company-culture-private-equity -intangible-value-creation-lever.aspx.

Datu, Jesus Alfonso D. "Beyond Passion and Perseverance: Review and Future Research Initiatives on the Science of Grit." *Frontiers in Psychology* 11 (January 27, 2021). https://www.frontiersin.org/ articles/10.3389/fpsyg.2020.545526/full.

Davidson, Paul. "Great Resignation: The Number of People Quitting Jobs Hit an All-Time High in November as Openings Stayed near Record." *USA TODAY* (January 4, 2022). https://www.usatoday.com /story/money/2022/01/04/great-resignation-number-people -quitting -jobs-hit-record/9083256002/.

Davis, Pete. *Dedicated: The Case for Commitment in an Age of Infinite Browsing*. New York: Simon & Schuster, 2021.

Deloitte. "Beyond Design Thinking: Part of the Business Trends Series." Deloitte Insights (April 16, 2015). https://www2.deloitte.com/us/en /insights/focus/business-trends/2015/beyond-design-thinking -business-trends.html.

Devenyi, Brittany. "The Psychology Behind First Impressions, and How It Affects Your Home Buying Choices." Livabl.com (August 11, 2014). https://www.livabl.com/2014/08/psychology-home-buying.html.

Dewar, Carolyn, Scott Keller, Vikram Malhotra, and Kurt Strovink. "Actions the Best CEOs are Taking in 2023." McKinsey & Company (March 15, 2023). https://www.mckinsey.com/ capabilities/strategy-and-corporate-finance/our-insights/ actions-the-best-ceos-are-taking-in-2023

Dhingra, Naina, Andrew Samo, Bill Schaninger, and Matt Schrimper. "Help Your Employees Find Purpose—Or Watch Them Leave." McKinsey (April 5, 2021). https://www.mckinsey.com/capa- bilities/people-and-organizational-performance/our-insights/ help-your-employees-find-purpose-or-watch-them-leave

Dishman, Lydia. "Intern Sushi Becomes Career Sushi, A Job-Hunting Site For Creative Professionals." *Fast Company* (May 20, 2014). https:// www.fastcompany.com/3030812/intern-sushi-becomes-career-sushi -a-job-hunting-site-for-creative-profe.

DMI. "The Difference between Being Busy and Being Productive—Digital Marketing Lesson—DMI." *Digital Marketing Institute*. Accessed February 7, 2023. https://digitalmarketinginstitute.com/resources/lessons /personal-skills_the-difference-between-being-busy-and-being -productive_fmwq.

"Don't Just Talk Transformation," Nobl.io. Accessed March 27, 2003. https://nobl.io/.

Dossetto, Fio. "The Quest for Better Collaboration: Principles, Cheat-sheets, and 10+ Tools We Use At Hotjar." *Hotjar Blog* (August 17, 2022). https://www.hotjar.com/blog/team-collaboration/.

Downard, Brian. "101 Best Leadership Skills, Traits & Qualities—The Complete List." *Brian Downard* (July 9, 2016). https://briandownard. com/leadership-skills-list/#effect.

Dweck, Carol. "Caution—Praise Can Be Dangerous." *American Federation of Teachers* (Spring 1999). https://www.aft.org/periodical/ american-educator/spring-1999/caution-praise-can-be-dangerous.

Edelman Trust Institute. *2023 Edelman Trust Barometer: Global Report*. Edelman Trust Institute (2023). https://www.edelman.com/ trust/2023/trust-barometer.

Ellis, A. P. J., West, B J., Ryan, A. M., and DeShon, R. P. "The Use of Impression Management Tactics in Structured Interviews: A Function of Question Type?" *Journal of Applied Psychology* 87, no. 6 (2002): 1200–1208. https://psycnet.apa.org/doiLanding?doi=10.1037 %2F0021-9010.87.6.1200.

Emmett, Jonathan, et al. "This Time It's Personal: Shaping the 'New Possible' through Employee Experience." McKinsey & Company (September 30, 2021). https://www.mckinsey.com/capabilities /people-and-organizational-performance/our-insights/this-time-its -personal-shaping-the-new-possible-through-employee-experience.

Enterprise Alumni. *2023 H.R. Statistics: Hiring, Retaining & Rehiring*. Enterprise Alumni (2023). https://enterprisealumni.com/research /hr-statistics.

Erica. "The Ultimate Guide to Values Based Recruitment." *Harver* (September 11, 2019). https://harver.com/blog/values-based-recruitment/.

Ferenstein, Gregory. "Read What Facebook's Sandberg Calls Maybe 'The Most Important Document Ever to Come Out of the Valley.'" TechCrunch (January 31, 2013). https://techcrunch.com/2013/01/31 /read-what-facebooks-sandberg-calls-maybe-the-most-important-document-ever-to-come-out-of-the-valley/#:~:text=2%20top%20 dog%2C%20COO%20Sheryl,over%203.2%20million%20views%20on.

Ferraro, Kathleen. "One Company's Trick to Getting 95,000 Hours Back? Canceling Meetings." StrideHealth.com (February 2, 2023). https://blog.stridehealth.com/post/stride-in-wsj.

Firstbird. "Firstbird—Employee Referral Platform." *Radancys Mitarbeiter-Werben-Mitarbeiter-Programm*, Firstbird.com. Accessed February 7, 2023. https://www.firstbird.com/en/how-it-works/.

Fischer, Brook. "12 Amazing Career Page Examples to Inspire Your Own." *My Company Name* (October 27, 2022). https://www.homerun.co/articles/career-pages-examples.

Forsyth, Donelson R. "The Psychology of Groups." *Noba*. Accessed February 7, 2023. https://nobaproject.com/modules/the-psychology-of-groups.

Fox, Michelle. "Companies Are Betting These Employee Benefits Will Help Them in the 'Great Reshuffle.'" *CNBC* (March 26, 2022). https://www.cnbc.com/2022/03/26/companies-bet-employee-benefits-will-help-them-in-the-great-reshuffle.html.

Fox, Michelle. "How to Convince Your Boss, Company to Institute a Four-Day Work Week." *MSNBC* (June 8, 2022). https://www.msnbc.com/know-your-value/business-culture/how-convince-your-boss-company-institute-four-day-work-week-n1296083.

Frazier, Ross, Naufal Khan, Gautam Lunawat, and Amit Rahul. "Products and Platforms: Is Your Technology Operating Model Ready?" McKinsey & Company (February 28, 2020). https://www.mckinsey.com.br/business-functions/mckinsey-digital/our-insights/products-and-platforms-is-your-technology-operating-model-ready.

Fresh Books. "How Many Hours Do People Work in a Year: Calculation." *FreshBooks* (August 18, 2021). https://www.freshbooks.com/hub/productivity/how-many-hours-do-people-work-in-a-year.

Fried, Jason. "Where We Came From," Basecamp.com. Accessed March 15, 2023. https://basecamp.com/about.

Gallup. "Employee Experience," Gartner.com. Accessed March 15, 2023. https://www.gallup.com/workplace/242252/employee-experience.aspx.

Gallup. "State of the Global Workplace Report." Gallup (June 15, 2021). https://www.gallup.com/workplace/349484/state-of-the-global-workplace.aspx?thank-you-report-form=1.

Gamble, Shane. "How Employee Engagement Leads to Customer Loyalty." Smile.io (April 2013). Updated on February 9, 2018. https://blog.smile.io/employee-engagement-leads-customer-loyalty/.

Gartner. "A Key Pandemic Lesson Learned: Invest in Your Talent." Gartner (July 7, 2021). https://www.gartner.com/smarterwithgartner/a -key-pandemic-lesson-learned-invest-in-your-talent.

Gartner. "Employees Increasingly Seek Value and Purpose at Work." Gartner (January 13, 2022). https://www.gartner.com/en/articles/ employees-seek-personal-value-and-purpose-at-work-be-prepared-to- deliver.

Gartner. "Gartner Glossary." Gartner. Accessed March 15, 2023. https://www.gartner.com/en/human-resources/glossary/employee -experience.

Gartner, "Gartner HR Research Finds 65 % of Women Report the Pandemic Has Made Them Rethink the Place of Work in Their Lives." Gartner (March 23, 2022). https://www.gartner.com/en/newsroom/ press-releases/03-23-22-gartner-hr-research-finds-sixty-five-percent- of-women-report-the-pandemic-has-made-them-rethink-the-place-of- work-in-their-lives

Gartner. "Gartner HR Research Reveals 82% of Employees Report Working Environment Lacks Fairness." Gartner (November 8, 2021). https://www.gartner.com/en/newsroom/press-releases/2021-08-11 -gartner-hr-research-reveals-eighty-two-percent-of-employees-report -working-environment-lacks-fairness.

Gartner. "Gartner Says U.S. Total Annual Employee Turnover Will Likely Jump by Nearly 20% From the Prepandemic Annual Average." Gartner (April 28, 2022). https://www.gartner.com/en/newsroom/04-28-2022 -gartner-says-us-total-annual-employee-turnover-will-likely-jump-by -nearly-twenty-percent-from-the-prepandemic-annual-average.

Gelles, David. "Billionaire No More: Patagonia Founder Gives Away the Company," *New York Times* (September 14, 2022). https://www .nytimes.com/2022/09/14/climate/patagonia-climate-philanthropy -chouinard.html.

Giang, Vivian. "A New Report Ranks America's Biggest Companies Based on How Quickly Employees Jump Ship." *Insider* (July 25, 2013). https://www.businessinsider.com/companies-ranked-by-turnover -rates-2013-7.

Ginn, Vance. "Overview of U.S. Economic Growth." Texas Public Policy Foundation (September 2, 2020). https://www.texaspolicy.com /overview-of-u-s-economic-growth/.

Glerum, Jaap, Sofie M. M. Loyens, Lisette Mijnia, and Remy M. J. P. Rikers. "The Effects of Praise for Effort versus Praise for Intelligence on Vocational Education Students." *Educational Psychology*, 40, no. 10

(June 2019): 1270–1286. https://doi.org/10.1080/01443410.2019
.1625306.

Goffee, Rob, and Gareth Jones. *Why Should Anyone Work Here?: What it Takes to Create an Authentic Organization*. Boston, Massachusetts: Harvard Business Review, 2015.

Goldberg, Emma. "The Magic of Your First Work Friends," *New York Times* (July 14, 2022). https://www.nytimes.com/2022/07/14/business/work-friends.html.

Google Trends. "Hybrid Working." Trends.Google.com. Accessed March 14, 2023. https://trends.google.com/trends/explore?date=2008-07-20%202022-08-20&q=hybrid%20working.

Google Trends. "Languishing." Trends.Google.com. Accessed March 14, 2023. https://trends.google.com/trends/explore?date=2008-07-20%202022-08-20&q=languishing.

Google Trends. "News." Trends.Google.com. Accessed March 14, 2023. https://trends.google.com/trends/explore?date=2008-07-20%202022-08-20&gprop=news&q=great%20resignation.

Google Trends. "Purpose." Trends.Google.com. Accessed March 14, 2023. https://trends.google.com/trends/explore?date=2008-07-20%202022-08-20&q=purpose.

Google Trends. "Side Hustles." Trends.Google.com. Accessed March 14, 2023. https://trends.google.com/trends/explore?date=2008-07-20%202022-08-20&q=side%20hustles.

Graham, Jesse, Peter Meindl, Spassena Koleva, Ravi Iyer, Kate M. Johnson. "When Values and Behavior Conflict: Moral Pluralism and Intrapersonal Moral Hypocrisy." *Social and Personality Psychology Compass* 9, no. 3 (March 5, 2015): 158–170. https://doi.org/10.1111/spc3.12158.

Grant, Adam. "Feeling Blah During the Pandemic? It's Called Languishing." *New York Times* (April 19, 2021). https://www.nytimes.com/2021/04/19/well/mind/covid-mental-health-languishing.html

Grenny, Joseph. "Great Storytelling Connects Employees to Their Work." *Harvard Business Review* (September 25, 2017). https://hbr.org/2017/09/great-storytelling-connects-employees-to-their-work.

Groschupf, Stefan. "What Makes a Great Company? Let's Talk Information Flow." *VentureBeat* (January 10, 2016). https://venturebeat.com/entrepreneur/what-makes-a-great-company-lets-talk-information-flow/.

Gulati, Ranjay. "When Employees Feel a Sense of Purpose, Companies Succeed." *Harvard Business School, Working Knowledge* (February

17, 2022). https://hbswk.hbs.edu/item/when-employees-feel-a-sense
-of-purpose-companies-succeed.

Hadley, Edward. "Design Thinking vs. Agile: Problem Finding + Problem
Solving." *Mendix* (November 29, 2022). https://www.mendix.com
/blog/design-thinking-vs-agile-combine-problem-finding-problem
-solving-better-outcomes/.

Hanson, Melanie. "U.S. Public Education Spending Statistics [2023]: Per
Pupil + Total." *Education Data Initiative* (October 28, 2020). https://
educationdata.org/public-education-spending-statistics.

Harper, Jane. "Why New Hires Quit Their Job Too Quickly?" *The HR
Digest* (May 25, 2016). https://www.thehrdigest.com/new
-hires-quit-job-quickly/.

Harter, Jim. "U.S. Employee Engagement Needs a Rebound in 2023," Gallup (January 25, 2023). gallup.com/workplace/468233/employee
-engagement-needs-rebound-2023.aspx#:~:text=Story%20Highlights
&text=After%20trending%20up%20in%20recent,2020%20to%20
34%25%20in%202021.

Harter, Jim. "U.S. Employee Engagement Slump Continues." Gallup (April
25, 2022). https://www.gallup.com/workplace/391922/employee
-engagement-slump-continues.aspx.

Hastwell, Claire. "The 6 Elements of Great Company Culture." *Great Place
To Work* (August 19, 2021). https://www.greatplacetowork.com
/resources/blog/6-elements-of-great-company-culture.

Heath, Dan. *Upstream: The Quest to Solve Problems before They Happen.*
New York: Avid Reader Press, 2020.

Heidari-Robinson, Stephen, and Suzanne Heywood. "Getting
Reorgs Right." *Harvard Business Review* (November 2016).
https://hbr.org/2016/11/getting-reorgs-right#:~:text=The%20
Problem,day%2Dto%2Dday%20work.

Henderson, Rob. "The Hidden Power of Conformity." *Psychology Today*
(September 4, 2019). https://www.psychologytoday.com/us/blog
/after-service/201909/the-hidden-power-conformity.

Hogue, Joseph. "The Psychology of Buyer's Remorse and How to Beat It."
Finance Quick Fix (April 26, 2021). https://financequickfix.com
/psychology-buyers-remorse/.

Hotchkiss, Michael. "Todorov Explores the 'Irresistible Influence of First
Impressions.'" Princeton University (October 16, 2017). https://www.
princeton.edu/news/2017/10/16/todorov-explores-irresistible
-influence-first-impressions.

HRTechX. "The Story of the Netflix Culture Deck." HRTechX. Accessed May 3, 2023. https://www.hrtechx.com/2021/05/25/the-story-of-the-netflix-culture-deck/.

Huhman, Heather R. "It's Science, Baby! Proving the Power of Positive Reinforcement at Work." *Entrepreneur* (October 16, 2017). https://www.entrepreneur.com/article/302489.

IBM. "What Employees Expect in 2021." IBM Institute for Business Value. (2021). https://www.ibm.com/thought-leadership/institute-business-value/en-us/report/employee-expectations-2021.

Indeed. "The Complete Guide to Researching a Company." *Indeed Career Guide* (April 17, 2017). https://www.indeed.com/career-advice/finding-a-job/the-complete-guide-to-researching-a-company.

InfoSurv. "It Takes Two: Engaged Employees and Satisfied Customers [Infographic]." InfoSurv Research. Accessed March 15, 2023. https://infosurv.com/it-takes-two-engaged-employees-and-satisfied-customers/.

James Clear. "Core Values List: Over 50 Common Personal Values." James Clear.com. Accessed February 7, 2023. https://jamesclear.com/core-values.

Jobvite. *2018 Job Seeker Nation Survey: Researching the Candidate-Recruiter Relationship*. Jobvite (2018). Accessed February 7, 2023. https://www.jobvite.com/wp-content/uploads/2018/04/2018_Job_Seeker_Nation_Study.pdf.

Kansas State University. "Employees Who Are Engaged in Their Work Have Happier Home Life." *Science Daily* (August 25, 2009). https://www.sciencedaily.com/releases/2009/08/090824115911.htm.

Kantor, Jodi, Karen Weise, and Grace Ashford. "Inside Amazon's Employment Machine." *New York Times* (June 15, 2021.) https://www.nytimes.com/interactive/2021/06/15/us/amazon-workers.html.

Kaplan, Robert E., and Robert B. Kaiser. "Stop Overdoing Your Strengths," *Harvard Business Review* (Febraury 2009). https://hbr.org/2009/02/stop-overdoing-your-strengths.

Keller, Scott. "Attracting and Retaining the Right Talent." McKinsey & Company (November 24, 2017). https://www.mckinsey.com/business-functions/people-and-organizational-performance/our-insights/attracting-and-retaining-the-right-talent.

Kelley, Susan, and Cornell Chronicle. "Woulda, Coulda, Shoulda: The Haunting Regret of Failing Our Ideal Selves." *College of Arts & Sciences* (May 24, 2018). https://as.cornell.edu/news/woulda-coulda-shoulda-haunting-regret-failing-our-ideal-selves.

Kim, Annie. "2022 Teacher Spending Study." Savings.com (August 1, 2022). https://www.savings.com/insights/teacher-spending-study.

Kivetz, Ran, and Itamar Simonson. "The Effects of Incomplete Information on Consumer Choice." *Journal of Marketing Research* 37, no. 4 (2000): 427–448. https://doi.org/10.2307/1558513.

Klucharev, Vasily, et al. "Reinforcement Learning Signal Predicts Social Conformity." *Neuron* 61, no. 1 (Jan. 2009): 140–151. https://doi.org/10.1016/j.neuron.2008.11.027.

Koetsier, John. "Why Every Amazon Meeting Has at Least 1 Empty Chair: Three People, Five People, 15 People? No Matter What Size the Meeting, Every Amazon Event Has One Extra Seat," *Inc.* (April 5, 2018). https://www.inc.com/john-koetsier/why-every-amazon-meeting-has-at-least-one-empty-chair.html.

Krauss Whitbourne, PhD, Susan, and ABPP. "5 Ways to Spot the Hypocrites in Your Life." *Psychology Today* (March 1, 2016). https://www.psychologytoday.com/us/blog/fulfillment-any-age/201603/5-ways-spot-the-hypocrites-in-your-life.

Lattice Team. "Lattice Research Reveals Great Resignation Trends," Lattice.com (April 12, 2022). https://docs.google.com/document/d/1z5B2U3DjZOZAa80MydoOUv6YCWTQ6U_qiOkMSKUAmgg/edit#.

Law, Jackson White. "Wondering What the Most Common Year of Marriage Ends in Divorce?" *Arizona Divorce Lawyers & Family Law Attorneys—JacksonWhite Law* (January 22, 2019). https://www.jacksonwhitelaw.com/arizona-family-law/what-year-of-a-marriage-is-divorce-most-common/.

Leary, M. R. "Impression Management - an Overview." *International Encyclopedia of the Social & Behavioral Sciences* (2001). https://www.sciencedirect.com/topics/psychology/impression-management.

Lee, Andy. "Leaders Need to Excel at Learning from Experience. Mindfulness Can Help," LinkedIn (March 2, 2020). https://www.linkedin.com/pulse/leaders-need-excel-learning-from-experience-mindfulness-andy-lee/.

Lee, Sophia. "What Is Employee Experience?" CultureAmp.com. Accessed on March 15, 2023. https://www.cultureamp.com/blog/what-is-employee-experience.

Lencioni, Patrick M. "Make Your Values Mean Something." *Harvard Business Review* (July 1, 2002). https://hbr.org/2002/07/make-your-values-mean-something.

Lerner, Harriet. "Learn the Real Reason Why Marriages Fail." *Psychology Today* (November 5, 2018). https://www.psychology

today.com/us/blog/the-dance-connection/201811/learn-the-real
-reason-why-marriages-fail.

Lieberman, Charlotte. "Why Your Procrastinate (It Has Nothing to Do With Self-Control)." *New York Times* (March 25, 2019). https://www .nytimes.com/2019/03/25/smarter-living/why-you-procrastinate-it -has-nothing-to-do-with-self-control.html.

Liedtka, Jeanne. "Why Design Thinking Works." *Harvard Business Review* (September-October 2018). https://hbr.org/2018/09/why-design -thinking-works.

Lightman, Alan. *Einstein's Dream*. New York: Pantheon Books, 1993.

Liston, Katie. "Workplace Culture and Communication: How One Affects the Other." *ContactMonkey* (December 23, 2020). https://www.contact monkey.com/blog/workplace-culture-and-communication.

Liu, Jennifer. "1 in 4 Workers Quit Their Job This Year—Here's What Companies Are Getting Wrong about Retention." *CNBC* (October 14, 2021). https://www.cnbc.com/2021/10/14/1-in-4-workers-quit-their- job-this-year-according-to-new-report.html.

Liu, Jennifer. "People Spend More than Half Their Day Doing Busy Work, According to Survey of 10,000-plus Workers." *CNBC* (April 6, 2022). https://www.cnbc.com/2022/04/06/people-spend-more-than-half-of -the-day-on-busy-work-says-asana-survey.html.

Lonczak, Heather S. "Positive Reinforcement in the Workplace (Incl. 90+ Examples)." PositivePsychology.com (April 9, 2019). https://positive psychology.com/positive-reinforcement-workplace/.

Lord, C., L. Ross, and M. Lepper. "Prior Bias and Attitude Change—Death Penalty." *Journal of Personality and Social Psychology* 37 (1979): 2098– 2109. https://faculty.babson.edu/krollag/org_site/soc_psych /lord_death_pen.html.

Lumbert, Samantha P. *Conformity and Group Mentality*. Rochester Institute of Technology (November 2005). http://www.personalityresearch.org /papers/lumbert.removed.

Lusty, Kendra. "Employee Engagement & Loyalty Statistics: The Ultimate Collection." *Access Perks* (August 17, 2022). https://blog.accessperks. com/employee-engagement-loyalty-statistics-the-ultimate-collection.

Luthens, Fred, and Suzanne J. Peterson. "360-Degree Feedback with Systemic Coaching: Empirical Analysis Suggests a Winning Comi- nation." *Management Department Faculty Publications* 147 (2003). https://digitalcommons.unl.edu/cgi/viewcontent.cgi?article =1156&context=managementfacpub.

LVMH. "Inside LVMH," LVMH.com. Accessed March 15, 2023. https://www.lvmh.com/group/lvmh-commitments/transmission-savoir-faire/inside-lvmh/.

Madgavkar, Anu, et al. "Performance through People: Transforming Human Capital Into Competitive Advantage." McKinsey Global Institute (February 2, 2023). https://www.mckinsey.com/mgi/our-research/performance-through-people-transforming-human-capital-into-competitive-advantage.

Mandriota, Morgan. "The Results Are In: How Many People Actually Tell the Truth on Their Dating Profile?" Top10.com (December 6, 2022). https://www.top10.com/dating/dating-survey.

Manta, Irina D. "The Case for Cracking down on Tinder Lies." *Washington Post* (November 16, 2018). https://www.washingtonpost.com/outlook/the-case-for-cracking-down-on-tinder-lies/2018/11/16/d3eb0b98-e2de-11e8-b759-3d88a5ce9e19_story.html.

Marfice, Christina. "Busy vs Productive — Which Are You?" *Superhuman Blog* (May 3, 2022). https://blog.superhuman.com/busy-vs-productive/.

Martensson, Johan, et al. "Growth of Language-Related Brain Areas after Foreign Langugae Learning," *NeuroImage* 63, no.1 (October 15, 2012): 240–244. https://www.sciencedirect.com/science/article/abs/pii/S1053811912006581.

Martin, Andre. "The Case for Inspiration." *Dialogue Review* (August 21, 2022). https://dialoguereview.com/the-case-for-inspiration/.

Mathieu, Cynthia. "Chapter 4: Performance Appraisal: How to Stop the Dark from Rising." *Dark Personalities in the Workforce: ScienceDirect* (2021). https://www.sciencedirect.com/science/article/pii/B9780128158272000041.

Matz, David C., and Wendy Wood. "Cognitive Dissonance in Groups: The Consequences of Disagreement." *Journal of Personality and Social Psychology* 88, no 1 (February 2005): 22–37. https://www.researchgate.net/publication/8098586_Cognitive_Dissonance_in_Groups_The_Consequences_of_Disagreement.

Maurer, Roy. "Promotions Got a Boost in 2021." *SHRM* (January 26, 2022). https://www.shrm.org/hr-today/news/hr-news/pages/promotions-rise-2021.aspx.

Maverick, J. B. "S&P 500 Average Return." Investopedia. Last updated February 15, 2023. https://www.investopedia.com/ask/answers/042415/what-average-annual-return-sp-500.asp.

McCall, Morgan W., Michael M. Lombardo, and Ann M. Morrison. *The Lessons of Experience: How Successful Executives Develop on the Job*. New York: Free Press, 1988.

McKinsey. "The Future of Work after COVID-19." McKinsey & Company (February 18, 2021). https://www.mckinsey.com/featured-insights /future-of-work/the-future-of-work-after-covid-19.

McLaren, Samantha. "10 Creative Job Advertisements and Hiring Posts." *LinkedIn Talent Blog* (January 22, 2023). https://www.linkedin.com/ business/talent/blog/talent-acquisition /creative-job-posts-and-ads-that-will-inspire-yours.

McLaren, Samantha. "Employees Stay 41% Longer at Companies That Use This Strategy." *LinkedIn Talent Blog* (March 4, 2020). https://www. linkedin.com/business/talent/blog/talent-management /employees-stay-41-percent-longer-at-companies-that-do-this.

McLeod, Saul. "Asch Conformity Experiment." *Simply Psychology* (February 8, 2023). https://www.simplypsychology.org/asch-conformity.html.

McLeod, Saul. "Operant Conditioning: What It Is, How It Works, and Examples." *Simply Psychology* (March 14, 2023). https://simplypsychology.org/operant-conditioning.html.

Mehta, Ravi. "Set Better Product Goals with NCTs—Reforge." *Reforge* (February 9, 2022), https://www.reforge.com/blog/ set-better-goals-with-ncts-not-okrs.

Mercer. "Employers Increased Investment in Benefits during Pandemic but Many Employees Did Not Feel Supported." *Mercer* (December 7, 2021). https://www.uk.mercer.com/newsroom/ employers-increased-investment-in-benefits-during-pandemic-but-many-employees-did-not-feel-supported.html.

Merritt, Jen. "The History of Shopify." *Full Fat Commerce* (January 10, 2022). https://fullfatcommerce.com/blog/a-history-of-shopify.

Michaelson, Christopher. "The Importance of Meaningful Work." *MIT Sloan Management Review* (January 1, 2010). https://sloanreview.mit .edu/article/the-importance-of-meaningful-work/.

Miller, Claire Cain. "The 24/7 Work Culture's Toll on Families and Gender Equality." *New York Times* (May 28, 2015). https://www.nytimes .com/2015/05/31/upshot/the-24-7-work-cultures-toll-on-families -and-gender-equality.html.

Miller, Jeremy. "This Compound Growth Calculator Predicts When You'll Double." *Sticky Branding* (December 4, 2018). https://stickybranding .com/compound-growth-how-to-double-the-size-of-your-business/.

Milne, A. A. *Winnie-the-Pooh: Classic Gift Edition*. New York: Dutton, 1926.

Mito. "Random Clever Person." Mito.hu. Accessed on March 15, 2023. https://mito.hu/jobs/random-clever-person/.

Mohan, Ronita. "Why Learning New Skills Is good for Your Confidence." ThriveGlobal.com (July 8, 2019). https://community.thriveglobal.com/why-learning-new-skills-is-good-for-your-confidence/.

Moneywatch. "It's Official: Recession Began in February, Ending Longest U.S. Expansion Ever." *CBS News* (June 9, 2020). https://www.cbsnews.com/news/united-states-recession-started-february/.

Moyle, Penny, and John Hackston. "Core Characters under Great Stress: The Grip Experience." The Myers Briggs Company (April 28, 2016). https://eu.themyersbriggs.com/en/Knowledge-centre/Blog/2016/April/Core-Characters-under-great-stress-the-grip-experience.

Murray, Alan. "Purpose, or 'Purpose-Washing'? A Crossroads for Business Leaders." *Yahoo* (November 11, 2020). https://www.yahoo.com/video/purpose-purpose-washing-crossroads-business-220000567.html.

Musser, Chris, and Gerard Taboada. "Use Internal Communications to Execute a Winning Strategy." Gallup (July 9, 2020). https://www.gallup.com/workplace/313367/internal-communications-execute-winning-strategy.aspx.

National Center for Education Statistics. "Fast Facts: Expenditures," NCES.ed.gov. Accessed March 27, 2023. https://nces.ed.gov/fastfacts/display.asp?id=75.

Nelms, Danny, Sarah Tucker, Glen Spinner, and Wiliam Mahan. *2022 Retention Report: How Employers Caused the Great Resignation*. Work Institute (2022). https://info.workinstitute.com/hubfs/2022%20Retention%20Report/2022%20Retention%20Report%20-%20Work%20Institute.pdf.

Neufeld, Dorothy. "The World's Most Influential Values, in One Graphic." *Visual Capitalist* (November 5, 2020). https://www.visualcapitalist.com/most-influential-values/.

Newport, Cal. "Why Are So Many Knowledge Workers Quitting?" *New Yorker* (August 16, 2021). https://www.newyorker.com/culture/office-space/why-are-so-many-knowledge-workers-quitting.

Newton, Ruth. "The Psychology of Conformity or Why Do We Have the Need to Fit In?" *Learning Mind* (October 2, 2018). https://www.learning-mind.com/psychology-of-conformity/.

Nichols, Hannah. "Job Dissatisfaction Has Negative Health Effects by Age 40." *Medical News Today* (August 22, 2016). https://www.medicalnewstoday.com/articles/312458.

Noba. "Knowledge Evolved." Noba. Accessed 7 Feb. 2023. https://nobapro
ject.com/.

Oakes, Kevin. "Let Your Top Performers Move Around the Company." *Harvard Business Review* (August 20, 2021). https://hbr.org/2021/08
/let-your-top-performers-move-around-the-company.

Ochs, Nola. "The yearning for study was always . . ." AZ Quotes. Accessed
on March 15, 2023. https://www.azquotes.com/quote/1300491.

O'Reilly, Tim., et al., "You're Not the Customer; You're the Product." Quote
Investigator (July 16, 2017). https://quoteinvestigator.com/2017
/07/16/product/.

Paychex. "Employee Benefits Trends for 2023: What Are the
Future Trends?" Paychex.com. Last updated December 20,
2022. https://www.paychex.com/articles/employee-benefits/
employee-benefits-trends.

Parker, Kim, and Juliana Menasce Horowitz. "Majority of Workers Who
Quit a Job in 2021 Cite Low Pay, No Opportunities for Advancement, Feeling Disrespected." Pew Research Center (March 9, 2022).
https://www.pewresearch.org/fact-tank/2022/03/09/majority
-of-workers-who-quit-a-job-in-2021-cite-low-pay-no-opportunities-
for-advancement-feeling-disrespected/.

Parker, Kim, et al. "COVID-19 Pandemic Continues to Reshape Work in
America." Pew Research Center's Social & Demographic Trends Project
(February 16, 2022). https://www.pewresearch.org
/social-trends/2022/02/16/covid-19-pandemic-continues-to-reshape
-work-in-america/.

Parker, Priya. *Together Apart Podcast.* https://www.priyaparker.com
/together-apart.

Patel, Alok, and Stephanie Plowman. "The Increasing Importance of a Best
Friend at Work." Gallup (August 17, 2022). https://www.gallup.com
/workplace/397058/increasing-importance-best-friend-work.aspx.

Paycor. "The Biggest Cost of Doing Business: A Closer Look at Labor
Costs." *Paycor* (December 8, 2022). https://www.paycor.com/
resource-center/articles/closer-look-at-labor-costs/.

Pendell, Ryan. "The World's $7.8 Trillion Workplace Problem." Gal-
lup (June 14, 2022). https://www.gallup.com/workplace/393497/
world-trillion-workplace-problem.aspx.

Pew Research Center. "Section 3. How Americans View Their Jobs." *The
State of American Jobs Report.* Pew Research Center, October 6, 2016.
https://www.pewresearch.org/social-trends/2016/10/06/3-how
-americans-view-their-jobs/.

Pieter, H. and Sashen N. "What Percentage of McDonald's, Walmart's, Safeway, Etc. Operating Budget Is Spent on Labor Hiring? If We Can Get an Idea of 5 of the Large Hourly Employers That'd Be Ideal. How Much Money Are These Companies Spending on Hiring?" *Wonder* (March 14, 2017). https://askwonder.com/research /percentage-mcdonald-s-walmart-s-safeway-etc-operating-budget -spent-labor-hiring-7yyf5la6y.

Platts, Chris. "Realistic Job Preview: 7 Great Examples to Inspire You." *ThriveMap* (November 20, 2020). https://thrivemap.io/ realistic-job-preview/.

Pugh, Marie-Reine. "These 10+ Onboarding Statistics Reveal What New Employees Really Want in 2023." Bamboo HR (January 25, 2023). https://www.bamboohr.com/blog/onboarding-infographic/ #point-two.

PwC. "Putting Purpose to Work: PwC." PwC. Accessed February 7, 2023. https://www.pwc.com/us/en/purpose-workplace-study.html.

PwC. "PwC Pulse Survey: Next in Work," PWC (2021). Accessed March 10, 2023. https://www.pwc.com/us/en/library/pulse-survey/future-of -work.html

PwC. "Striking Gaps between Consumers', Employees' and Employers' Definitions of 'Trust' Creates Complex Challenge for Businesses, According to PwC Survey: PwC." PwC. Accessed 7 Feb. 2023. https:// www.pwc.com/us/en/about-us/newsroom/press-releases/ complexity-of-trust.html.

Qualtrics. "What is EX? Your Ultimate Guide to Employee Experience." Qualtrics.com. Accessed March 15, 2023. https://www.qualtrics.com /experience-management/employee/employee-experience/.

Quantum Metric. "Join Our Team," QuantumMetric.com. Accessed March 15, 2023. https://www.quantummetric.com/careers/.

Ranosa, Rachel. "Unhappy at Work? Your Health May Suffer." Human Resources Director (February 10, 2020). "https://www.hcamag.com /us/specialization/workplace-health-and-safety/unhappy-at-work -your-health-may-suffer/213123.

Red Bull. "Talent Communities." RedBull.com. Accessed March 15, 2023. https://jobs.redbull.com/us-en/talent-communities.

Rosenberg, Wallace. "The Purpose Gap - Corporate Reporting." *PwC UK Blogs* (October 22, 2020). https://pwc.blogs.com/corporatereporting /2020/10/the-purpose-gap-october-2020.html.

Sanders, Daisy Melamed. "The Psychology of Divorce and the Pursuit of Happiness." *Psycom* (February 26, 2020). https://www.psycom.net /divorce.

Sarasohn, Eliza. "Raj Choudhury on 'Work from Anywhere'—and Why the Future of Work is Borderless." Future Forum (December 15, 2021). https://futureforum.com/2021/12/15/raj-choudhury-on-why-the-future-of -work-is-borderless/.

Schleckser, Jim. "How Many Direct Reports Should You Have?" *Inc.* (March 5, 2019). https://www.inc.com/postitbrand/identi-fy-your-teams-productivity-styles-and-improve-collaboration.html.

Schutz, Bart. "Belongingness & Conformity." *Wheel of Persuasion* (June 6, 2013). https://www.wheelofpersuasion.com/technique/belongingness -conformity/.

Schwantes, Marcel. "The Surprising Reason Why So Many Employees Quit within the First 6 Months." *Inc.* (July 25, 2019). https://www.inc.com /marcel-schwantes/surprising-reason-why-employees-quit.html.

Scott, Shelby B. et al., "Reasons for Divorce and Recollections of Premarital Intervention: Implications for Improving Relationship Education." *Couple Family Psychology* 2, no. 2 (2013): 131–145.

Sharot, Tali. "What Motivates Employees More: Rewards or Punishments?" *Harvard Business Review* (September 26, 2017). https://hbr.org/2017/09/ what-motivates-employees-more-rewards-or-punishments.

SHRM. "Developing and Sustaining Employee Engagement." SHRM.org. Accessed March 15, 2023. https://www.shrm.org/resourcesandtools /tools-and-samples/toolkits/pages/sustainingemployeeengagement .aspx.

Sigall, PhD, Harold. "Buyer's Remorse." *Psychology Today* (August 17, 2017). https://www.psychologytoday.com/us/blog/wish-ful-thoughts/201708 /buyer-s-remorse.

Slack Team. "The Great Executive-Employee Disconnect." Slack (October 5, 2021). https://slack.com/intl/en-in/blog/news/the-great-executive -employee-disconnect.

Slattery, Ciara. "Top Employee Onboarding Programs." *Kallidus* (March 1, 2022). https://www.saplinghr.com/top-employee-onboarding -programs#1.

Sleek, Scott. "The Science of Sameness." *APS Observer* 29 (November 2016). https://www.psychologicalscience.org/observer/the-science-of -sameness.

Smith, Charlene. "Fitting In: The Neuroscience Of Conformity." *Brain World*." *Brain World* (May 6, 2021). https://brainworldmagazine.com /fitting-in-the-neuroscience-of-conformity/.

Softstart. "4 Companies Who Nailed the New Employee Onboarding Experience." Softstart.app (May 19, 2022). https://softstart.app/blog/ best-employee-onboarding-examples/.

Somers, Meredith. "10 Smart—Not Soft—Skills for Leaders." *MIT Sloan* (August 15, 2022). https://mitsloan.mit.edu/ ideas-made-to-matter/10-smart-not-soft-skills-leaders.

Spiceworks. "Five Reasons Why the Four-Day Workweek Is Worth a Shot." *Spiceworks* (July 18, 2022). https://www.spiceworks.com/tech /it-careers-skills/articles/four-day-work-week-employee-productivity/.

Staff, Leading Effectively. "4 Unexpected Lessons Learned from Hardships & Adversity." *CCL* (July 17, 2020). https://www.ccl.org/articles/leading-effectively-articles/4-lessons-learned-from-hardship-adversity/.

Staff. "New Offices for the Hybrid Era? Many Companies Are on Board," *News Tribune* (March 6, 2022). https://www.newstribune.com/ news/2022/mar/06/new-offices-for-the-hybrid-era-many-companies -are/.

Stallen, Mirre, and Alan G. Sanfey. "The Neuroscience of Social Conformity: Implications for Fundamental and Applied Research." *Frontiers in Neuroscience* 9 (2015). https://doi.org/10.3389/fnins.2015.00337.

Stieg, Cory. "People Keep Mistaking Doll Chairs for Human Ones on Amazon, and the Reviews Are Hilarious." *Good Housekeeping* (September 2, 2016). https://www.goodhousekeeping.com/life/money/news/a40264 /amazon-fails-tiny-chairs/.

Street, Farnam. "Carol Dweck: A Summary of the Two Mindsets." *Farnam Street* (March 2, 2015). https://fs.blog/carol-dweck-mindset/.

Student Experience Research Network. "Carol Dweck." *Student Experience Research Network*. Accessed February 7, 2023. https://studentexperiencenetwork.org/people/carol-dweck/.

Studypool. "Methods of Employee Onboarding in Patagonia Discussion." Studypool.com. Accessed March 15, 2023. https://www.studypool .com/discuss/26488722/discussion-5893.

Suellentrop, Austin, and E. Beth Bauman. "How Influential is a Good Manager?" Gallup (June 2, 2021). https://www.gallup.com/clifton strengths/en/350423/influential-good-manager.aspx.

Sull, Donald, Stefano Turconi, and Charles Sull. "When It Comes to Culture, Does Your Company Walk the Talk?" *MIT Sloan Manage-*

ment Review (July 21, 2020). https://sloanreview.mit.edu/article/
when-it-comes-to-culture-does-your-company-walk-the-talk/.

Tailored Thinking. "The History of the Job Description." TailoredThink-
ing.co.uk (August 10, 2021). https://tailoredthinking.co.uk/blog
/2021/8/10/job-descriptions#:~:text=They%20were%20originally%
20produced%20as,necessary%20to%20perform%20those%20
activities.

Tappe, Anneken. "A Record 4.5 Million Americans Quit Their Jobs in
March." *CNN* (May 3, 2022).

Tayeb, Zahra. "Apple Is Now Valued More Than Alphabet, Amazon and
Meta Combined." *Business Insider* (November 3, 2022). https://mar-
kets.businessinsider.com/news/stocks/apple-alphabet-amazon-meta
-market-value-cap-trillion-big-tech-2022-11.

Teach for Australia. "The Power of Praise: Effort vs. Intelligence." *Teach
For Australia* (May 6, 2015). https://teachforaustralia.org/the-power
-of-praise-effort-vs-intelligence/.

The Conference Board. "One Third of Those Who Changed Jobs Make
30% More." *The Conference Board* (February 28, 2022).
https://www.conference-board.org/press/One-Third-of-Those-Who
-Changed-Jobs-Make-More.

"The Knowledge Work Demand Index by Braintrust." Braintrust. Accessed
February 7, 2023. https://www.usebraintrust.com
/knowledge-work-demand-index.

Thrash, Todd M. and Andrew J. Elliot. "Inspiration As a Pyschological
Construct." *Journal of Personality and Social Psychology* 84, no. 4
(2003): 871–889. https://psycnet.apa.org/record/2003-02410-016.

Thrive Map. "Pre-Hire Assessments for High Volume Hiring." *ThriveMap*
(February 10, 2022). https://thrivemap.io/pre-hire-assessments-for
-high-volume-hiring/.

Trivedi, Isha. "Faculty-Pay Survey Records the Largest One-Year Drop
Ever." *Chronicle of Higher Education* (June 22, 2022). https://www.
chronicle.com/article/faculty-pay-survey-records-the-largest
-one-year-drop-ever.

Tu, Marianna, and Michael Li. "What Great Mentorship Looks Like in a
Hybrid Workplace." *Harvard Business Review* (May 12, 2021). https://
hbr.org/2021/05/what-great-mentorship-looks-like-in-a-hybrid
-workplace.

Tucker, Elissa. "The Employee Experience—Is There Value Behind the
Buzz?" *The APQC Blog* (April 10, 2019). https://www.apqc.org/blog
/employee-experience-there-value-behind-buzz.

Tunguz, Tomasz. "How Quickly Does Headcount Scale in the Fastest Growing Software Businesses?" TonTunguz.com (November 29, 2017). https://tomtunguz.com/headcount-growth/.

Twaronite, Karyn. "The Surprising Power of Simply Asking Coworkers How They're Doing." *Harvard Business Review* (February 28, 2019). https://hbr.org/2019/02/the-surprising-power-of-simply -asking-coworkers-how-theyre-doing.

Udemy. "Q1 Global Workplace Learning Skills Index." *Udemy Research* (April 21, 2022). https://research.udemy.com/featured_infographic /q1-workplace-learning-skills-index-2/.

University of Minnesota. "Best Methods for Making Group Decisions." University of Minnesota Extension. Accessed Feb. 7, 2023. https:// extension.umn.edu/leadership-development/best-methods-making -group-decisions.

US Bureau of Labor Statistics. "Number of Quits at All-Time High in November 2021 : The Economics Daily." US Bureau of Labor Statistics (January 6, 2022). https://www.bls.gov/opub/ted/2022/number-of- quits-at-all-time-high-in-november-2021.htm.

US Bureau of Labor Statistics. "Table 2. Percent of Employed Wage and Salary Workers 25 Years and over Who Had 10 Years or More of Tenure with Their Current Employer by Age and Sex, Selected Years, 2012-2022." *2022 A01 Results*. Accessed February 7, 2023. https:// www.bls.gov/news.release/tenure.t02.htm.

US Bureau of Labor Statistics. "Table 4. Quits Levels and Rates by Indus- try and Region, Seasonally Adjusted." *2022 M12 Results*. Accessed February 7, 2023. https://www.bls.gov/news.release/jolts.t04.htm.

Valdes-Dapena, Carlos. "How One Global Company Cracked the Code on High Performance Collaboration and Teamwork." John Hunt Publish- ing (March 22, 2019). https://www.johnhuntpublishing.com/blogs /changemakers/the-five-principles-of-mars-inc/.

Van Velsor, Ellen, Cynthia D. McCauley, and Marian N Ruderman. *The Cen- ter for Creative Leadership Handbook of Leadership Development*. Third Edition. San Francisco, CA: Jossey-Bass, 2010.

Van Vulpen, Erik. "The Realistic Job Preview Explained: 5 Tips to Do It Right." Academy to Innovate HR (June 15, 2020). https://www.aihr .com/blog/realistic-job-preview/.

Veylan, Bhavani. *Are Your New Hires Quitting?* Recruiting.com. Accessed February 7, 2023. https://www.recruiting.com/blog/are-your-new- hires-quitting/.

Viteles, Morris S. *Industrial Pyschology*. WW Norton & Company, 1932.

Vozza, Stephanie. "This Is Why New Hires Leave within the First 90 Days." *Fast Company* (June 19, 2018). https://www.fastcompany.com /40583243/this-is-why-new-hires-leave-within-the-first-90-days+.

WARC. "PwC Identifies Purpose 'Gap' That Must Be Closed." *WARC* (November 11, 2020). https://www.warc.com/newsandopinion/news /pwc-identifies-purpose-gap-that-must-be-closed/en-gb/44344.

Ware, Bronnie. *Regrets of the Dying—Bronnie Ware* (January 7, 2018). https://bronnieware.com/blog/regrets-of-the-dying/.

Westfall, Chris. "The Economy Is Strong, So Why Do Over 46% Of Americans Have to Do This to Make Ends Meet?" *Forbes* (May 29, 2019). https://www.forbes.com/sites/chriswestfall/2019/05/29/us-economy -strong-side-hustle-gig-freelance-career/?sh=414a0ad0117f.

Whippman, Ruth. "Happiness Is Other People." *New York Times* (October 27, 2017). https://www.nytimes.com/2017/10/27/opinion/sunday /happiness-is-other-people.html.

"Who Originally Suggested That 'If You're Not Paying for the Product, You Are the Product'?" *Quora*. Accessed February 7, 2023. https://www. quora.com/Who-originally-suggested-that-if-youre-not-paying-for- the-product-you-are-the-product.

Wigert, Ben, and Heather Barrett. "Performance Management Must Evolve." Gallup (August 31, 2020). Updated May 26, 2022. https:// www.gallup.com/workplace/318029/performance-manage- ment-evolve-survive-covid.aspx.

Wikipedia. "Nola Ochs," Wikipedia.com. Last modified February 3, 2023. https://en.wikipedia.org/wiki/Nola_Ochs.

Wilkie, Dana. "The Executive View: Moving into 2022, Antidotes to the 'Great Resignation.'" *SHRM* (January 14, 2022). https://www.shrm .org/executive/resources/articles/pages/executive-view-the-great -resignation-.aspx.

Wilkinson & Finkbeiner, LLP. "Divorce Statistics and Facts." Wilkinson & Finkbeiner, LLP. Accessed February 7, 2023. https://www.wf-lawyers .com/divorce-statistics-and-facts/.

Wisniewski, Benedikt, et al. "The Power of Feedback Revisited: A Meta-Analysis of Educational Feedback Research." *Frontiers in Psychology*, 10 (2019). https://doi.org/10.3389/fpsyg.2019.03087.

Witters, Dan, and Jim Harter. "In U.S., Life Ratings Plummet to 12-Year Low." Gallup (April 14, 2020). https://news.gallup.com/poll/308276 /life-ratings-plummet-year-low.aspx.

Woodward, Michael. "The Psychology of a First Impression." *Psychology Today* (May 9, 2017). https://www.psychologytoday.com/us/blog /spotting-opportunity/201705/the-psychology-first-impression.

Wooldridge, Scott. "90% of Employers Say They're Investing More in Mental Health Programs." BenefitsPro.com (January 5, 2022). https:// www.benefitspro.com/2022/01/05/90-of-employers-say-theyre-investing-more-in-mental-health-programs/?slreturn =20230214162905

World Economics. "United States GDP: $21.478 Trillion." WorldEconomics.com. Accessed March 27, 2023. https://www.worldeconomics.com /GrossDomesticProduct/Real-GDP-PPP/United%20States.aspx.

Work Institute. "Employee Retention Solutions & Engagement Solutions—Work Institute." Workinstitute.com (September 9. 2022). https://workinstitute.com/problems-we-solve/first-year-turnover/.

Wrongski, Laura, and Jon Cohen. "Nine in 10 Workers Who Have a Career Mentor Say They Are Happy in Their Jobs." *CNBC* (July 16, 2019). https://www.cnbc.com/2019/07/16/nine-in-10-workers-who-have-a -mentor-say-they-are-happy-in-their-jobs.html.

Yip, Jeffrey, and Meena Wilson. "Learning from Experience," in *The Center for Creative Leadership Handbook of Leadership Development*. Third Edition, ed. By Ellen Van Velsor, Cynthia D. McCauley, and Marian N. Ruderman. San Francisco, CA: Jossey-Bass, 2010.

Ysa, K. "The Crucial Difference Between Fitting In and Belonging." *Mind Cafe* (July 22, 2021). https://medium.com/mind-cafe/the-crucial -difference-between-fitting-in-and-belonging-cbc3da9d2f4a.

Zenger, Jack. "The Feedback Conundrum: Does Positive Or Negative Feedback Help You Most?" *Forbes* (March 21, 2014). https://www.forbes .com/sites/jackzenger/2014/03/21/the-feedback-conundrum-does -positive-or-negative-feedback-help-you-most/?sh=7eb00c821ad0.

Zip Recruiter. "The Job Market Outlook for Grads." ZipRecruiter. Accessed February 7, 2023. https://www.ziprecruiter.com/grad-report.

NOTES

Introduction

1. Pendell, "The World's $7.8 Trillion Workplace Problem."
2. Collins, "Job Unhappiness Is at A Staggering All-Time High, According to Gallup."
3. Ranosa, "Unhappy at Work? Your Health May Suffer."
4. Nichols, "Job Dissatisfaction Has Negative Health Effects by Age 40."
5. Sull, Turconi, and Sull, "When It Comes to Culture, Does Your Company Walk the Talk?"

Chapter 1

1. Newport, "Why Are So Many Knowledge Workers Quitting?"
2. Slack Team, "The Great Executive-Employee Disconnect."
3. Brower, "Finding a Job Is Tougher Now."
4. Jobvite, *2018 Job Seeker Nation Survey*.
5. Braintrust, "The Knowledge Work Demand Index by Braintrust."
6. Andre, "112 Employee Turnover Statistics: 2023 Causes, Cost & Prevention Data."
7. Nelms, Tucker, Spinner, and Mahan, *2022 Retention Report*.
8. Lattice Team, "Lattice Research Reveals Great Resignation Trends."
9. Tappe, "A Record 4.5 Million Americans Quit Their Jobs In March."
10. PwC, "PwC Pulse Survey: Next in Work."
11. Gallup, "State of the Global Workplace Report."
12. Edelman Trust Institute, *2023 Edelman Trust Barometer*.
13. HRTechX, "The Story of the Netflix Culture Deck."
14. Ferenstein, "Read What Facebook's Sandberg Calls Maybe 'The Most Important Document Ever To Come Out Of The Valley.'"
15. Harter, "U.S. Employee Engagement Needs a Rebound in 2023."
16. Moneywatch, "It's Official: Recession Began in February, Ending Longest U.S. Expansion Ever."
17. Maverick, "S&P 500 Average Return."
18. Davis, *Dedicated*, 8.
19. Davis, *Dedicated*, 14.
20. Davis, *Dedicated*, 247.
21. Parker and Horowitz, "Majority of Workers Who Quit a Job in 2021 Cite Low Pay, No Opportunities for Advancement, Feeling Disrespected."

22. Westfall, "The Economy Is Strong, So Why Do Over 46% Of Americans Have to Do This to Make Ends Meet?"
23. Brower, "The Power of Purpose and Why It Matters Now."
24. Brower, "The Power of Purpose and Why It Matters Now."
25. Ferraro, "One Company's Trick to Getting 95,000 Hours Back? Canceling Meetings."
26. Birkinshaw and Cohen, "Make Time for the Work That Matters."
27. Martin, "The Case for Inspiration."
28. McKinsey, "The Future of Work after COVID-19."
29. McKinsey, "The Future of Work after COVID-19."
30. Ariella, "27 US Employee Turnover Statistics [2023]."
31. Staff, "New Offices for the Hybrid Era? Many Companies Are on Board."
32. Parker, *Together Apart Podcast.*

Chapter 2

1. Belli, "Here's How Many Years You'll Spend at Work in Your Lifetime."
2. Campbell, "We've Broken Down Your Entire Life into Years Spent Doing Tasks."
3. Ware, *Regrets of the Dying—Bronnie Ware.*
4. Gallup, "State of the Global Workplace Report."
5. World Economics, "United States GDP: $21.478 Trillion."
6. Tayeb, "Apple Is Now Valued More Than Alphabet, Amazon and Meta Combined."
7. National Center for Education Statistics, "Fast Facts: Expenditures."
8. Harter, "U.S. Employee Engagement Slump Continues."
9. Grant, "Feeling Blah During the Pandemic? It's Called Languishing."
10. Abramson, "Burnout and Stress Are Everywhere."
11. Abramson, "Burnout and Stress Are Everywhere."
12. Chatterjee and Wroth, "WHO Redefines Burnout as a 'Syndrome' Linked to Chronic Stress at Work."
13. Chatterjee and Wroth, "WHO Redefines Burnout as a 'Syndrome' Linked to Chronic Stress at Work."
14. Pieter and Sashen, "What Percentage of McDonald's, Walmart's, Safeway, Etc. Operating Budget Is Spent on Labor Hiring?
15. Mercer, "Employers Increased Investment in Benefits during Pandemic but Many Employees Did Not Feel Supported."
16. Wooldridge, "90% of Employers Say They're Investing More in Mental Health Programs."
17. Gartner, "A Key Pandemic Lesson Learned: Invest in Your Talent."

18. Paychex, "Employee Benefits Trends for 2023: What Are the Future Trends?"
19. Matz and Wood, "Cognitive Dissonance in Groups."
20. Buckley, "What Happens to the Brain During Cognitive Dissonance?"
21. Paychex, "Employee Benefits Trends for 2023: What Are the Future Trends?"
22. Cooks-Campbell, "What Is Cognitive Dissonance and How Do You Reduce It?"
23. Cooper, "Cognitive Dissonance."
24. Psychology iResearchnet, "Basking in Reflected Glory."
25. Carr et. al., "The Value of Belonging at Work."
26. Twaronite, "The Surprising Power of Simply Asking Coworkers How They're Doing."
27. Heath, *Upstream*.
28. Belli, "Here's How Many Years You'll Spend at Work in Your Lifetime."
29. Belli, "Here's How Many Years You'll Spend at Work in Your Lifetime."

Chapter 3
1. Keller, "Attracting and Retaining the Right Talent."
2. Keller, "Attracting and Retaining the Right Talent."

Chapter 4
1. Wilkinson & Finkbeiner, LLP, "Divorce Statistics and Facts."
2. Graham et al., "When Values and Behavior Conflict."
3. Kaplan and Kaiser, "Stop Overdoing Your Strengths."
4. Moyle and Hackston, "Core Characters under Great Stress."
5. Suellentrop and Bauman, "How Influential is a Good Manager?"
6. Anderson, "The Pros and Cons of Following a Boss to a New Company."
7. Goffee and Jones, *Why Should Anyone Work Here?*, 2.
8. Grenny, "Great Storytelling Connects Employees to Their Work."
9. Grenny, "Great Storytelling Connects Employees to Their Work."

Chapter 5
1. Kivetz and Simonson, "The Effects of Incomplete Information on Consumer Choice."
2. Kivetz and Simonson, "The Effects of Incomplete Information on Consumer Choice."
3. Lord et al., *Prior Bias and Attitude Change—Death Penalty*.

4. Ellis et al., "The Use of Impression Management Tactics in Structured Interviews."
5. Artz, Goodall, and Oswald, "If Your Boss Could Do Your Job, You're More Likely to Be Happy at Work."
6. Artz, Goodall, and Oswald, "If Your Boss Could Do Your Job, You're More Likely to Be Happy at Work."
7. Allas and Schaninger, "The Boss Factor."

Chapter 6

1. Brown, *Braving the Wilderness*, 160.
2. Manta, "The Case for Cracking down on Tinder Lies."
3. Mandriota, "The Results Are In."
4. Coletta, "Top Tips for Strenghtening EX in 2023 from Patagonia's Former CHRO."
5. Buckingham and Goodall, "Why Feedback Rarely Does What It's Meant To."
6. Zenger, "The Feedback Conundrum: Does Positive or Negative Feedback Help You Most?"
7. Koetsier, "Why Every Amazon Meeting Has at Least 1 Empty Chair."
8. Gelles, "Billionaire No More: Patagonia Founder Gives Away the Company."
9. Valdes-Dapena, "How One Global Company Cracked the Code on High Performance Collaboration and Teamwork."
10. Lee, "Leaders Need to Excel at Learning from Experience"; McCall, Lombardo, and Morrison, *The Lessons of Experience*.
11. Musser and Taboada, "Use Internal Communications to Execute a Winning Strategy."
12. Musser and Taboada, "Use Internal Communications to Execute a Winning Strategy."
13. Lightman, *Einstein's Dream*.

Chapter 7

1. Lerner, "Learn the Real Reason Why Marriages Fail."
2. Lerner, "Learn the Real Reason Why Marriages Fail."
3. Sanders, "The Psychology of Divorce and the Pursuit of Happiness."
4. Scott et al., "Reasons for Divorce and Recollections of Premarital Intervention."
5. Sanders, "The Psychology of Divorce and the Pursuit of Happiness."
6. Sanders, "The Psychology of Divorce and the Pursuit of Happiness."
7. Sanders, "The Psychology of Divorce and the Pursuit of Happiness."

8. Campbell, "We've Broken Down Your Entire Life into Years Spent Doing Tasks."
9. Sanders, "The Psychology of Divorce and the Pursuit of Happiness."
10. Chamorro-Premuzic, "Does Money Really Affect Motivation?"
11. Chamorro-Premuzic, "Does Money Really Affect Motivation?"
12. Chamorro-Premuzic, "Does Money Really Affect Motivation?"
13. Google Trends, "Purpose."
14. Google Trends, "News."
15. Google Trends, "Hybrid Working."
16. Google Trends, "Languishing."
17. Google Trends, "Side Hustles."
18. Rosenberg, "The Purpose Gap - Corporate Reporting."
19. Gulati, "When Employees Feel a Sense of Purpose, Companies Succeed."
20. Birkinshaw and Cohen, "Make Time for the Work That Matters."
21. Michaelson, "The Importance of Meaningful Work."
22. Gartner, "Gartner HR Research Finds 65 % of Women Report the Pandemic Has Made Them Rethink the Place of Work in Their Lives."
23. IBM, "What Employees Expect in 2021."
24. Dhingra et al., "Help Your Employees Find Purpose—Or Watch Them Leave."
25. Liu, "People Spend More than Half Their Day Doing Busy Work, According to Survey of 10,000-plus Workers."
26. Marfice, "Busy vs Productive — Which Are You?"
27. Wikipedia, "Nola Ochs."
28. Ochs, "The yearning for study was always . . ."
29. Martensson et al., "Growth of Language-Related Brain Areas after Foreign Langugae Learning."
30. Mohan, "Why Learning New Skills Is Good for Your Confidence."
31. Campbell, "Six Surprising Benefits of Curiosity."
32. Beres, "Mentally Challenging Yourself Curbs Anxiety and Depression, New Research Shows."
33. Mohan, "Why Learning New Skills Is Good for Your Confidence."
34. Madgavkar et al., "Performance through People: Transforming Human Capital into Competitive Advantage."
35. Yip and Wilson, "Learning from Experience."
36. Staff, "4 Unexpected Lessons Learned from Hardships & Adversity."
37. Liedtka, "Why Design Thinking Works."
38. InfoSurv Research, "It Takes Two: Engaged Employees and Satisfied Customers [Infographic]."

39. Gamble, "How Employee Engagement Leads to Customer Loyalty."
40. SHRM.org., "Developing and Sustaining Employee Engagement."
41. Birkinshaw and Cohen, "Make Time for the Work That Matters."
42. Lieberman, "Why Your Procrastinate (It Has Nothing to Do With Self-Control)."
43. Thrash and Elliot, "Inspiration As a Pyschological Construct."

Chapter 8

1. Milne, *Winnie-the-Pooh*.
2. Luthens and Peterson, "360-Degree Feedback with Systemic Coaching."
3. McLeod, "Operant Conditioning."
4. Cameron and Pierce, "Reinforcement, Reward, and Intrinsic Motivation: A Meta-Analysis."
5. Tu and Li, "What Great Mentorship Looks Like in a Hybrid Workplace."
6. Wrongski and Cohen, "Nine in 10 Workers Who Have a Career Mentor Say They Are Happy in Their Jobs."
7. Whippman, "Happiness Is Other People."
8. Whippman, "Happiness Is Other People."
9. Patel and Plowman, "The Increasing Importance of a Best Friend at Work."
10. Goldberg, "The Magic of Your First Work Friends."
11. Patel and Plowman, "The Increasing Importance of a Best Friend at Work."
12. Patel and Plowman, "The Increasing Importance of a Best Friend at Work."
13. Block, *The Answer to How Is Yes*, 28.
14. Coleman and Coleman, "Don't Take Work Stress Home with You."
15. Coleman and Coleman, "Don't Take Work Stress Home with You."
16. Miller, "The 24/7 Work Culture's Toll on Families and Gender Equality."
17. Witters and Harter, "In U.S., Life Ratings Plummet to 12-Year Low."
18. Kansas State University, "Employees Who Are Engaged in Their Work Have Happier Home Life."

Chapter 9

1. Gartner, "Gartner Glossary."
2. Gallup, "Employee Experience."
3. Tucker, "The Employee Experience—Is There Value behind the Buzz?"
4. Lee, "What Is Employee Experience?"
5. Qualtrics, "What is EX? Your Ultimate Guide to Employee Experience."

6. Fried, "Where We Came From."
7. Merritt, "The History of Shopify."
8. Dewar, Keller, Malhotra, and Strovink, "Actions the Best CEOs Are Taking in 2023."
9. Hotchkiss, "Todorov Explores the 'Irresistible Influence of First Impressions.'"
10. Devenyi, "The Psychology behind First Impressions, and How It Affects Your Home Buying Choices."
11. Devenyi, "The Psychology behind First Impressions, and How It Affects Your Home Buying Choices."
12. Stieg, "People Keep Mistaking Doll Chairs for Human Ones on Amazon, and the Reviews Are Hilarious."
13. Dossetto, "The Quest for Better Collaboration: Principles, Cheatsheets, and 10+ Tools We Use at Hotjar."
14. Chouinard, "Earth Is Now Our Only Shareholder."
15. Mito, "Random Clever Person."
16. Apple, "Careers at Apple."
17. Quantum Metric, "Join Our Team."
18. 37 Signals, "37 Signals Manifesto."
19. Red Bull, "Talent Communities."
20. LVMH, "Inside LVMH."
21. Tailored Thinking, "The History of the Job Description."
22. Viteles, *Industrial Psychology*.
23. Van Vulpen, "The Realistic Job Preview Explained."
24. Platts, "Realistic Job Preview."
25. Vozza, "This Is Why New Hires Leave within the First 90 Days."
26. Nobl.io, "Don't Just Talk Transformation."
27. Nobl.io, "Don't Just Talk Transformation."

Chapter 10

1. Anderson, *From Recruitment to Onboarding, What Is the True Cost of Hiring Employees?*
2. Tunguz, "How Quickly Does Headcount Scale in the Fastest Growing Software Businesses?"
3. Gartner, "Gartner Says U.S. Total Annual Employee Turnover Will Likely Jump by Nearly 20% from the Prepandemic Annual Average."
4. Anderson, *From Recruitment to Onboarding, What Is the True Cost of Hiring Employees?*
5. Slattery, "Top Employee Onboarding Programs."
6. Slattery, "Top Employee Onboarding Programs."

7. Studypool.com., "Methods of Employee Onboarding in Patagonia Discussion."
8. Softstart, "4 Companies Who Nailed the New Employee Onboarding Experience."
9. Schleckser, "How Many Direct Reports Should You Have?"
10. Schleckser, "How Many Direct Reports Should You Have?"
11. Harter, "U.S. Employee Engagement Slump Continues."
12. Bersin, "The Death of the Performance Appraisal."
13. Wigert and Barrett, "Performance Management Must Evolve."
14. Baker, "6 Predictions for the Future of Performance Management."
15. Gartner, "Gartner HR Research Reveals 82% of Employees Report Working Environment Lacks Fairness."
16. Sarasohn, "Raj Choudhury on 'Work from Anywhere'—and Why the Future of Work is Borderless,"
17. Davis, *Dedicated*, 4.
18. Davis, *Dedicated*, 4.
19. McLaren, "Employees Stay 41% Longer at Companies That Use This Strategy."
20. McLaren, "Employees Stay 41% Longer at Companies That Use This Strategy."
21. Cerullo, "Unnecessary Meetings Can Cost Big Companies $100 Million a Year, Report Finds."
22. Bennett, "Talent Marketplace Platforms Statistics 2022."
23. Heidari-Robinson and Heywood, "Getting Reorgs Right."

ACKNOWLEDGMENTS

Over the years, many have contributed to the ideas and insights found in this book. First, there is the publishing team at IT Revolution, Margueritte and Gene Kim, Anna Noak, and Leah Brown. Thank you for taking a chance on me, remaining in my corner throughout the writing process, and making the book better than I could have imagined. Second, there are the 65+ leaders who agreed to be interviewed. Though they will remain nameless to honor the honesty and rawness they shared about their *right fit* and *wrong fit* experiences, I wanted to thank them for raising their hand, finding time in their busy lives to speak with me, and for offering beautiful insights that shaped this book and will undoubtedly help other talent to find a place where they can shine.

There is also a select group of friends, colleagues, and contributors who shaped the book and the content within it. First, there is Madison Stamen, who was a primary researcher, reviewer, and contributor to the book. Her enthusiasm, deft pen, and unbridled curiosity provided both "ah ha's" related to the text and an extra boost of energy that kept me pushing forward when things got hard. Then, there were my early readers, Nicholas Borjeka, America Bliss, Drew Fifield, Wyatt Taubman, and Sandy Speicher. Thank you for your care, your careful consideration of the text, your laser focused ideas of how to make it stronger, and your endorsement that this book was worth writing and sharing with the world. Last, I would be remiss to not thank my PR team at Finn led by Adrienne Fontaine. You believed in the book from the first moment and were unwavering in helping it to find its audience.

Finally, to my wife, Julie Duke. She has created the space for me to have both a beautiful career and the time to write this book. Her love for me and her belief in my ability has been unwavering since the moment we met. She has been there every step of the way, standing beside me, cheering me on, and giving me the inspiration to be a better man, a better husband, a better father, and a better writer. While I have spent my days helping leaders to develop themselves and build great companies, she has tirelessly and without fanfare helped our family to build a life that is pure magic. I am so lucky to have her. This book is dedicated to her.

To all of those listed above and the countless other leaders, friends, and colleagues who are in my orbit and have shaped my thinking, I will be forever in your debt.

ABOUT THE AUTHOR

Andre Martin is an organizational psychologist and talent management executive with 20+ years of experience in talent development, executive team development, employee engagement, culture change, c-suite assessment and succession planning, innovation/design thinking, strategy development, and employee experience design. He has worked at or with Nike, Disney, Target, Mars Inc., Google, and more. He is also a father, a husband, and a wildly curious learner who is dedicated to ensuring iconic brands become iconic companies.

DISCOVER MORE TITLES FROM
IT REVOLUTION

Helping Technology Leaders Succeed for 10 Years

Discover books, resources, and more at ITRevolution.com.